SUNK
WITHOUT
TRACE

OTHER TITLES OF INTEREST

TOTAL LOSS
Dramatic First-Hand Accounts of Yacht Losses at Sea
3rd edition
Paul Gelder
978 0 7136 8783 5

Dramatic first-hand accounts of yachts lost at sea through collision, fire and explosion, exhaustion and crew failure, navigational blunders, dismastings and severe storms. A bestseller since first publication, this is a compelling thought-provoking read.

LEFT FOR DEAD
The Untold Story of the Tragic 1979 Fastnet Race
Nick Ward, with Sinead O'Brien
978 1 4081 2816 9

The tragic and inspirational account of Nick Ward's survival against all the odds in the 1979 Fastnet. Updated for the new edition with the gripping account of Nick's 2009 Fastnet triumph – finally rounding the rock after 30 years.

DISASTERS AT SEA
Dag Pike
978 0 7136 8878 8

Based on the author's experience, the book features a mosaic of accounts dealing with a wide range of yachts, motorboats and commercial vessels which have encountered difficulty at sea. They are all analysed in a useful yet entertaining way.

FATAL STORM
The Inside Story of the Tragic Sydney to Hobart Race
Rob Mundle
978 1 4081 0700 3

Telling the story of the 1998 Sydney to Hobart yacht race, this book details the history of the race, the excitement of the start and the thrill of competition. It contains extensive interviews with officials, survivors and rescue service personnel.

DEADLIEST CATCH
Desperate Hours
978 1 4081 0623 5

This is the authorised book of the hit TV series featuring the harrowing struggles of fishermen on the wild and freezing Bering Sea – it's the perfect storm but for real.

PAUL GELDER

SUNK
WITHOUT
TRACE

30 DRAMATIC ACCOUNTS OF
YACHTS LOST AT SEA

ADLARD COLES NAUTICAL
LONDON

TO MY WIFE ANNE, WHO HAS KEPT ME AFLOAT, BOTH ASHORE, WHERE
A TIDE OF PAPERWORK THREATENS TO OVERWHELM ME, AND OFFSHORE
WHERE, AS THEY SAY, 'WORSE THINGS HAPPEN AT SEA...'

Published by Adlard Coles Nautical
an imprint of A & C Black Publishers Ltd
36 Soho Square, London W1D 3QY
www.adlardcoles.com

Copyright Paul Gelder 2010

First edition published 2010

ISBN 978-1-4081-1200-7

A CIP catalogue record for this book is available from the British
Library.

This book is produced using paper that is made from wood grown
in managed, sustainable forests. It is natural, renewable and
recyclable. The logging and manufacturing processes conform to
the environmental regulations of the country of origin.

Typeset in 10.5 on 12.5pt Adobe Garamond Pro
Printed and bound in UK by Cox and Wyman Ltd

Note: *while all reasonable care has been taken in the publication of
this book, the publisher takes no responsibility for the use of the
methods or products described in the book*

CONTENTS

PREFACE

Disaster at sea comes in many disguises. This collection of 30 dramatic accounts of yachts lost at sea covers several decades, and crosses the Atlantic to the Pacific and Indian oceans, venturing to Australia and New Zealand, as well as the Caribbean, America's East Coast and closer to home in Holland and the UK, including the Solent, Suffolk and Scotland.

Most of the stories date from the 1970s to the 1990s and involve a wide variety of craft, from cruising yachts, ranging in size from 23ft to 45ft, as well as Open 60 ocean-racing yachts, multihulls (both catamarans and trimarans), sloops, yawls, gaff-cutters and a barge yacht.

The disasters include storms – in one case a terrifying hurricane of 130 knots – as well as equipment failure, involving, among other things, broken anchor chain, failed bilge pumps, an unsecured mast and broken rudders. There are also incidents of faulty navigation – resulting in deadly encounters with reefs and harbour entrances.

There are fires, explosions, capsizes, encounters with UFOs (unidentified floating objects), a yacht which sinks in mid-Atlantic after being struck by a whale and yachts that spring mystifying leaks and slowly sink, despite the desperate efforts of crew to find or fix the leak. Finally, there is the human element as sheer exhaustion or seasickness take their toll on skipper or crew.

Advice from the long-suffering skippers involved in these tragic tales varies from 'never change the colour of your boat' to unselfishly questioning their own judgement or preparation before putting to sea.

If your yacht was dismasted, would you have the tools the cut away the rig? As one skipper found, 'a mast becomes a horrific hammer which can puncture a hole in your hull'. If your rudder dropped off, would you have the equipment and the ingenuity to fix things and create an emergency steering system? When did you last check your liferaft and lifejackets?

Do you carry a knife? Three skippers in this book survived, thanks to having a handy knife – in one case, he had to cut his personal lifeline, when it became a death line, trapping him on a capsized yacht. In two other cases, it was needed to cut the painter on a liferaft which threatened to sink, dragged along by the yacht they had just abandoned.

How secure is your anchor chain? In one incident grippingly described in these pages, the anchor chain broke after been 'sawn' through by coral. In another, the chain ran out of the anchor locker and disappeared overboard when the bitter end lashing simply snapped. The yacht was a total loss.

For the single-handed sailor aboard a badly-leaking monohull, there is the dreadful conundrum of choosing between pumping for your life, stopping to search for the cause of the leak, or abandoning ship while there is still time to launch the liferaft and collect essentials. In the case of Peter Tangveld (*Mystery Collision, Miraculous Survival*), he had no liferaft aboard his 32ft yacht *Dorothea*. Instead, he made a remarkable 55-mile voyage to safety in his 7ft plywood dinghy.

Self-sufficiency, self-reliance and self-preservation are absolute essentials of good seamanship. Qualities that, in this modern age, seem endangered by too many of our rule-makers.

You have to admire the resourcefulness, pluck and fortitude of the 30 skippers and their crew on these unlucky yachts. They include legendary sailors, like the late H W Tilman and Malcolm Robson, as well as acclaimed contemporary writers, like Peter Nichols, author of *Voyage for Madman* and *Evolution's Captain*.

Nichols had wanted to be a writer since he was in his 20s. But it took the sinking of his leaky, engineless 27ft wooden boat, *Toad*, to inspire the memoir of the twinned sinkings of his boat and first marriage as described in *Sea Change*, his first highly praised book from which our extract is taken. As Nichols dryly observes aboard his sinking boat with her unstoppable leak: 'The bilge is V-shaped, so what looks half full is probably only a quarter full. I normally see half a glass of water as half full, but I have just become a fervent half-empty man.'

Malcolm Robson's laconic account of abandoning his 38ft cutter, *Banba IV*, reminds us of the rewards of maintaining a calm and phlegmatic grace when confronted with crisis. Faced with his sinking yacht 450 miles away from the nearest land, Robson did his sums: 'Total fuel about 90 hours in calm…. Total Trinidad rum: about three cases… say your prayers, lads, and away with prohibition!'

Spotting a rescue ship on the horizon, he called the crew aft, read them chapter 23 of *Hornblower*, put on lifejackets and sent up a red flare, announcing: 'Passports and money only!' since once near the freighter, it would be 'Jump!' and then would come the crashing of rigging, splintering of planks, etc. Robson's trousers fell down at the critical moment, but all were saved.

Peter Combe, the only crew member aboard the ill-fated *Windstar*, describes his skipper as 'a man of astounding imperturbability and apparent nonchalance' who seemed sublimely and blithely content to sail on, so long as there seemed to be water under his keel.

There are some truly remarkable accounts in these pages, plucked from yacht club journals and newsletters. Some appeared in earlier editions of the book *Total Loss* and deserve not to be lost to the passage of time. Herein lies courage, wit and dogged determination, all wrapped up and recorded with literary verve. More importantly, there are some thought-provoking and indispensable lessons from which any modern sailor can learn the art or survival – saving lives, if not yachts.

We go to sea for adventure and as one survivor says in this book: 'If you can't cope with this, then don't go to sea. But don't get in a car either, and don't cross the road to get your morning paper!'

PAUL GELDER

ACKNOWLEDGEMENTS

Like any collection of stories, this book could not have been compiled without the assistance and generosity of many people who were willing to share their tales of disaster at sea so that others might learn some of the lessons.

Happily, no lives were lost in any of these dramatic disasters and the skippers and crew survived even if their vessels did not.

There are stories here that never made the pages of *Total Loss*, a sister volume of first-hand accounts of losses at sea. And there are stories that were squeezed out of the third edition of that anthology as new disaster accounts took their place. But those stories deserved not to be lost and forgotten. I have added new, extended lessons where appropriate.

The late Jack Coote, who wrote the first edition of *Total Loss* more than 20 years ago, acknowledged Julian van Hasselt and the late Peter Tangvald (whose story, *Mystery Collision, Miraculous Survival*, appears in chapter 16) for their contribution in preliminary research into many of the accounts in these pages.

The editors of sailing magazines on both sides of the Atlantic have also given permission to use extracts from their publications, including Andrew Bray, editor of *Yachting World*.

I am particularly indebted to the author Peter Nichols for his permission to use an excerpt (chapter 4, *The Leak that Wouldn't Stop*) from his book, *Sea Change*, a heartfelt account of his single-handed voyage across the Atlantic in a leaking wooden boat. It's one of the most intimate, in-depth and thoughtful survival stories I have read and justifiably launched Nichols' career as a successful author. I am also grateful to Jack Gush for his gripping shipwreck tale, *Bluewater Castaways*, which gives a unique insight into the celebrated solo sailor Tom Follett. It took Ross Ireland 22 years before he could share his traumatic story, *The End of the Affair*, about the loss of his beloved 42ft classic Nicholson wooden sloop, *Inkoosaan*, which was dropped from a ship's crane. I would also like to thank Geoffrey Toye for his story *Storm Force 10 in the Irish Sea* about the loss of *Gwendoline*.

Solo sailors Isabelle Autissier (chapter 5, *Sea Dark Sky Crying*) and Josh Hall (chapter 15, *When Fear Came in Waves*) both gave me valuable time to interview them about their ordeals in the Southern Ocean, where both their yachts sunk within a few weeks of each other.

I was assisted on my own 'voyage' through these 30 traumatic tales by Janet Murphy, editorial director at Adlard Coles, and Hannah Leech, my book editor. I am also grateful for help from Jane Fenton at *Yachting Monthly*. Finally, I am indebted to my wife Anne for her patience on the 'lost weekends' while this book was taking shape, as well as her encouragement. She's 'bailed me out' metaphorically, more than once!

one

THE END OF THE AFFAIR

Yacht	*Inkoosaan* (Nicholson 42 wooden sloop)
Skipper	Ross Ireland
Bound from	Palma, Majorca to Muscat, Oman
Date of loss	March 1988
Position	approx. 120 miles from the Egyptian Port of Berenice

It's taken 22 years for Ross Ireland to tell the story of his brief and traumatic love affair with his first yacht, Inkoosaan, *a Nicholson 42, which he lost in a tragic accident in 1988.*

WAS IT LOVE AT FIRST sight, or just a moment of boat owner insanity? I really wanted a Contessa 32 but in March 1985, I mysteriously ended up buying *Inkoosaan*, a classic 42ft wooden cruising yacht.

That summer I took a five month sabbatical to sail her from Ireland across the Bay of Biscay, to Spain, Portugal and the Mediterranean. *Inkoosaan* (Afrikaans for 'little chief' or 'little master') was a one-off, designed by John Nicholson and built in 1953 by Clare Lallow's yard, in Cowes, of Burmese teak on oak frames. Maybe it was the exposed, varnished planking and frames in the forecabin that turned my head. As well as being beautiful her hull was black and, as the old saying has it, 'Black boats never go to Hell'.

That March we were both 32 years old, which made me relatively young and inexperienced, while *Inkoosaan* was getting quite old and tired. We ended that summer's voyage in Palma, Majorca. It had been eventful. Halyards broke, blocks parted and sails split. We sprang a leak in the middle of the English Channel and were nearly dismasted in Portugal, where a dredger ran a steel wire across the main channel at Figuera da Foz. But I was learning fast, or so I thought, and *Inkoosaan* was getting a new piece of kit in every port. At the end of our first summer together I put her to bed in the marina in Palma and went back to work in Muscat in the Oman.

Two years later, after a succession of big bills and poor workmanship and many frustrating trips to Majorca, I decided to bring *Inkoosaan* closer to home and arranged a mooring in Muscat harbour. In October 1987 we set off on the first leg of the journey, to the Egyptian city of Port Said at the entrance to the Suez Canal. A faulty alternator meant we lost engine power and couldn't charge the electrics. We sailed by paraffin lamp and sat out the frequent calms.

We left *Inkoosaan* at Port Said Yacht Club until the following March, when we began the second leg of the voyage to Muscat. I had an experienced crew via Crewseekers and two friends from Muscat, Steve and his girlfriend Maija.

Once we cleared the canal we sailed south in the sunshine. We passed the Straits of Ghulab and entered the Red Sea. Nothing broke, parted or split. Apart from some minor seasickness we were enjoying a great sail. But 100 miles further south we had a problem.

At 0500 on Friday, 18 March, one of the crew woke me to say we had lost steerage. The wheel felt okay, but there was a clunking sound under the cockpit floor and whichever way I turned the wheel, nothing happened. The clunk was the steering box moving under the floor.

As dawn broke, the seriousness of our position and the words of a shipwright in Palma came back to haunt me. I'd been warned that the steering gear box was fastened by coach or carriage bolts, which could work loose, causing a steering failure. I accepted his advice to change them for through-bolted fastenings with external pads, but I'd run out of time and money, having just spent a small fortune on painting the hull white and new cushion covers. But I always made sure that the wheel was lashed securely in port.

In Port Said, *Inkoosaan* had been moved while I was away and when I returned, the wheel was untied. How long had her rudder been flopping from side to side over the winter? Why hadn't I checked the bolts? Why hadn't I replaced them? Why hadn't I listened to the man in Palma? Self-blame and recrimination were overwhelming me.

We dropped the sails, put out a Mayday on the VHF radio, and being British, made a cup of tea to calm us while we discussed our situation. Wallowing in a lumpy sea and a 20 knot breeze, everyone was sick. I'd read a bit about rudderless sailing but never practised it. We were well offshore, 120 miles from the nearest feasible Egyptian port of Berenice. If we got close and contacted a local fishing boat I wondered what sort of salvage terms would be agreed and then reneged upon.

We had plenty of fuel, food and water, maybe we could fashion a jury rudder and get into Berenice ourselves for repairs? It was when I went below looking for tools (and inspiration) that I discovered we were sinking. Dashing back to the cockpit, it dawned on me that, of course, the rudder stock would sooner or later fall through its skin fitting, leaving a neat round hole in the hull. Grabbing an armful of tools and bungs, I yelled to Maija to change the Mayday from 'drifting without steerage' to 'sinking'. The tone of her voice turned from a calm monotone into a scream for help as I began unscrewing floorboards.

Half an hour later, bung in place and boat pumped dry, I sat in the cockpit trying to regain my breath and composure. We tried making a jury rudder by lashing boards to the end of the spinnaker pole and tying it to the stern. But the person on the end of the pole was lifted off his feet – you can't steer a 15 tonne yacht that way. While we were rethinking our strategy, a response to our Mayday came over the radio from the watch officer of an oil tanker. Although this was before the days of GPS, I had a satellite navigation system which gave a position every few hours from passing, rather than geo-stationary satellites. We were able to give our position to within a mile or so. The Scandinavian-owned VLCC (Very Large Crude Carrier) soon appeared on the horizon.

We took a bearing on the ship and told them where to look for us. Even with binoculars they couldn't see us, nor could they pick us up on their radar. They didn't even see the parachute distress flare we launched a little later. We used an orange smoke flare on the foredeck, but the breeze blew away the smoke. Finally, as they got closer, we launched another parachute flare, which they saw.

Less than an hour after we first saw her, the tanker was alongside.

She approached us to windward, so we were sheltered from the swell. They lowered a line and towed us gently at 3–4 knots about halfway along their hull. If they had stopped they would have turned to wind and the swell would have had us bouncing against her side.

In ballast, the ship's deck was about 60ft above us. A rope ladder was lowered and I climbed on deck to be met by an officer who invited me to join the captain on the bridge. It was about midday by now, seven hours since we lost steerage. I was grateful to be on the air-conditioned bridge, where the captain explained he was under orders to cruise at optimum speed for fuel efficiency to Khorfakkan, at the entrance to the Arabian Gulf, in the UAE.

He had not radioed the oil company he was chartered by for permission to stop, as he didn't expect it would be given. But he was willing to help us, providing we agreed not to discuss the matter with the media or draw attention to him or his ship. Obviously, I agreed.

The tanker's deck crane was rated for 15 tonnes and *Inkoosaan*, fully laden, probably weighed about 17 tonnes. The captain said he could spare another couple of hours if we wanted to try and lift her aboard and he would then 'drop us off' in Muscat, where we could pre-arrange a tow into port. I had friends there who could help.

Towing *Inkoosaan* behind the tanker at 14 knots for 2,000 miles was not an option. The alternatives were to cut her adrift (a potential danger to shipping), scuttle her, or use the ship's more powerful radio to arrange a tow to the nearest port in Egypt, still about 120 miles away. But would our new rescuers be able to find us? The tanker could not wait around. Would the rescuers claim the boat as salvage, or demand a very inflated fee? It was not a difficult decision to accept the captain's offer of a crane lift.

First a stairway was lowered down the side of the tanker's hull so we could get up and down to *Inkoosaan* more easily to transfer crew and personal possessions aboard the tanker. Then canvas lifting strops were lowered by the deck crane. We disconnected the fore and back-stays and pushed the strops into position under the hull – not easy as we were still being towed at 3–4 knots. The stairway was hoisted out of the way.

The crane took the strain and as the strops stretched and settled in position we realised we wouldn't have enough height to clear the tanker's rail. We lowered her again and rearranged things so the crane hook was lower. Satisfied it might work this time, we climbed back up the rope ladder to the deck. The heat and activity taking its toll, we were, by now, very tired. *Inkoosaan* was lifted clear of the water, the strops creaked and groaned as they took the load. The crane slowly lifted her up the side of the tanker. She swung and bumped her way higher until she was almost at the rail. Then, suddenly, one of the strops broke and *Inkoosaan* fell. Seventeen tonnes dropping 50ft makes quite a splash!

I felt numb – too exhausted to feel much emotion. Somehow I think I'd been expecting her to fall. As I looked down, I saw the cabin roof had collapsed, along with the mast, but she was still afloat and still attached alongside the tanker.

A brief and slightly bewildering conversation followed with the officer in charge of the lift. Did we carry any electronic emergency signalling devices that might need to be disabled to prevent a full-scale rescue alert? Did the liferaft have a hydrostatic release?

With *Inkoosaan* severely damaged and her hull full of water, the officer was explaining to me that I would have to scuttle her. A bosun's chair was hooked to the crane and I was lowered back into her cockpit. The saloon was flooded with several feet of water. As waves broke over the side, more water ran into the cabin. The yacht's freeboard was only a couple of feet now and, even in the lee of the tanker, waves were washing aboard. Finding and opening a seacock underwater was difficult and it was clear *Inkoosaan* would sink soon enough in open sea. I climbed back into the chair and gave the signal to be hoisted up.

We cut *Inkoosaan* adrift. Three years to the month since I had first set eyes on her in Carrickfergus, my love affair with her ended so abruptly. I walked to the stern rail and watched my boat slide past and recede into the waves as the tanker steamed back on course. Sitting low in the water and with no mast she was soon lost from view. My tears didn't help.

We spent a week on the tanker, eating, drinking, jogging round the deck and playing table tennis. The captain and his crew looked after us very well. The chief engineer gave me a tie with the shipping line's logo, which I've kept but never worn.

It was over ten years before I could easily discuss what happened.

The question I was asked most often was 'Did the insurance pay up?' which, thankfully, it did. But not before asking me to write to the tanker's owners holding them responsible for the loss – I refused.

The most important question should have been 'Was anybody hurt?' – which no one ever asks. Thanks to fate, kindness and the competence of the tanker's crew, no lives were lost or injuries sustained.

■ LESSONS LEARNED

- Never change the colour of your boat – it's considered unlucky.
- Always lock or secure the wheel or tiller with the rudder amidships when not in use.
- If you are planning to cruise long distances, or outside areas that are geared up to service sailing boats, you need to be as technically self-sufficient as possible. Make sure your boat is structurally and mechanically sound. A surveyor's report isn't enough. Get to know your boat's systems well. The steering gear can be a common cause of problems.
- Practise rudderless sailing. Do you have a plan for a jury steering system in case of a broken, lost or disabled rudder? Consider fitting a windvane self-steering unit and choose one that combines an emergency rudder, then you'll have a permanent spare.
- In the event of a Mayday situation, has your liferaft been serviced regularly? Do you have an EPIRB? Fit a decent radar reflector.
- Always keep a good lookout and fit an AIS receiver. They are cheap, and with ships travelling at up to 25 knots one of the best bits of safety kit you can have.
- Remember, a liferaft is a tiny dot in the ocean for any approaching rescue ship. Carry lots of distress flares or a Very pistol and cartridges.

BLUEWATER CASTAWAYS

Yacht	*Arcularius V* (35ft US Kaiser Gale Force loop)
Skipper	Tom Follett
Crew	Jack and Lella Gush
Bound from	Playa Blanca, Lanzarote Island in the Canary Island to Fort Lauderdale, Florida
Date of loss	2 February 1986
Position	off Great Inagua in the outer Bahama group of islands

Jack Gush tells the story.

IT WAS A RESTLESS SORT of night. For some reason, which I could not define, I had a strong premonition that all was not well. Twice during Lella's watch from 0400 to 0600 I got up, went to the cockpit and asked her if she was steering the courses Tom had given her.

Tom Follett, our American skipper, claimed to be familiar with the area and had laid off a series of courses to take us from Ambergris Cay in the outer Bahamas, round the southern limit of the vast Caicos Bank and then north-west to Acklins Island, a passage of 200 miles.

We were delivering *Arcularius V*, a 35ft sloop, from Vilamoura in Portugal to Fort Lauderdale, Florida, and were now nearing the end of what had been a harmonious and successful voyage.

The three of us were following our customary night watch routine, two on and four off. Normally, I had only to put my head to the pillow to fall into a deep and dreamless sleep. But that night sleep would not come. Before we set sail from the shelter of Ambergris Cay, Tom had spent a long time poring over the chart. The islands along our route were low-lying and the currents between them strong and unpredictable. In those days, 1986, there was no GPS, and even if there had been Tom certainly wouldn't have had one. Tom had his chart, his compass and his sextant – his wrist watch was his chronometer.

Tom was short, thick-set, with cropped grey hair, a smattering of white stubble and very blue eyes – which readily took on a mischievous twinkle.

He was a celebrated single-hander and had made several solo Atlantic crossings, including taking part in the 1968 Ostar (Observer Singlehanded Transatlantic Race (see footnote), in which he came third. It was typical of Tom that he sailed in one of Dick Newick's somewhat unconventional proas. He took the longer southern route and came third. Tom was Spartan – to say the least.

Lella and I (in our late fifties) were amateurs. We planned one day to make an ocean voyages of our own. We had signed on with Tom to get further experience and also because he had misled us over the size of *Arcularius V*. We had crossed the Atlantic with him in his own boat, a 28ft Hereshoff, again with just a chart, a sextant and Tom's wrist watch, and he knew we had had enough of small boat sailing. This time, in his invitation to join as crew, he wrote that the *Arcularius* was a 53ft sloop – a luxurious yacht, he said: but when we got to Playa Blanca, Lanzarote, we found that she was only 35 ft.

'What happened?' I asked Tom.

The mischievous twinkle appeared. 'I reversed the digits,' he replied. 'I had to; I knew you wouldn't come otherwise...'

Towards the early hours I must have dozed off. It seemed to me that I had hardly slept at all when there was a tremendous crash and a jolt from underneath that shook the yacht from truck to keelson. Then, to my relief, she seemed to sail on, but only to strike again and yet again.

As I struggled up, I could hear Lella calling for Tom from the cockpit and by the time I came into the saloon from the forward cabin his stubby figure was ahead of me, mounting the companionway steps. By this time the yacht had come to rest on her beam ends. As I climbed into the cockpit, I could hear the roar of the breaking seas. Lella had been thrown about and was bruised but not injured. The next wave sent spray all over us and the yacht lifted and then pounded, but she had stopped driving across the reef, or whatever we had hit.

The time was 0520. The moon had gone down and the night was pitch black. Tom discovered that on our lee side, where the stanchions were half awash, we were in 2ft of water. Breaking seas hit hard on the weather side of the yacht and broke over us into the cockpit. We were soon drenched, but at least the water was warm.

We were not sure what we had hit or where we were, and it was too dark to see anything. So we went below to await daylight and assess our situation. The yacht still lifted and pounded in an alarming manner, but more than half an hour was to pass before we heard the ominous cracking and splitting of the glass fibre hull. Water then started to trickle in and was soon slopping round our feet.

In the meantime, we drank some rum and sent out a Mayday on the VHF radio, though we knew we were in a sparsely populated area and were certain our call would go unanswered.

As I perched as best I could on the upper side of the saloon in dripping oilskins, sipping the rum, I was overcome by a feeling of deep disappointment. What had been a happy, harmonious voyage had ended in a shambles. Cushions, clothes, bedding and books had tumbled onto the lee side, and already Tom's bunk and much of his gear was half under water. Lella was up forward, attempting to pack our clothes into a large red canvas bag. As soon as she opened a locker on the upper side, everything fell out on top of her; the lower side was already under water.

At the first glimpse of light, Tom and I were in the cockpit straining our eyes shorewards. Gradually we could make out the land, low-lying and sandy, about 300 yards away. We decided it must be one of the Inaguas, either Great or Little Inagua, two islands that form part of the outer Bahama group. We were on a reef on which the seas were breaking heavily. The Trade Wind was blowing steadily at 20 knots. The reef was insufficient to give much of a lee and the sea inside it was choppy.

Tom climbed gingerly over the lee rail and stood up to his thighs in the water. He decided, unwisely I thought, to try to wade ashore and make a reconnaissance. I insisted on putting a line round his waist and paying out as he went. This was just as well, for after a few yards he disappeared with the waves over his head. A raised hand appeared, which I took to be the signal to haul him back to the comparative safety of the yacht. Lella had always been unable to swim, perhaps due to negative buoyancy.

In all her years of sailing Lella has never learnt to swim, so it was decided that Tom should now row her ashore to terra firma in our inflatable. We could see that there was a long, sandy beach running off to the south, backed by low scrub and stunted palm trees. Before Tom left, we inflated our six-man liferaft and attached it to a stanchion that was not quite under water.

While Tom was away, I began to gather up the gear and provisions we would need as castaways, and load them into the liferaft. At the angle at which the yacht lay, buffeted by the seas, moving around was something of an acrobatic feat and progress was slow and wet. I was concerned only with our immediate future. I collected tins of food, two 25-litre jerry cans of fresh water, a sail to serve as a tent, an awning as a groundsheet, a small camping stove, spare gas containers, plenty of lines, a ball of twine and an axe. I did not forget the tin opener, the cutlery, a sharp knife, matches, mugs, loo paper, soap, the binoculars, a torch, a few tools and some fishing gear. But I discovered later that I left behind my wallet, containing money and credit cards, though more than once my hand must have been within inches of it. Subconsciously, I must have been aware that for the time being other things were of more pressing importance.

Tom returned after a hard row against wind and sea. I could see he was grey with fatigue. We loaded the bag Lella had thoughtfully packed into the liferaft. The interior of the yacht was now chaotic. The water was over the batteries, which were giving off acrid fumes. We sloshed about and gathered up our documents: the ship's papers, insurance policy and our passports.

We attached the laden liferaft to the inflatable with a short line.

By the time we were ready to cast off, the inflatable dinghy was full of water from the spray that came right over the yacht, but we climbed in and, while Tom rowed, I bailed with a saucepan. Downwind it was relatively easy going.

On the beach we took stock of our situation. It was now daylight and we found we were on the east side of Great Inagua. The island's northern extremity, a low sandy headland, was only a few hundred yards away. The green scrub and the sprinkling of stunted palms covered the island as far as the eye could see. Just north of us, the beach ran into rocks that continued as far as the headland. The reef ran roughly north-south, parallel to the beach, about 300 yards offshore. Inside the reef were a number of nasty-looking coral heads, which became more prominent at Low Water.

We were clearly miles from anywhere, in a lonely sea-area, and it might be days before we were rescued. We began to carry the gear from the liferaft up to the scrub and organise a camp. The beach was littered with exactly the kind of bamboo poles that were needed to make the framework of a tent. The ball of twine came in handy for the lashings and the lines became guys for the tent poles.

Finally, we pulled the liferaft up to higher ground, from where we hoped its orange canopy might be spotted by a passing vessel. In it we left our scant emergency gear: a few flares, a torch and two small cans of water. The bushes round the tent soon became decorated with our wet, bedraggled clothing. At about noon we crowded into the tent to get out of the heat. I made a salad with a few bits and pieces, but none of it was eaten. We each had a drink of water and began to discuss our situation.

The island of Great Inagua is pear-shaped and is about 65 miles long. There is one settlement, Matthew Town, at its southern end, near extensive saltings. We were at the northern end, the tip of the pear. The rest of the island is uninhabited. None of us was enthusiastic about a 60-mile walk through the prickly scrub, carrying a load of provisions. The alternatives were to try to get to Matthew Town in the inflatable, or stay where we were in the camp. I seemed to remember reading somewhere that as a general rule castaways are better off to remain encamped in one place and try to attract attention.

In the afternoon, Tom rowed out to the yacht, still on the reef, to get our charts to help make a better assessment of our position. Lella and I set off with binoculars to reconnoitre our immediate surroundings and walked up to the sandy headland. We could see where the reef petered out at the point. Had our course been 50 yards to the east, we would have cleared both reef and headland and sailed between the two Inaguas. We could see Little Inagua about five miles away, also uninhabited. A current in the night setting strongly to the south-west had put us several miles off course.

We sat down and minutely scanned the interior through the binoculars for any sign of human activity, however small. About two miles away rotting trees protruded at crazy angles from a big lake or swamp, which we judged to be salt water, or at least brackish. As we walked slowly back to the camp we came across some dung, dried out but not that old. But what sort of animal? We have never before studied dung with such keen interest.

Our first night in the camp was a misery. Tom, perhaps out of respect for our privacy, chose not to sleep in the tent, but under the bushes. Lella and I lay down in our oilskins using our other clothes as a makeshift pillow. We had thought that because the ground was sandy it would be soft, or at least yielding, but we soon found it as hard as concrete. The wind got up and swung to the north-east, so that the tent became a wind tunnel and the sail flapped noisily. The palm fronds rustled, and more than once I thought of the dung and the wild animals that must be somewhere about. Two or three times in the night I got up and went down to the beach. I peered seawards, but there were no lights, only darkness and wind.

At dawn I found Tom standing above the beach, gazing out to sea. He had not slept either. The yacht now lay over, her mast in the water. The previous afternoon, Tom had found the cabin flooded and had been unable to rescue our charts. It looked as if we would not salvage much more from the yacht, though things that floated might get washed ashore. The tide was out and the beach was devoid of foot-prints. A flock of sandpipers, unafraid of humans, tripped uncon-cernedly across the sand, only feet away from us.

We made coffee on the tiny stove and then moved the tent. This time we were more thorough. We chose a sheltered hollow, uprooted all the bushes and stacked them as a windbreaker and wild animal fence. We gathered palm fronds and made a mattress of them, several inches thick. We collected driftwood and made a galley protected from the wind, and with shade for our tins of food.

We calculated we had food for at least 20 days, plus 40 litres of water, which we intended to ration with great care. Though there were probably animals about, we could not count on finding fresh water.

In the afternoon I donned mask and flippers, hoping there were no sharks about. I swam lazily among the coral heads, some with rusty antlers. There were mounds of mustard-coloured brain coral 3 feet high; waving fans, long-spined urchins and dead men's fingers – all in a confusion of colour. And there were fish everywhere. We were not likely to die of starvation, I thought, as I swam among them. I had no gun and began to ponder the question of catching them. We had a few hooks and we had our dinghy, or perhaps I could fashion a spear.

That evening, we cooked ourselves a decent meal: a tin of stew and a tin of sweetcorn. Except for our torches, which we were anxious to conserve, we had no form of lighting, so before it got dark, at about 1900, the meal had to be cooked and eaten. It was not clear whether it was supper or high tea. We washed it down with sips of water.

After breakfast the next morning Tom went for a walk to explore to the south, and I set about making further improvements to the camp. Lella later went to the beach to wash the dishes in the sea. Suddenly, I heard her shouting, 'There's a ship, there's a ship!'

As I ran, it seemed an incredible stroke of good fortune that a vessel had come into these waters so soon.

But sure enough, there she was, about 2 miles away to the south, outside the reef, the black shape of a small ship. Lella ran to our tent and came back with a mirror. I placed her on the beach a few yards away, facing the sea, so that the ship appeared to me to sit on the top of her head. I trained the mirror until the flash fell on her back and then moved it up to the top of her head, and then flashed it repeatedly up and down. After a couple of minutes I stopped and we waited, straining our eyes for any sign of response. Tom had walked along the beach in that direction. Would they see him?

'It's going further away,' Lella said, despair in her voice. I tried to line up the distant boat with some part of the reef to discern which way it was moving, but without a definite result.

I started flashing the mirror again. Watching carefully, I noticed that the ship was approaching. For the moment I said nothing to Lella. I wanted to be certain.

Then everything seemed to happen at once. We saw Tom striding back along the beach, and a small wooden boat appeared inside the reef, powered by an outboard, with two men in it, moving quickly towards us. We stared in disbelief.

Tom and the men in the boat arrived at about the same time. The two men, one inky black and the other brown, both dressed in tattered shorts, spoke Spanish; a language with which we have no difficulty.

They explained that they were from the Dominican Republic, fishing illegally in these waters. They had seen Tom on his walk and our signals, but had come to explain that they could not help us. If caught by the Bahamas police they would go to prison. The brown one stressed this by crossing his wrists, as if handcuffed. But surely, we replied, they were not going to leave us on the beach, two men and a woman, to die of thirst.

They spoke of their poverty. They had not yet started fishing. In a few days time, with their catch, if they were lucky, they would return to Santa Domingo. They were sorry, they could not help us.

Could they take just one of us to Matthew Town, we asked. It was a long way off, they answered. They would lose fishing time. We replied that we would be prepared to pay their expenses.

I saw them glance towards the reef and our stricken yacht, as if to assess our financial standing. They then moved away, towards the bow of their boat, and conferred among themselves. After a few minutes they came up with their figure – 5,000 US dollars.

We received this figure in stony silence. The wavelets slapped gently against our legs. I think that all of us were aware that we were about to bargain in earnest, perhaps for our lives, but we were not going to pay a ridiculous price. We put our heads together at the stern of the boat.

Our offer was for them to take Tom to within a few miles of Matthew Town at night and land him on the beach. For this we were prepared to pay 200 dollars. They conferred among themselves for quite some time, and eventually came up with a figure of 500 dollars, a tenth of their original asking price, and as I pointed out to Tom, not a bad figure when worked out on a per person basis.

Tom went back to the camp to get ready. Lella and I stayed talking to the fishermen. We thought it wisest not to let them see our stores. I asked them about the wild animals. There were wild donkeys, they told us, hundreds of them, and they could be aggressive. We ought to watch out for them, they said. There were also wild cattle and boar.

Tom returned and we said goodbye, and they took him out, through the reef, to where their fishing boat lay rolling horribly.

Left to ourselves, Lella and I settled down to camp life. We continued to ration ourselves as regards both food and water. As I pointed out to Lella, it was not certain when, or if, Tom would return. The fishermen might not take him to Matthew Town; they might take him to Santa Domingo, in which case he would be weeks getting back to us. Or they might suspect that he had more than 500 dollars on him, which he had, cut his throat and toss him overboard.

In the days that followed there was plenty to do. Again we improved the camp and thickened up the surrounding prickly bushes, our wild donkey defence. We left the inflatable handy on the beach in case the donkeys came in force; in which case we planned to row out a short distance, on the assumption that they could not swim.

The mattress of palm fronds was now over a foot thick and was, Lella declared, as comfortable as our mattress at home. But often I could not sleep. This may have been because, without lighting, we went to bed so early. But I would lie awake, listening to the rustling palms, and a plan began to form in my mind to get us out of our predicament if Tom failed to return.

This plan entailed cutting a path through the scrub and carrying the dinghy to the lee side of the island, where the sea was flat calm. This would take Lella and I some time, perhaps two or three days, but we could cover the distance in stages, returning to the camp every evening. We could then sail down the 70 miles to Matthew Town on lee side, anchoring or beaching the boat at night.

Our inflatable was a Tinker and could be sailed, except that its centreboard, mast, and sail were under water in *Arcularius V*. But its rudder and tiller unit had, by a stroke of luck, already been washed ashore. It would not be too difficult to make a centreboard, and, with the bamboos lying around, a mast.

Beach-combing soon became an important part of our daily routine. Early every morning and last thing before our evening meal, we carefully searched the beach, and were usually rewarded for our pains. One day we found a box of a dozen eggs, which we had bought in the supermarket in San Juan, Puerto Rico – only two eggs were broken. Another time it was an almost full bottle of good quality

Spanish olive oil, which we had transported from the Canary Islands. These were important additions to our stores.

And one evening I found one of our sails in a bag, half buried in the sand. It was *Arcularius*'s cruising chute and was of very light material, exactly what we wanted. Our escape plan in the dinghy was now beginning to materialise. I rather fancied the idea of sailing into the harbour at Matthew Town, two castaways who had struggled back to civilisation on their own initiative.

Though we did not put our plan into effect for the moment, while we waited for Tom, the idea of it buoyed our morale and we discussed it endlessly. However, it was not to be. Three days later, early in the morning, Lella sighted a vessel. This time she walked calmly into the camp and said matter-of-factly, 'There's a white boat of some sort, lying off the headland.'

We took the binoculars and hurried along the now well-worn path. The binoculars were not necessary. A small boat had already come through the reef on the lee side of the headland, and the several people in it were now landing. Among them we could see Tom's white-haired head.

Soon the police, armed with hefty-looking rifles, were pushing through the scrub towards us, like an assault force. Some of them were exceptionally tall and fit-looking. The local chief of police, we were to find, was among them. They were all black.

We led them to the camp where, with tongue in cheek, we said, 'Coffee, gentlemen?' To our pleasure, our invitation was readily accepted.

When the coffee was drunk, they dismantled our camp and all our gear, now quite a considerable amount, was carried off, balanced on their heads or brawny shoulders. We did not quite realise that we were never to see most of it again.

Tom, it turned out, had not been taken to Matthew Town. The fishermen had put him ashore about 10 miles north of it, and in the night he had walked along the beach, stumbling over rocks and removing mosquitoes from his face in handfuls.

We were loaded into the small boat, which then headed towards the reef under the power of its big outboard. The breaks in the reef were, I could see, shallow and the sea was breaking heavily on them. I covered our cameras and warned Lella to hold on. We hit the gap just as a sea broke. It swept us from stern to stern and half filled the boat, to the delight of the police.

The rescue boat was called *Foxy Lady* and was a typical flybridge, sport-fishing boat, though in filthy condition. On the way to Matthew Town the skipper stopped and let her drift. With two of the police he jumped into the small boat, having first tossed in their underwater fishing gear. They zoomed off towards a dazzling beach about a mile away, and half an hour later, when they returned, in the bottom of the boat were two large lobsters and about five kilos of fish.

Once cleaned, scaled and chopped up the lot went into a blackened pot, along with tomatoes, peppers, potatoes and spices. One of the policemen, the smallest one, was cook. The result was the most delicious bouillabaisse I have ever eaten. Afterwards, sitting in the sun, watching the island slip lazily by, knowing we would soon come to Matthew Town, it was difficult to stay awake.

AUTHOR'S FOOTNOTE

Tom Follett, the skipper, was in his sixties and a celebrated single-handed sailor who came a remarkable third in the 1968 OSTAR (Observer Single-handed Transatlantic Race from Plymouth, England, to Newport Rhode Island, USA) in *Cheers*, a 40ft LOA proa. She was designed by the multihull guru Dick Newick. Tom's time across the Atlantic was 27 days and 13 minutes. He later told Jack Gush that, having passed the race's pre-start scrutiny checks, he pumped his water tank dry to save weight and be faster!

Jack recalls: 'We elected to sail with Tom having been told *Arcularius* was 53ft LOA. But when we got to the Canaries to start the trip, we found that *Arcularius* was 35ft. Tom explained that he had reversed the digits to make sure we would come!'

In Great Inagua, the local chief of police wrote the following report. (Jack Gush helped him a little) 'TO WHOM IT MAY CONCERN: I certify that on 3 February 1986, at Matthew Town, Great Inagua, Captain Thomas Follett, who had been rescued by fishermen, reported to me that the yacht *Arcularius V* had struck a reef and sunk at the north-east extremity of this island, 60 miles from Matthew Town and uninhabited.

He further reported that the crew of the yacht, Mr John B Gush and Mrs Lella Gush were in a makeshift camp near the sunken vessel.

On 5 February 1986, with two of my policeman, I rescued Mr and Mrs Gush and brought them safely to Matthew Town in the boat *Foxy Lady*.

They reported that they had lost nearly all their personal possessions in the sea. In my opinion, the yacht is a total loss and these possessions will never be recovered.'

FOOTNOTE

Jack Gush's first cautious sailing was some 45 years ago in the Mediterranean. Later, with his wife, Lella, the couple 'sold up and sailed... with not one regret'. They sailed thousands of miles in their own 43ft steel cutter-rigged sloop, *Jackella*. They left Gibraltar in 1988, and sailed, via the Canaries, to the Gambia, Brazil and the Caribbean islands, before transiting the Panama Canal into the Pacific. Here they 'dawdled' across the ocean, exploring the Galapagos, Marquesas, Tahiti, and other islands, before arriving in the Bay of Islands, New Zealand, in 1990. Later they sailed to Australia and lived ashore for some years in Tasmania. The couple now live in Spain and have downsized to a smaller yacht.

■ LESSONS LEARNED

- The inescapable lesson learned is never to sail at night in any area of low-lying coral reefs.
- That night, in that area, the crew of *Arcularius* should not have weighed anchor and set sail. A dark moonless night with low lying islands, (somewhat like the Tuamotu islands in the Pacific, known as 'the Dangerous Archipelago'), combined with strong unpredictable currents proved to be a treacherous mix. But on this long delivery they were already considerably behind schedule and the skipper, Tom, was anxious to move on.

- Today, of course, with navigation by GPS, there would not have been a problem. Tom laid off his courses with considerable care, and allowed for the current. They were hand-steering, two hours on, two off, and perhaps they weren't always bang on course. As it was, they were unlucky and just hit the tip of Great Inagua: had they been 200 yards to the east they would have been in safe water.

three

STORM SURVIVORS

Yacht	*Rushcutter* (30ft Harmonic class sloop)
Skipper	Anthony Lealand
Crew	Annette Wilde
Bound from	Wellington, New Zealand to Sydney, Australia
Date of loss	19 April 1978
Position	190 miles W of Auckland, New Zealand

Annette Wilde and Anthony Lealand, both from Christchurch, New Zealand, had undertaken the task of delivering the 30ft Rushcutter, *a boat of the Harmonic class, to Sydney for her owner. They had examined her in Wellington and considered it was a reasonable proposition to sail her the 1,200 miles across the Tasman Sea. Anthony Lealand tells the story:*

THE DISASTER REALLY STARTED WHEN we spent ten days waiting around for a chart, which the Post Office lost, and our beacon battery, already a year on order. When the new battery arrived, our beacon refused to light its test lamp, but after a day of tests and phone calls to Auckland it was decided that the beacon worked, although the test lamp was at fault. I made a little test unit to take with us for future checks, and this was heat-sealed in polythene bags along with our over-age batteries which still tested 'good'.

We had stripped our own yacht *Valya* of all her navigational equipment, our sailing necessities, and a good selection of tools, and with this ponderous load of excess baggage we flew to Wellington on 3 April, leaving a friend to live in our house, water our cat and feed our plants.

Rushcutter had not been sailed seriously for a year, so right away we had a year's accumulation of rust and stiffness to set to rights. Owner Charles Troup had left us a detailed list of things he knew of to attend to and, with what we considered necessary, it was 11 days before we were ready to clear.

We started with a morning's work cleaning out a bilge full of engine oil, dropped by a recently broken oil line. I regarded this as very important for there was no depth to her bilge and it would need only a splash below to have the whole slimy lot swilling around above the cabin sole.

At the masthead I found the reason for the jib halyards needing a winch even to move them. Severe corrosion of the alloy sheaves was bulging the $^3/_{16}$-inch stainless sheave box. To remove the sheaves was difficult as the mast fabricator had bolted the sheave pin in and then welded on mounting flanges, completely blocking the pin's removal.

I did not understand the reason for the severe corrosion until we found the alloy sheave had a bronze bearing. Aluminium in contact with bronze and salt water is severely corroded – a fact well known since 1895 when *Defender*, an America's Cup yacht, was built with bronze hull and aluminium topside plating. She was broken up after six years, so severe was the action.

Our next surprise was to find the available replacements constructed in the same way. Oh well, we greased them well and considered that they would last the two weeks to Australia.

A day at Shelly Bay slipway saw *Rushcutter* fitted with ply dead-lights and a spare rudder. The shipwrights and manager took an interest in the work and we were able to get through a long list of minor items, leaving finally with a big handful of assorted nails and a spare sheet of ply for luck.

We had lashed down the liferaft aft in the cockpit. Over this on a board, athwartships, was our new Sestrel compass. The board was held by headless screws so it could be pulled away should we want to get at the liferaft. *Valya*'s chronometer seemed to like its new lodgings, and for the first time in its life settled to a steady rate. We were in some difficulty over our emergency aerial, a 13ft-long helical whip we had made in Christchurch. This had been lost in transit, but Ted (Annette's brother) brought it down just in time for our safety inspector's visit.

Wellington Customs were kind enough to come to the marina to issue our clearance, which made departure easy. It is a nuisance to have to clear from some foul commercial berth with piles a boat length apart.

As we beat out of Wellington, we marvelled at the improvement in the mast, now solidly wedged. Her mast, stepped through the deck, had been rubber wedged on our sail some days before, and shook about in a lively manner. Of course the solid wedges now rendered the bendy mast gear inoperative but did mean we no longer had 6ft of unstayed mast thrashing about below.

We were perhaps an hour late catching the tide at Sinclair Head, but with full main, a fresh southerly, and an indicated 8 knots, we felt more than happy. That is till I went below and found all our clothes, bunks and sleeping bags sodden. In the beat out of Wellington the deck joints of the inboard chain plates had obviously hosed water everywhere. It continued to leak even now, running downwind. Murmuring rude words I climbed into the pipe berth, still in my waterproofs, which we were to wear till rescued. This was my first acquaintance with a pipe berth, and I found it a damn good bunk, even though *Rushcutter*'s were a little narrow.

Annette was tight-lipped about the wet below. She feels that boats with deck leaks just ought not to be allowed. I suppose we were rather spoiled on *Valya* with no deck leaks and a diesel heating stove to dry our gear while off watch.

Rushcutter hustled on, a delight to sail. Occasionally, the full quarters would catch on a wave, but she needed no more than a firm hand to bring her back. There was no sign of loss of control.

By now life below was pretty foul. The main hatch was a cunning contrivance of the cabinetmaker's art, for surely no shipwright could have made it. Every slosh that landed on it was delivered below by the hatch's forward slope to dribble across the deckhead, fill galley lockers, soak the charts and eventually wipe out the beacon receiver. What the hell, the sailing was good!

On Sunday, *Rushcutter* was changed to cutter rig, using the storm jib as a staysail. The sheet from this ran through roller-bearing blocks to the tiller's windward side and was balanced by a red rubber tube from leeward. She steered herself well, though as the wind drew aft, the staysail would have to be backed. Self-steering by this method seems to have a lot in its favour, not least of which is rapidly learning about the balance and steering of the boat. It will not, of course, put you about or hold you on a course with an unbalanced rig while you change sail. But it is very powerful with a breeze in the open sea.

Monday night saw a rising easterly wind which soon had us clearing the deck of lashed-down sails and, for the caution of it, putting the deepest reef in the main. Just as well, for the easterly had us swishing along in perfect control, dodging breaking seas in the confused turmoil that the rapidly rising wind caused. *Rushcutter* sometimes banged solidly up forward, but she had thumped more heavily beating out of Wellington, so we felt no worry.

Charles had mentioned he felt it unwise to let her thump, but to reduce sail when we had such good control seemed a pity. We had good visibility with a near full moon behind clouds. By the time the moon was setting the wind was dropping, which was just as well for it is less funny to dodge seas in the darkness.

By dawn the wind was light and the seas pleasantly regular. We jilled along quietly that day, doing a lot of sleeping but confident that *Rushcutter* was more boat than she perhaps looked. The cabin was pleasantly light too, for as the easterly had risen I had whipped out the deadlights and spiked them on with 3-inch roofing nails. It seemed a little dramatic and I wondered how I was going to explain the splinters to Charles.

The seas that came rolling in from the south late that day had me thinking we needed even less sail than the deep-reefed main. As the trysail had only a little less area than the main reefed, I hanked on the storm jib. This proved a dubious arrangement. Hanked on the topmast stay, and so having a very long sheet, it vibrated badly, shaking the whole rig, and unless the wind was taken a long way round on the quarter, it would bang from tack to tack with great wrenching thumps.

But now the wind was so strong that we were overpowered and broaching badly on the crests. The storm jib came down, leaving us still overpowered by the yacht's windage alone on the crests but dead and down to 3–4 knots in the troughs. Big seas filled the cockpit. We had never taken serious water from astern into a cockpit before, but, as other commentators have said, in the conditions in which it comes aboard, it is thrown out just as quickly. Which was just as well, for *Rushcutter* had a large cockpit.

By midnight I was worried. The wind was from the south and steady storm force, but seas came from WSW and SE as well. They were each about 20ft high with the top 6 feet breaking, which they did fairly frequently. *Rushcutter* was piggishly slow to answer in the troughs but a handful on the crests.

Around 0130 on Wednesday morning I asked Annette to send out a PAN PAN call saying that if we did not call up within 24 hours it could be presumed we were in trouble. Unfortunately, it was just past the silence period. Indeed, the set did not load up well, no doubt as a result of the salt water sloshing over the deck, the aerial lead-in, and the lower backstay insulator. At 0140, as *Rushcutter* slid off the back of a southerly wave, broaching a little to port, from the port beam came a classic breaker. *Rushcutter*, dead in the water, would not turn and to my surprise rolled right over. I came up on her port side, my lifeline taut at water level, to see her floating high and very stable upside-down. My lifeline was short to avoid being flung some distance and injured. Now as *Rushcutter* settled I was slowly spending more time under water and as my knife had been flung from around my neck, I knew that shortly I would drown. I rapped on the hull for Annette but heard no reply. Just previously, Annette had been contemplating a tedious wait for a silence period when *Rushcutter* started pouring the contents of the lockers over her and she saw the whole cabin slowly revolve around her. Water gushed in the gap between the washboards and hatch slide, and perhaps through the ventilator and where the mast was.

She scrabbled at the hatch trying to open it and get out, but the water was soon over her head as she bent to it. Hearing my rapping she saw the water rolling about, and with a quick understanding of the situation blundered back and forth in time with the water, until a good roll built up. *Rushcutter* came up so fast I did not know what had happened until I found myself in the cockpit roaring for a knife to release myself from the tangle of sheets, halyards and safety harness. Annette was similarly yelling for me to open the hatch and let her out. In her hand was the carving knife which had jammed the hatch.

We turned to find the mast gone at deck level, about 2 feet of water below, and the liferaft in its slick glassfibre case surging alongside.

It was agreed in an instant not to waste time getting it on board, for it was a six-man raft weighing well over 100lb, and I would have had to go into the water to get a line securely around it. At any instant we expected to be slammed again; *Rushcutter*'s stability and self-righting were seriously in doubt now she had taken so much water below.

We pulled yards of string from the liferaft, till it popped open and was full in an instant. Annette leapt in gratefully, for although totally in control she had been thoroughly freaked when trapped below. I cut free our water bottles and bag of emergency gear, passing these to Annette, who lashed them into the liferaft. One bottle had been holed, and so I left it. There was another below but the boom of a nearby sea had me in the raft in an instant. The line was cut, *Rushcutter* went behind a wave and we did not see her again.

Inside the raft we had to shout to make ourselves heard, for the canopy flogged with an insane rage. Its door, something one would hesitate to fit to a pup tent, could not be closed properly, as the foolish, stiff plastic domes just kept popping open.

Then a great crushing roar slammed us into numbness. The raft was very full of water, on its side, and the door torn. By moving our weight inside we righted her and then bailed, using a cut-open gallon water bottle. We had poured its contents into the 5-gallon bottle, which was not completely full, purposely so that it would be easy to handle and float.

We had just finished stabbing holes and lashing the door shut when we were hit again. This time the canopy burst open on the opposite side. Again we bailed, stabbed holes and lashed, and again we went over.

This time the raft stayed upside-down. Annette did not know where she was and I was spluttering in the little air under the raft trying to get my arm out of one of the rope handles. Annette decided which way was up and told me to cut the rope. The water-activated light inside the raft must have been obscured by the torn canopy. Without this light we would have been totally lost in the black tangle and drowned blindly.

Diving outside the raft, I did not think of anything tied to that rope. It must have been very dark now for I did not see the raft's water-ballast bags whose existence I knew of. Instead, I clawed my way on to the bottom, holding handfuls of the rubber, put my feet in the girdling rope and threw myself backwards. Annette slid in as the raft surfaced, awash, and bailed till I could be dragged aboard safely. At this stage the canopy had pulled away completely from the raft, the glue line having failed. We were not flipped again, just filled by roaring seas. Perhaps the loss of the canopy contributed to our stability.

Dawn brought us the sight of huge seas marching from the south, and still small steep cross-seas making crests tumble and break. With light we felt we had come out of a minute-to-minute survival situation, and started to make things shipshape. It was then I saw our 5 gallons of water had gone, cut away by me when I freed my arm.

With our weight at one side of the raft, it took up an attitude with the remains of the door side of the canopy across the wind. We, in the lee of this, had tightened up all our belts and buckles and with an aluminised plastic foil blanket around us were reasonably warm.

It was impossible to keep the raft dry; sloshes and occasional big seas came on board, slamming the canopy tube down on us. I had the beacon out, tied to my wrist, and we kept a constant lookout for breaking seas. I folded the aerial at any hint of one, as aerial length is critical for transmission of a signal. I doubt that we could have survived the night had we been alone, or with anyone else but each other. There were so many occasions when we had to know exactly what the other was doing without even talking or with just a few brief words.

We sat in silence, from time to time bailing as seas hit, and licking the salt splashes off the beacon's aerial insulator. From time to time the wind would rise, and in an instant the wavetops would be hissing and breaking. Around 1000 hrs (a guess, for we had no watch), I saw a vapour trail overhead. Annette, who had lost her glasses, could only just see it. It cheered us greatly.

Lunch was tinned peaches. And I can thoroughly recommend them. Easy to swallow, sweet and wet. Later we tried a lifeboat biscuit. Scientifically designed they may be with no protein and high in calories, but they are such a foul brew, forming a great sticky glob in our mouths, that we gave up eating them.

Early that evening I snapped out of a doze to see a flashing red light above us in the sky. But by the time I had a red parachute flare in my hand, I could not see it. Surely I had seen it? Perhaps I had seen a star scintillate strongly. Some time later Annette woke me to point out another flashing red. If she, without glasses, could see it, I was convinced, and I had two parachute flares fired before I realised the plane could be 20–30 miles away as it was fairly low on the horizon.

Annette slept now and I held the beacon as high and as far out as I could, keeping it away from the salty wet canopy which would absorb the signal. Every time the tattered canopy started to shiver with a rise in the wind we both felt a sick apprehension that it would continue to rise, treating us to another night of breaking seas.

Dawn brought considerable cheer to Annette for she recognised a stable Tasman sky. It also brought me water, which I was craving. We had caught a little water in the showers the previous day, about a quarter cup each. Most had been wasted in waiting for the salt to be rinsed off the canopy. Torn and tied as the half left was, it caught water rather well.

Anyway we punctured the first of our 6-pint tins of water, drank, and then spent about half an hour devising a way of holding the rest so it did not spill. The beacon we lashed to the canopy support tube.

I had been having hallucinations for some time and we decided that I was dehydrated, not because of lack of water but because of all the salt I had drunk while admiring *Rushcutter*'s underwater sections.

We had not drunk much in the last couple of days on *Rushcutter*, for it had really been too rough to bother making the innumerable cups of tea I normally fill my day with. So it was with the measured precision of a drunk that I carefully knelt up to listen to a plane sound I heard. I decided it was the wind.

Fish had been bumping under the raft, so we set to trailing a lure and then pulling it in with inviting tugs. From time to time I checked the beacon's output with our tester, finding the needle still flicking high. I had to put a strong conscious effort into ignoring flaring red and blue blobs which crossed my vision. Even the shiny black raft floor was bad to look at, reflecting a writhing image of the sky.

Annette was still her quiet self, not even very hungry or thirsty. Our next can of peaches was again a winner, but the fishing was not going too well. We could not have eaten the fish had we caught it, for fish is very high in protein, needing lots of water to digest. We were going to just suck the juices out for water. It was just when the sea around the raft was starting to resemble a marine safari, for there were so many fish, that Annette heard the low throaty roar of a real piston and propeller aeroplane. We could not see him, low though he was, because of the cloud and blinding sun, and after our last waste of flares we were excessively cautious. Then, sighting the Orion, we had smoke and parachute flares ready for his next run.

Leaving us marked with a sonar buoy and smoke candles, the Orion went to fetch a Japanese refrigerated freighter, the *Toyu Maru*, which was 20 miles off. They were alongside us in an hour and a quarter, crossing very close upwind of us, with a ladder and boarding nets out. The raft leapt over the bow wave, leaving us wishing we had lifejackets for this last bit. I grabbed a thrown monkey's fist and twirled it on to the raft. Annette meanwhile held her weight central in the raft to stop the floor bulging up and sucking the raft down, which happens when flexible rafts are towed. Thumping into the ship's side threw me on to the ladder, which I started to climb, my legs hardly able to support my weight. Below me as I climbed I could see Annette climbing too.

■ **LESSONS LEARNED**

- The actions of skipper Anthony Lealand and his wife, Annette, display the importance of preparations before a setting off on any long passage. *Rushcutter*'s shallow bilge was pumped out to clear any engine oil. In bad conditions, as the skipper observed, a splash of oil below would have turned the cabin into a slimy ice rink.

- Lealand also checked the aluminium halyard shaves at the masthead and found them corroded where they had been in contact with the bronze bearings and salt water. It's always good seamanship to make a thorough check of your boat from masthead to keel.

- *Rushcutter* was fitted with ply deadlights and a spare rudder. The crew set sail with assorted nails and a spare sheet of plywood 'just in case'. When the wind increased, Lealand 'whipped out the deadlights and spiked them on with three in-roofing nails. There are lots of examples of yacht crews being able to get themselves out of trouble because they had the forethought to take along spare timber and nails to make repairs – or even a new rudder. In 2009, the crew of a 25ft yacht crossing the Atlantic made three jury rudders to get themselves to St Lucia in the Caribbean without need of rescue.

- A knife, along with a torch, is an essential item for a sailor to have handy when he's on watch. It also needs to be secured with a lanyard. Lealand nearly drowned when *Rushcutter* rolled over and he lost his knife which he wore around his neck. He was trapped underwater by his lifeline, which had been shortened to avoid him being flung too far overboard. When the yacht righted herself, Lealand landed back in the cockpit and Annette handed him a carving knife to cut himself from the tangle of sheets, halyards and safety harness.

- When the two crew took to the six-man liferaft their weight was not enough to keep it stable and it flipped over. Liferafts are designed to be stable when used to recommended capacity. For two-handed cruising, a six or eight-man liferaft is as much of a liability as six people in a three-man raft.

- These days with EPIRBS, rescue from a liferaft is more likely to be a matter of hours or days than weeks. But what additional provisions would you take in a liferaft or emergency grab bag? Spare water containers are essential. Lealand observed that the lifeboat biscuits, though scientifically designed and high in calories, were such a foul brew that they gave up eating them. He recommended the tinned peaches – 'easy to swallow, sweet and wet.'

THE LEAK THAT
WOULDN'T STOP

Yacht	*Toad* (27ft engineless, wooden sloop, built in 1939)
Skipper	Peter Nichols
Bound from	Falmouth to Maine, USA
Date of loss	27 July 1978
Position	300 miles NE of Bermuda

JULY 22

At 0500, just before dawn, the alarm wakes me. Swinging my feet off the bunk, I touch water before floor.

Real panic. Before I know it, I'm up in the cockpit pumping for all I'm worth – so frenziedly that part of my mind is wondering about the age and strength left in the sun-faded rubber diaphragm C-clamped on the pump's exterior. I have a spare, but it would rattle me further if this broke and I had to repair it right now. Pump-pump-pump-pump-pump-pump.

After a while – I've forgotten to count or look at my watch – I look down the companionway: water's no longer visible over the wet floorboards. I slow down a bit and catch my breath. Several deep breaths. What a way to wake up!

I start thinking: I was in the lee bunk – the lower side of the boat now that it's well heeled with wind in the sails for the first time in weeks. Water just under the floor when the boat is becalmed and upright would overflow on the lee side when moving and heeled. No need for panic. But water over the floorboards is above the threshold of my peace of mind.

Five minutes later I know with certainty there's a hell of a lot more water coming in now. Still no suck from the bilge and I've been at it for ten minutes at least. I stop and go below and pull up a floorboard. The bilge appears half full. Jesus Christ.

Up in the cockpit I pump like a mad metronome. Of course, I think, the bilge is V-shaped so what looks half full is probably only a quarter full. I normally see half a glass of water as half full, but I have just become a fervent half-empty man.

Another five minutes until I hear the sucking of air from bilge. I go below, up into the bow, and what I see is a waking nightmare that makes my gut feel suddenly full of ice: water is welling in, steadily, along half the seams in the hull below the waterline on both sides. The inside of the planking up here looks as if a hose is being played across it. I pull sails, duffel bags, coils of rope, wildly away from the hull to see how far aft this continues. Not far, thank God, not too far: it stops about 6 feet or so back from the stem. The planking is dry aft of this. The water's getting under the sheathing, of course, and coming in through the seams, which haven't been caulked for a decade at least. You can't caulk them if you can't get at them, but the water sure can. I stare for a few minutes, trying to think – of what I don't know. Through the hatch light overhead I can see that it's dawn. I go aft and start making coffee.

Okay. I can still pump it out, I can keep it below the floorboards. But no question about it now: the faster I sail, the more water comes in. However, we're doing about 5 knots now, we won't go much faster than this, so maybe it'll stabilise at this rate.

Not a hope. The leak got progressively worse over the last two weeks while we were practically sitting still. It will get worse and worse, faster and faster, and I know why now: the water will work away at the old caulking and force its way aft. It's a race against time.

But aren't we moving well!

I think of the Al Italia joke that a Pan Am flight attendant once told me: an announcement from the cockpit: 'We gotta good news, anda bad news. The bad news is we're lost. The good news is, we're makinga great time.'

Later in the morning, the liquid crystal digital display on my short-wave radio starts fragmenting: batteries are low. I change them, but when I turn the radio back on, it is silent. A second moment of raw panic this morning. Absurdly, this seems far worse than the leak. The prospect of life without my radio makes me feel lonelier than Robinson Crusoe. The radio is my Man Friday, my contact with the rest of the species. Auntie BBC, jazz from the VOA in the evenings, this is the company that has kept me from feeling utterly alone.

I pull the batteries – brand new Duracell – out of the radio and look at the contact points inside the battery compartment. Nice and shiny, no sign of corrosion. The batteries, fresh from their plastic packaging, look good too. I put them back, slowly, firmly, with the intense telepathic message: You will work now. I put the lid back on. Turn the radio on. Nothing.

I unscrew the back of the radio and pull it off, revealing the inscrutable Japanese interior. I might as well be looking at an atomic bomb. I see no sign of corrosion, which I could expect after years on board. I pick the radio up and turn it upside down: nothing falls out, which is good, but then I realise that if it had I wouldn't know where it came from to put it back.

I feel a terrible cascading fear. I'm undermined, no doubt, by the other, realistically greater problem, but I am undone by the silence from my radio. I feel myself reverting to the baby state I escaped into on the dope boat: I want to blubber and appeal to someone, 'Pleeee-assse! More than 1,000 miles to go, 10 to 15 days. Cut off from the world. Absolutely, completely, out-of-touch alone.'

Almost whimpering, I climb into the cockpit and start pumping. Pump-pump-pump. The voyage seems too grim now. Suddenly it's no longer fun. I look around at the empty ocean and realise, with a sharpness I've never felt before, how alone I am. Just myself and a leaky boat in the middle of the ocean. Alone, alone, all, all alone.

But isn't this really what you've wanted all along? A real test? To see if you can take it? This now, at last, a survival situation, mentally and physically. It's perfect. It's going to take everything you've got. Are you going to cave in now, as you did once before, on the *Mary Nell*, when someone else was looking after you, or are you going to rise to this? If you set out across an ocean in a boat like *Toad*, eager for a whiff of danger and sensation but unprepared to face just such a scenario, you're just a ******* dilettante. This is real. Life or death. Are you up to it, or not?

1800: Fixed the radio. It had to be the batteries. I tried one from another pack – noise erupted. The sound is big, clear and glorious. Listening rather smugly to Jazz Hour.

JULY 24

Twenty-second day out of Horta.

We have been tearing along all night with the main slightly reefed, and at 0200 I go out on deck to roll the reef deeper. It is windier than an hour ago. Maybe because of the large dark rain cloud passing astern of us.

Below, I am unable to go back to sleep, feeling we are still over-canvassed and hearing the sloshing in the bilges. An hour later the cloud is gone and the wind is the same, about a steady 20 knots. I go forward and drop the genoa. I sit astride the bowsprit in the dark, bunching up the genoa and tying it to the whisker stays. I grip the 4-inch-wide teak spar with my thighs like a bronco rider. My feet on the bobstay dip in and out of the warmish water as the bow rises and falls. I'm still not wearing a harness, not yet, it's not at all bad out. Just a lot different from what it has been for so long. And there is so much noise now: waves tumbling over themselves, and *Toad*'s insistent charging through them, and the steady cataract sound of the white water tumbling along both sides of the hull.

The boat is much happier under reefed main and staysail. Me too. I go below and fall asleep.

Still blowing this morning. Amazing difference from a few days ago. At noon we'll clock a good run at last. America is 1,000 miles away but seems infinitely closer. I feel it now just over the horizon. I picture it, New England in August: clams, lobsters. station-wagons, sneakers and tattered sweatshirts; and toothsome American girls, strong, corn-fed, happy, impossibly normal. I imagine bringing *Toad* alongside some grey-bleached dock festooned with floats, stacked with lobster pots, and meeting one of these splendid, freckly girls. The ordinariness of it makes it seem so far beyond my reach.

At 0900 I notice a new sky. It is still blue and sunny, but high up there is now a lot of streaky cirrus.

If clouds appear as if scratched by a hen,
Get ready to reef your topsails then.

I get out Alan Watt's weather lore book and find this sky in Photograph 2: 'Sky which means deterioration. The warm front of a depression is probably on its way… the wind will increase … rain is likely later.'

The sea is up, too, after several days of this wind, confused and lumpy. A southerly swell now dominates over a steady procession of smaller waves from the north-west. *Toad* is being knocked about, slapped on the nose by the north-westerly lumps. But we are still making good progress, moving at 5 knots, heading north-westerly, straight for Maine.

However, Maine is still about 1,000 miles away. I have been thinking of making for Bermuda, now 400 miles due west. But with the wind up and from the south-west, I can't push *Toad* any closer to Bermuda than we're heading. When and if the wind shifts or drops, we will head that way.

A lot of water below, and more, always more, coming in. I pump now when I'm not doing anything else.

At local noon, 1330, my sights show we have made 112 miles in the last 24 hours. The log mileage is 121, so there is some current with the north-westerly swell which has set us back 10 or 11 miles.

At 1500 and again at 1600, I roll up more of the main on to the boom. *Toad* is equipped with a roller-reefing gear that pulls the mainsail down and rolls it around the boom. Operated by a ratchet and pawl, it does its job quickly and neatly. I can roll up half the mainsail in about a minute. The remainder sets well on the mast, maintaining a taut, efficient airfoil shape. I can roll it down to storm-sail size in two minutes. There is a photograph of this gear in Hiscock's book, *Cruising Under Sail*. Turner's roller-reefing gear, it's called, manufactured in the 1930s. It works much faster than the modern system, laughably known as 'jiffy' reefing, for its supposed speed of operation, which is what I found on all the new boats I've skippered or delivered.

Later in the afternoon I tune in to the short-wave weather forecast given by the US Coast Guard station 'November Mike November' in

Portsmouth, Virginia, to see if they mention this weather. Two gales are moving east off the eastern seaboard, but that's way north, around 45° north.

And at 1800 I roll up still more of the main. The wind – finally admit it – is much, much stronger now. It's blowing about 30 knots – a gale. We are being knocked and slammed about now. It is impossible to think of getting any closer to Bermuda at the moment.

No matter how much I pump, water is now constantly sloshing over the floorboards. It has become wet and grimly depressing below. Gallons of water pouring without let-up into an old boat bouncing around in the middle of the ocean without a proper liferaft undermines your confidence, I find. I'm used to seeing an ocean of water outside but a lot of it inside the boat, where by essential principle it's supposed to be dry, can get you down.

Just keep pumping. The Coast Guard forecast doesn't mention any weather system around here, so maybe it'll quieten down again soon. We'll go to Bermuda or maybe still poop on to Maine. It's hard to adjust to the fast-changing reality of life aboard: I keep thinking everything will be okay.

JULY 25

Haven't slept much. That sloshing noise. I worry about drifting off and letting too much water come in. When I do doze I dream we're sinking. Waking is hardly less nightmarish, with water above the floorboards.

The rain predicted by Watts' weather book comes in the night, with a low dark caving-in of cloud and those spatial hallucinations that make me feel we are turning and hobby-horsing through great amorphous rooms. The strangest sensation, not unpleasant, but so strong tonight, probably because this is the lumpiest sea and weather of this voyage so far, and because I'm tired and it's easy, even a relief, to get carried away into it.

I have to watch myself. I know from all my book reading of sailors at sea and my own encounters with exhaustion that this is when you make mistakes. You let things go, let yourself and your boat down. I have to be vigilant. I have to eat to keep strong, and somehow I have to sleep. I have to sleep soon too, otherwise I risk getting so tired that when I wake up there will be too much water in the boat and I'll have lost the battle. Later this morning I'll nap.

We are converging with shipping lanes between northern Europe and ports in the Gulf of Mexico. We would never be seen by any lookout aboard a ship in such conditions. Nor would *Toad* be spotted on radar with all the wave clutter. And we've stopped moving now, so if I did see a ship looming up out of the murk, it would take long minutes to attempt evasive manoeuvres. I'm relying on the statistical unlikelihood of collision. We are hove-to, staysail backed and the reefed main sheeted flat amidships, bobbing quite comfortably, pointing west, probably making a knot of leeway to the north-west, which is where we want to go. I want to see if heaving-to, reducing our motion, slows the water coming in. Can't tell yet. It's four o'clock in the morning.

Under way again at 0800. Tried napping, and maybe dozed a little but not too much. Just as much water coming in, so we might as well keep going and we're making good time in the right direction. The wind is still 28 to 30 knots.

A lot of water, in fact, is coming in. More than yesterday. It is unhinging to have this much water coming in and no visible hole in the boat. I pump all the time now when I'm not doing anything else vital. Sleep is vital, but I can't seem to manage it. The floor is continually under water now. I wade through the interior of the boat. Yet I seem to be able to keep it at around that level.

Local noon is 1335, and I'm lucky enough to get a sight of the sun for latitude. Earlier this morning I managed two quick snapshots of a hazy but sufficiently distinct orb through cloud. We're at 35° 18' N, 52° 45' W. Eighty-three miles since noon yesterday, which is good for being hove-to and slowed down. This boat sails well.

Marking my pencilled 'X' on the chart, I find we are again at one of those spots on the ocean where I've been before. Two years ago, on 16 July, J and I were just 3 miles away with the cats aboard *Toad*, bound for the Azores. A year ago, on 28 June, we were 5 miles away on *Sea Bear*, a Moody 33, which we delivered from Florida to England.

But on this afternoon we're being knocked about too much, and tons of water are filling the boat, so I heave-to again, feeling for the first time, a little desperate, unsure if I am able to handle what's happening. I want to keep moving, get closer to Bermuda, but moving seems to make the leak worse – although, finally, it's hard to tell. My attitude is changing fast. For a while, around teatime, that English ritual so suggestive of warmth and cosiness that I observe most days at sea, I lose my nerve and think about putting out a Mayday call. It's not warm and cosy at all aboard the boat now, but wet and loud and ******* terrifying.

Never mind, then, have a nice cup of tea.

''Ere, 'ave a nice cuppa tea, luv,' I say aloud in my best East Ender charlady accent. ''At's right, put the kettle on. Lovely! An' a bit of that bread – why don't you toast it, luv? You got this bleedin' oven wiv a grill, use it! Go on! Give yourself a lit'le treat, then. All you bin froo. Yes, lovely! An' a bit of that jam. A proper tea! ''At's it!'

Whoever she is, she's wonderful. She makes me a lovely tea.

I should sleep. I'm tired – you're exhausted, *you've got to sleep* – but I'm afraid to let myself go all the way, because I don't know at what point, if I stop to sleep, the water coming in will become too much ever to get ahead of again. If 'x' amount is coming in now and I can keep ahead of it, can I pump out enough water after 'y' minutes of sleep? I don't know the answer, and I'm too terrified to get it wrong. And behind that is the fear that once asleep I simply won't hear the alarm.

This evening I do a marathon stint at the pump, getting glimpses of solid floorboard for a few minutes. Then I turn on the radio and hear McCoy Tyner on the Jazz Hour. I make spaghetti. Looking around the cabin, I'm intensely glad J isn't here tonight to see this water sloshing over the floor, to see *Toad* reduced to this. To fear for it now as I do.

JULY 26

Spend most of the day in the cockpit. In my foul-weather gear, my harness on now because I'm getting some sleep, sitting upright over the pump, back against the cabin, nodding off between strokes. Rocked and bounced to sleep. Getting real sleep too, must be, because I'm dreaming vividly. Dreamed we were approaching the Azores. Woke up once and saw Maine ahead, for sure, all those granite shores and fir

trees. Straight out of *Wooden Boat* magazine. Eggemoggin Reach, I
guessed. Thought about getting up and going forward to unlash the
anchor and then it wasn't there and I realised we still had about 800
miles to go. A lot of dreams like that all day.

Hove-to. No sailing. Boat full of water, although I can go below
and wade around pretty easily.

I put the battery (a Die Hard car battery, which powers my tape
deck and VHF radio) into the cooler, which is floating where the
engine would be. I have to keep it dry, keep the VHF radio working.

No sun today, so no position. No one makes me tea either. Not
that sort of day. Or else she's on holiday.

Odd, but there's this white stuff in the water today, all around the
boat, particularly as we roll in the swell. Little white bits, like chunks
of barnacle you scrape off the hull when you haul out, only a little
smaller. In the water around the boat. Waves cleaning the hull? The
stuff sinks slowly. I watch it go down. Bits of something.

I think it's windier today, if anything. A real gale, over 30 knots.
The seas are up from yesterday – but they would be, after days of this.

Might try the radio later, put out a call, see if anyone's there.

An endless night, pumping when I'm not dozing. Pump-pump-
pump. Back and forth, back and forth, a rhythm building, like pros-
tration for prayer. It's cloudy, but through the cloud comes the dim
illumination from a new moon somewhere above, giving the night
shape and texture.

JULY 27

At dawn I see a ship off to the north, four or five miles away. Very
hazy, dawn light and misty air, but it stays there and keeps going like a
real ship while I stand up and watch it.

I go below and call it up on the VHF.

'Hello ship at about 35° 43' N, 53° 03S W, this is the sailing yacht
Toad several miles off your port beam. Do you read? Over.'

An answer, from a Dutch ship. He claims it's not him I see because
he doesn't see me anywhere off his port beam, or on radar. He tells me
I'm probably seeing another ship. I don't care. I have rehearsed what I
want to say.

I am in a severely leaking condition. I am en route to Bermuda. I may have to abandon ship. Would you please radio the US Coast Guard and let them know my position and situation, and ask them to alert shipping in this area to keep a good lookout in case I have to abandon ship?'

The Dutch ship will have a short-wave transmitter. My VHF will transmit no further usually than you can see from its aerial at the top of the mast: maybe 20 miles, possibly further at sea in good conditions.

'You need to get off now?'

I'm not prepared for this question.

'Yacht, you want to abandon ship now?'

'No thanks. I'm hoping to make it to Bermuda. But my boat is leaking, and I may have to abandon ship later.'

'Ja, okay.'

I wait a little while, then call back to see if he got through, but I get no answer. I call several more times without a response. I go back on deck and look to the north-west, but the ship is gone. It's still blowing about 30 knots.

Immediately, I start thinking I should have said, 'Yes, I'm sinking, I have to get off now. Please save me.'

What constitutes sinking? I wonder. Is *Toad* sinking? Even now, this is almost a new concept. It has a leak, but is it sinking? How bad is it? How accustomed to it have I become?

What if I don't see another ship?

When do I let go?

I pump for a long time, but there is still water over the floor below. I go down to find something to eat. No bread left. There is some muesli. I haven't made a proper meal for several days. I look in the lockers around the galley, not really seeing what I'm looking at. Didn't I have some peanut butter?

I drift, standing in the galley, holding on while the boat lurches back and forth, my mind blank.

'Hello, *Toad*!' An incredibly cheery voice on the radio, which I've left on. 'Little boat *Toad*!' An Indian accent. 'Hello! Hello! Hello!'

I pick up the mike. 'Yes, hello. This is *Toad*.'

'*Toad*, yes! Good morning! How are you?'

How am I? 'I am leaking, thank you. How are you?'

'Oh, yes, you are leaking!' A definite chuckle. 'That is what we are hearing! But we are fine, thank you! Very good, very good!'

The Indian accent, beloved of comics and mimics in England, is thick, and irrepressibly cheerful. It sounds like Peter Sellers, escaped from *The Party* and running amok on the high sea. If I were anywhere else – hearing this on the phone, say – I would know it was a joke.

And even here I say, 'Who is this?'

'We are the ship *Laxmi*. We are calling to see if you need help. How are you, really?'

'Where are you?'

'We are here!'

We are here is not a position a professional seaman would be likely to give. The sense of joke compounds, turns surreal.

'I mean what is your position, please?'

'But we are right here, *Toad*! Look! Look out the door, please!'

Still holding the mike, I step up on the galley counter and look out – a ship is right behind us, on top of us. I could whack a badminton birdie on to its deck. Big, black, rusty, a cargo ship of some sort. *Laxmi* written on its bow. The bridge towers overhead, and eight or ten grinning Indians are crowding the rail above my head, waving as if I were Prince Charles. I can hear them shouting: 'Hello *Toad*!' I wave back.

'You see!' says the laughing voice on the radio, 'We are here!'

We all wave for a while.

'Well, do you want to come with us?'

That question again. Get off or wait? For what? It's still blowing. I'm not doing well. I'm tired and dopey. And I don't think the leak is going to slow down when the wind drops. I've reached a crossroads.

'Where are you going?' I ask.

'We are going to Burma!'

'Burma?'

'Yes, Burma! You know, next door to India!'

What a thought! What might be waiting for me in Burma?

Perhaps I could turn into a Somerset Maugham character, become an old Burma 'hand'.

Manage a rubber plantation, wear baggy shorts and pith helmet and start drinking a lot of gin.

Here at the crossroads, *Laxmi* is unmistakably the less travelled road, forking towards Burma. And, with some disappointment in myself, I fail to rise to the occasion.

'No, thanks, *Laxmi*. I'm trying to get to the States. Or Bermuda.'

'You are sure?'

'Yes, thanks.' And now I'll always wonder.

I ask *Laxmi* to radio the Coast Guard in Portsmouth, Virginia, to tell them about me and my situation. They promise to do this and, with lots of waving and wide white smiles, they steam off to the south-east.

Will this be the last ship I see? I'm sure not. It's the second I've seen in an hour. We must be bang in the middle of the shipping lane.

A little later *Laxmi* calls back. They're in touch with the Coast Guard, who are asking for an ETA in Maine or Bermuda. Eight to ten days, or three or four for Bermuda, I tell my pal aboard *Laxmi*. In our last exchange, he gives me a position check, which puts me considerably further to the north-east than where I think I am. One of us is about 40 miles off.

The sun appears at 1030 and I get two LOP (line of position) snapshots with my sextant. I work them out and find that I am, in fact, where I thought I was. I believe in my navigation, and wonder whether *Laxmi* will make Burma after all.

With the sun comes a sudden dramatic moderation of wind and weather. By noon it's a nice day, blowing about 12 knots, the sea is still lumpy, but it's time to crack on more sail, which will steady us and get us moving. I'm invigorated. I feel wide awake.

I go up on deck and unroll all of the main. Then I go out on the bowsprit, sit down on it and start untying the genoa.

My feet and legs and the bobstay chain are plunging in and out of the water as *Toad* rises and falls in the leftover swell. At the lower edge of my vision I suddenly register a large dark shape in the water immediately beneath my feet. I'm back on deck, well inboard, saying out loud, 'Jesus Christ!' before I know it. It was huge, dark brown and bobbing at my feet with a curious undulating motion, as if sniffing me.

I lean over the edge of the deck and look down. My God, what is that? The weirdest creature I've ever seen, huge too: flat, ragged torn, waving in the water.

It's the sheathing. Delaminated from the bow, hanging off the hull in a long wide flap of heavy cloth, brown with dried resorcinol glue, waving up and down in the water with the motion of the waves. I move out onto the bowsprit again to get a better look and see the same waving flap down the other side of the boat too. The Cascover has delaminated at its joint at the bow and peeled back down both sides of the boat, at least halfway back, as far as I can see. Great obscene flaps waving from amidships. How long has it been like this?

I see those white bits in the water again, and now I know exactly what they are: old caulking, dried and brittle, washing out of the seams.

Dizzy, with a cold feeling in my stomach, I rush below and look at the hull up forward. Plain as day, sea water is pouring in, welling arterially, through most seams, as far back as the saloon, and farther. White bits of old caulking have also been pushed in and are lying on the planking and down the sides of the frames. Everywhere. Haven't I seen this until now? Known, without looking overboard, how bad it was? I don't know. If I saw it, I pushed away its meaning.

I don't know if I've been holding my breath, but now I can't breathe. I rush topside again.

I sit in the cockpit. I'm feeling dizzy. Hard to breathe. I sit, holding on. Minutes pass.

The boat, I realise – I knew it all along – is quite sound. All those sister frames, and the new laminated floor frames I put in just two years ago before we left Florida. The boat is as strong as ever. But the sheathing is off, the caulking gone or going from half the seams in the hull's planking. The boat has turned into a colander.

Nothing I can do about it… is there? A hole I could patch: I could saw up the plywood beneath the bunks and nail it over ten holes. But this… I think of Robin Knox-Johnston caulking *Suhaili*'s leaking seam underwater with a complicated patch. Eight feet of seam on both sides of the boat. What would he do here with the equivalent of 40 15ft-long kerfs sawn through the hull? And certain to lengthen.

Toad is gone. I know this absolutely as I sit here in the cockpit on what is now becoming rather a nice day. The sun is out, the sea is going down.

Knowing this, I look at the boat around me. The teak vent boxes I built on the cabin roof. The stainless steel guard-rail stanchions I installed. The winches, the rigging. The new compass Martin and I hooked up. The slight imperfection beneath the paint on the cabin side that I know is my plug of a hole made by Henry's useless depth gauge. I look up and down the boat and I cannot see an inch of it that I haven't remade according to my idea of what would make *Toad* the best it could be. Now I know that the leak will not get better but worse, that I can't keep ahead of it, that I must get off, save my life, and let *Toad* sink.

I have never thought of *Toad* as a 'she', the way many think of their boats. To me *Toad* doesn't have gender, but it is certainly something far more than the sum of its wood and bits and pieces. With every screw and bolt and pass of a paintbrush that J and I gave it, this boat made these its own, and added something of itself. It has absorbed more love into its fibres than any amount of paint or varnish, until this has become part of its matrix. What *Toad* is to me now is a thing that was made and lives from that love.

And I believe *Toad* loves me back.

So as I sit in the cockpit and look at it with tears pouring down my face, I am careful to keep quiet. I don't say anything. I'm not going to tell it what is going to happen now.

I sheet the main amidships, heaving-to, and wait for local noon. I get a latitude sight. I work out our position with unusual care, thinking about our drift since the morning LOP sights.

At 1400 I put out my first Mayday call on VHF. I say into the mike, according to international radio etiquette: Mayday, Mayday, Mayday. This is the sailing yacht *Toad* at 36° 08' N, 53° 12' W, requesting assistance. Mayday, Mayday, Mayday. This is the sailing yacht *Toad* at 36° 08' N, 53° 12' W, requesting assistance.'

No reply. I repeat it a few more times, then stop. I haven't been heard. Probably no ship within range. I'll wait an hour and try again. I'll do this every hour on the hour, but for no more than two or three minutes, to conserve battery power. I know this part of the ocean. I know this is a shipping lane. I've spoken with two ships already this morning. Another will come along. I cling positively to this thought so I don't have to think about getting into the dinghy and sailing for Bermuda. I think, instead, of what to take when a ship comes along to take me off. I start to pack. This is a good time to go through my wardrobe and get rid of a few things.

I don't have a suit, but I do have a blazer, wool, and I stuff it into a sail bag. I'll pull it out when I have my next shower. I have a number of shirts, out of which I select two Brooks Brothers button-downs, and several T-shirts. A pair of venerable jeans. Underwear, socks, a hankie Martin gave me. I hope this will do. I have no idea what this next boatless phase in my life will bring, or what I will have to become in it, or how often I will have to shower with my blazer.

I look around at my books, About 100 of them stuffed into the shelves above the saloon berths, over the chart table, in the back of the galley. Years of selecting and collecting. Mostly they are books about boats and the sea. How to design them, build them, sail them. By the designers, builders and sailors I most respect. Like William Albert Robinson, whose 70ft brigantine *Varua* is my favourite boat in all the world. Robinson circumnavigated in a small ketch call *Svaap* in the 1920s, and then designed *Varua*, his 'ultimate' ship, with Starling Burgess, and in it he experienced the 'ultimate' storm:

> *'Again and again that night, I asked myself why I was there – and had no better answer than that perhaps this was the very thing that had drawn me into this voyage: an unexpressed urge to experience a real Cape Horn gale.'*

Robinson built *Varua* in his own shipyard in Gloucester, Massachusetts, starting construction in 1939 – the same year *Toad* was built – and then sailed to Tahiti, where he lived for the rest of his life. He wrote about this ship and his life sailing it around the Pacific, and through the Roaring Forties to Chile, in two of my favourite books, *Return to the Sea* and *To the Great Southern Sea*. But if I take them, what do I leave behind? *Skiff and Schooners; Boats, Oars and Rowing*; and *Spray*? All by R D 'Pete' Culler, who learned marline spike seamanship from a man 'who had learned his seamanship under men who had sailed with Nelson'. Bill Tilman's *Mischief in Patagonia*? My Knox-Johnston, Moitessier, Crowhurst books? *Sailing Alone Around the World* by Slocum? Chapelle's *Boatbuilding*, and *Yacht Designing and Planning*? … My Hiscocks, for ****'s sake?

It doesn't matter that I've read them all; they are my library, I refer to them constantly, for reassurance more than anything, to know that this world I've read about and want to be a part of exists, and I feel a chill intimation of a coming loneliness at the thought of leaving them all behind.

I take the Hiscocks, all nine of them; Eric's complete oeuvre, hardbacked, blue cloth, Oxford University Press. They are salt-stained, half ruined, broken-spined, dust jackets long disintegrated, the foundation of my library – and of who I am, for they describe all I want to do and the world in which I want to do it – and upon them I will build one more from scratch. The rest I hope I can find again.

At 1500 I make another Mayday call. No response – until, minutes after I've stopped and gone back to my packing for a new life, a clear static-free voice fills the cabin:

'Ship calling Mayday, this is the *Almeria Lykes*. *Almeria Lykes* responding to Mayday, come back.'

For all my desperate confidence of being picked up, relief floods me. I think: Wow, that was fast.

'Yes, *Almeria Lykes*, this is the sailing yacht *Toad*. I'm at 36° 08' N, 53° 12' W, and I am sinking. Over.'

The voice on the radio, a voice of calm, of authority, tells me that he is about 20 miles from my position. He is a container ship, on his way from Rotterdam to Galveston, Texas. He asks me how sure I am of the position I have given. Pretty sure, I reply, within a couple of miles – sure that if they come to that position I will see them. The voice responds that he is on his way. He will be here in an hour. He will remain standing by on the air.

I hang up the mike and look around *Toad*'s saloon. After six years, an hour more. After an immeasurable moment I resume packing. I can, of course take more than these clothes, the Hiscocks, and the grab bag I had ready to take in the dinghy (in fact, I will leave my Neal's Yard peanut butter and Gibbon's *Decline and Fall* behind), but already I can see myself afoot in America. I have about 60 US dollars and an English Barclaycard Visa with a £100 limit. I will be starting my new life in a Texas bus station. I will have to hump everything, God knows how far, or for how long. I must travel light. I must be ruthless.

I am a sailor. This is how I hope to make my living. So I put my varnished sextant box into the cockpit. Into the sail bag, on top of my irreducible wardrobe, I cram all my charts, my Filofax with my Coast Guard 100-ton licence and my passport, oilskin jacket and pants and seaboots. In go the Hiscocks, camera, exposed film, envelopes of loose photographs, and my logbook of this voyage, the last entry reading:

> *1500 Mayday call replied to by* Almeria Lykes, *a container ship bound for Galveston. Gave him my position and he said he'd be here in an hour.*

My Seiko is on my wrist, and around my neck is my Azorean scrimshaw of *Toad*.

For J, I throw in her five hardback diaries.

On top of them I place the folder containing the novel I've been trying to write. I suspect it's not what I want it to be. I yearn to write something great and wonderful – much better than this novel – but I don't know yet what that might be.

I take my Olivetti typewriter up into the cockpit, put it next to the sextant box, look up and see the ship on the horizon. Black and square. It looks like a building. I go below and call him on the radio, tell him I see him, give him his bearing from me – let him work out the reciprocal, I'm too busy.

I go back up into the cockpit and start pumping, partly because I can't stand the sight of so much water below, also because I don't want *Toad* to sink before the ship gets here. I don't know how long it will take the ship to manoeuvre alongside, or how all that will work.

The ship is now about 3 or 4 miles away. He calls over the radio to tell me he's spotted me, made visual contact.

I watch it get bigger and bigger, its shape and details growing more definite. It's ugly, slab-sided, tier upon tier of containers – red, grey, blue, rust – stacked high above the black hull along its entire length. Almost no superstructure visible except the bridge at the very front, right up in the bow where it doesn't belong according to all the laws of ship aesthetics as I know them. The closer it gets, growing huger and uglier, the less it looks like a ship. Finally, it has the size and appearance of a mall nearing the end of construction: rectangular, black and 900ft long. It looks like Armageddon and it's coming to save me.

The ship approaches from windward, leaving us becalmed in a

short chop. His voice comes up out of the cabin, from my radio, to tell me that he's going to stop, drift down to me, throw me a line to fasten at *Toad*'s bow. He will then move ahead at his slowest speed, several knots, and we will be pulled in alongside the hull. He will drop a rope ladder, which I am to climb up.

Soon the ship is all I see. It drifts towards us, sideways, blotting out half the visible world. The black hull stretches from horizon to horizon along *Toad*'s starboard side and goes all the way up to the sky.

My hackles rise – no metaphor: the back of my scalp is contracting tightly. This is against all my small-boat sailor's instincts. I should clap on sail and get away from this monster that can mean only one thing to *Toad*: damage. The last time I was on a small boat this close to a larger one was with Bill on *Mary Nell* as the Russian lassoed us and pulled us in and *Mary Nell*'s masts both snapped like dry twigs.

Toad is half-turned towards this black wall, now about 15ft away. Instinctively, with no thought at all, I dance across the cabin top, over the foredeck, out onto the bowsprit. I stand on the very tip, holding onto the forestay. The back steel plate – pitted, dull and uneven up close – is closing fast. *Toad*'s angle is all wrong.

I look up for a moment: high above me, peering over the top of the hull, I see a man with long blond hair and a moustache. He's waving. Waving me back.

The ship is a foot away. I stick out my foot now, bracing the other on the bowsprit, to push it off, or push us off. Suddenly this is a collision, that's all I know.

And we collide: the tip of *Toad*'s bowsprit, 4 inches from my foot, meets the black wall. There's a crack – I'm flying through the air, still holding onto the forestay – and then I land back on the cabin top by the mast. The bowsprit is broken, snapped immediately on contact. The forestay, attached to the end of the bowsprit, under tension from the mast and rig, has whipped backwards carrying me with it like Tarzan on a jungle creeper. I land at the mast (which remains upright, held by the inner forestay, which was not set up when the mast fell backward in St Thomas harbour five years ago). I look at the jagged broken stump of sprit in the bow, and the other piece lying by my foot, and think about how to fix it … and then I pull myself away from this thought and push myself towards what must be done.

A shout from above: I look up again and the blond man swings a coil of line right above me, which as I watch turns into a helix as it falls through space and drops onto *Toad*'s foredeck. I fasten the end to the oversize bronze cleat on the foredeck that I took off the *Chris Craft* lying on the hard in the Lagoon one night years ago.

The small chop, the collision, perhaps even my attempt to push us off have caused us to drift away from the ship's hull. But now the ship begins to move slowly ahead. Tension straightens the line at *Toad*'s bow, and we are pulled forward and in against the black hull. *Toad*'s three-quarter inch larch planking smacks and bumps against the black steel and I just try not to think about it.

A bright orange rope ladder drops down over the side of the ship astern of us. Someone starts letting out the line holding *Toad* alongside and we are eased back along the hull until we are bobbing and thumping against the ladder. Small thin lines are dropped down into the cockpit where my bags are packed and ready.

The blond man is now about 30ft directly above me. I can hear him clearly. He tells me to tie my bags to the small lines. I do this and crewmen haul them up over the side. They are careful with the sextant, keeping it from banging into the steel on the way up. Four items altogether: a sail bag, the sextant, the typewriter and a Billingham overnight bag.

'Is that it?' the blond man asks me when they're up and out of sight.

'Yes, I'll be right up.' And I go below.

I look around. Apart from the water now at my knees, all looks normal aboard *Toad*. Very neat, just as I like it aboard a small boat crammed with years of collected belongings. The kettle on the stove. It's past teatime.

There remains an hour or two of daylight. I know what I must do. I take the bread knife, bend and crawl into the space behind the galley, where the engine would have been, and cut the one-and-a-half-inch-diameter plastic hose between the cockpit drain and its gate valve through the hull. Water begins to gush in, spouting. *Toad* must sink before dark. So no other yacht will smash into it, waterlogged but still floating, and sink with it. Full of love and memories, *Toad* is now an obstruction to safe navigation.

I climb back up into the cockpit, grab the orange polypropylene and start up the rope ladder. An unreal, dislocating sense of what I am doing, deserting and abandoning the thing I love – a suddenly familiar and reverberating sensation – weighing me down. About a 30ft climb.

I'm standing on the ship's high deck. The blond man – he's about six foot four, looks like a Viking, or a young Hulk Hogan – grabs my hand and shakes it, grinning.

'Hey, I'm Dan. How you doing?'

The other crewmen around me are also grinning. They introduce themselves. They are all American. This is an exciting episode in the middle of a monotonous trip for them. They're all thrilled.

I'm not sure what I say, but farther along the deck I see someone casting off the line to *Toad*'s bow. He drops it into the sea.

Dan speaks into a portable VHF he's holding in his hand. A moment later the ship shudders. It begins a long arcing turn around *Toad*, which I find I can't take my eyes off.

I'm walking along the deck behind Dan, who's talking to me, though I have no idea what he's saying. This is just like a dream: I observe, but I am completely detached, disembodied from the scene. We go forward, up steps, into the superstructure below the bridge. Inside we continue up steel stairs.

I'm shown into a stateroom, so vast as to confirm that this is a dream. A double bed, a bathroom en suite. It looks like a motel room, but bigger than most. Windows look out at the sea – I crane my head but I can't see *Toad*. Dan tells me to make myself comfortable, have a shower, and come up and meet the captain, who's on the bridge, one deck up, whenever I'm ready. The other guys bring in my four items of luggage, all I own in the world. Then they all leave.

Again, I look out the window but I can't see it. *Toad* is behind us somewhere, to port. I leave my stateroom and run – so, so dreamlike with the uphill roll of the ship against me, holding me back – down a long hallway to a door. Through it, I'm outside, on a wing far above the ocean. *Toad* is astern, a quarter of a mile away, maybe, looking not quite itself with its stump bowsprit, and conspicuously low in the water. But it still looks good, the paint and varnish glinting in the low sunlight.

Its bow is pointing straight at Maine.

POSTSCRIPT

On 2 August, after docking in Galveston, Nichols catches a bus to New York City and reflects:

'As the bus hums through the dark, I look out the window at the flat landscape and think of the sea. Now for the first time I begin to think of what *Toad* has done for me, and suddenly it becomes clear. *Toad* showed me that I could use scavenged inner-tube rubber to replace a diaphragm on a galley pump. That I could be a carpenter if I needed to be, or a navigator; that I could sleep for no loner than 30 minutes at a time for weeks on end. That after disgracing myelf years ago in a Bristol Channel gale, I could go back to sea alone and acquit myself well. For most of the last 40 days, *Toad* and I flew across the sea together as sleekly and happily as partners in a fairy tale: a boy riding on a magic dolphin. Through my shame and grief I find I'm proud of our fine voyage. The ending was simply how it finished, not the voyage itself.

What I will do now is find my way back to the sea.'

■ LESSONS LEARNED

- As many stories in this book graphically demonstrate, old wooden boats and leaks are a disastrous combination. Peter Nichols admits that *Toad*'s seams, hadn't been caulked for a decade at least. The old, brittle caulking simply washed out of the seams.
- As the boat turned into a colander, Nichols went on deck and saw the hull's sheathing had delaminated at the bow and peeled back down both sides of the boat... 'Great obscene flaps waving from amidships'. Heaving-to, to stop, or limit the ingress of water, is one method of slowing the flood of water. Another would be to deploy a collision mat, or a sail, over the damaged area. But in this case it was not an option.
- It takes an emergency like this to realise just how important the manual bilge pump is aboard a yacht. Bilge pumps are one of the most neglected and essential pieces of equipment on every

boat and the manual pump is the most important and of all. In these days of cheap electric bilge pumps, the hand-operated back-up is often forgotten, but as anyone who has sailed for more than a few years knows, electric units are not always reliable. The automatic float switch can jam, seize up, or just pack in. Motors can burn out and the connections corrode.

- A manual bilge pump, as Peter Nichols discovered, will give you valuable breathing time, more than doubling your pumping capacity and perhaps allow you to find and fix the leak, or in Nichols' case, prepare for an orderly evacuation.

- It's important to make sure your strum box (the filter in the bilge) does not get clogged by rubbish – matchsticks, clothes or plastic wrapping – and is accessible.

- It's often said that 'No-one bails faster than a drowning man with a bucket!' and in a recent test in *Yachting Monthly* magazine, the man with a bucket was the second fastest (54 litres a minute) to the best bilge pump (63 litres).

- Finally, Nichols' last act was to make sure his beloved vessel sank – so no other yacht would collide with the wreck and sink herself. Having pumped 'like a mad metronome' for five days, he finally cut the plastic hose on one of the seacocks, allowing the ocean that he had tried to keep at bay to gush in and finish what it had begun.

SEA DARK, SKY CRYING

Yacht	*Ecureuil Poitou Charentes 2*, 60ft cutter designed by Jean Berret with a canting keel, a beam of 17ft 8in and a draught of 14ft 10in
Skipper	Isabelle Autissier
Bound from	Cape Town to Sydney
Date of loss	28 December 1994
Position	920 miles SSE of Adelaide

Isabelle Autissier, the only woman competing in the 1994–95 BOC Challenge Round the World Single-handed Yacht Race, was forced to abandon her crippled yacht deep in the Southern Ocean, plucked by helicopter at the limits of rescue services.

IT TOOK JUST A SPLIT second and an unavoidable slam on the port side for Isabelle Autissier's dreams to suddenly come toppling down around her. A rigging screw on her yacht's main port shroud failed and the mast collapsed over the starboard side, snapped at the base.

It was 2 December and the 38-year-old French yachtswoman, a marine science professor and engineer, was halfway between Cape Town and the Kerguelen Islands on the seventh day of the second leg of the BOC Challenge Round the World Singlehanded Yacht Race.

Her 60ft rocket ship *EPC2* had streaked away down the Atlantic from the September start in Charleston, South Carolina, America, to win a decisive victory in the first leg of the race, leaving the men, her fellow competitors, 1,200 miles astern, battling in her wake for second place. Now she was the southernmost boat in the fleet of 14, reduced from the 18 competitors that had begun the epic race.

'I felt like I had been hit in the stomach. I thought "No. Not this. Not here." It was already over for me. But what was the use of yelling, shouting and crying for a victory that was completely lost?' Isabelle asked herself. She sent a message to Race HQ in Charleston: 'Dismasted. No danger immediately.' She was 1,200 miles from Cape Town, and lying at 48° 52' S.

There was no time to waste. A mast can become a horrific hammer of carbon fibre threatening to puncture the hull of a yacht. The winch at the foot of the mast was already starting to smash a hole in the deck. With hacksaw, pliers and a knife, Isabelle scrabbled about on her knees, cutting away the rig as the yacht rolled. She tried to save the boom, but it broke, dragged down by the weight of the mainsail. Ninety minutes later, she had cut away most of the rig and stood on the bare deck of her yacht. She had one complete spinnaker pole and half of a broken one.

'There are 5,000 miles left to Sydney. I feel so much like crying for my lost hopes. But this is the way racing goes.'

Fellow competitor David Adams, 65 miles away, diverted to her position, sailing at 11 knots in storm force winds. All day long in rough sea conditions and strengthening winds, Isabelle worked to set up a replacement rig. In an eloquent satcom message to her supporters in France, she described her plight: 'Thirty knots of wind, sea dark, sky crying. I'm working to clear off the deck and see what I can do. There is almost nothing left on deck. Nothing left of my dream. But I won't think about that now. I am safe …'

By evening she had managed to put the small pole at the mast foot, ready to use it as a support for raising the main 9m pole as her replacement mast the next day. Out of the mist and the darkness that night appeared the ghostly silhouette of David Adams' *True Blue*. He swept past riding the ocean swell under three reefs. Adams was a close friend as well as fellow competitor. More than anyone else in the race he would understand the emotional turmoil Isabelle was suffering.

As Adams passed to leeward, Isabelle could see his silhouette on deck.

'How are you Isa? Can I help?' he shouted at the shadowy figure of Isabelle on deck waving a torch. The mastless boat was, in Adams' words, 'rolling her guts out'.

'No Dave, just think about me. It's just so good to see you that's all. Good luck. Have a good race, see you in Sydney,' she yelled back.

Adams stayed on station for a while. Conversation was impossible. They could only talk in bursts of shouting. They switched to 'talking' for a while on their laptop computers, via Satcom-C.

'There was nothing I could do. There was no way Isabelle was going to get off and no point in my hanging around. If you accept outside help you are disqualified,' said Adams afterwards. Soon his blue hull faded away in the darkness.

But he was deeply affected. 'Isabelle didn't need my help so I carried on. But for two days I couldn't get anything together.'

For Isabelle, too, it was hard to keep up her spirits. 'Everything tastes like ashes and I am physically and mentally exhausted. What is the point in continuing a race already lost? But I already know I will carry on because one cannot quit like that. I am in the race until I cross the finishing line, no matter what it takes.'

As she slept that night it was blowing 40 knots and *EPC2* was drifting due south of two remote island outposts: Marion Island and Prince Edward Island. Coast Guard officials in South Africa had been notified and had an aircraft on standby alert.

'Perhaps the Indian Ocean doesn't want me,' thought Isabelle as she lay in her bunk. She had suffered a dismasting four years ago on this same leg of the BOC Challenge, south of Tasmania. On that occasion, the mast broke at the first spreader and she fashioned a jury rig and sailed into Sydney Harbour to step a new mast. She gained many admirers by going on to complete her circumnavigation.

At the crack of dawn next day, Isabelle began work afresh on erecting an emergency mast. Using her small 5m broken spinnaker pole, with a halyard rigged from the top, she raised the 9m pole. 'I am forgetting about the second leg. My goal is to arrive in Sydney with enough time to make preparations to start leg three with the others.'

Under two tiny headsails, Isabelle set course for Kerguelen Island, a remote French outpost some 1,200 miles away that was home to weather and scientific research stations.

Two days later, when the sun was out, she worked to reinforce the base of her new mast with epoxy glue and carbon fibre. She wound a length of small diameter rope around the mast and glued it together to add thickness at the foot. In the damp conditions, to help it dry, she made a tent around the mast and used her small emergency generator inside to add warmth. *EPC2* was averaging 4 knots and was expected to arrive at Kerguelen Island in 13 days. Sources in France found a replacement mast for her yacht on Reunion Island that was shipped to Kerguelen on a French cargo vessel.

Two weeks later, sailing under jury rig, Isabelle, dubbed 'Isabelle the Incredible', arrived at Kerguelen Island eager to re-rig her yacht with the replacement mast.

It was snowing hard and the winds were over 40 knots as *EPC2* was towed into the protected harbour by a French scientific vessel conducting studies in the Antarctic region.

After a three-day stop at Kerguelen, Isabelle had converted *EPC2* from a single-masted sloop into a double-masted yawl, using her spin-naker pole as a mizzen mast. Her new 13m main mast was from a much smaller Figaro solo yacht and a set of sails had been donated by French yachtsmen Philippe Poupon and Pierre Follenfant.

On the 20th day of leg two, Isabelle reported: 'I'm now at sea again. Everyone has been wonderful. Now I'm heading for Sydney as fast as I can.' Her new rig gave her the ability to fly 70 sq m of sail on an upwind heading and 153 sq m for reaching and running. Position reports showed she was averaging over 9 knots. Under her drastically shortened emergency rig, Isabelle reeled off a remarkable 24-hour run of 229 miles.

But 12 days later on 28 December, the 32nd day of leg two, Isabelle was averaging 8 knots under bare poles with the wind howling around her at 60–70 knots. The yacht had been laid over twice, creating chaos in the cabin, but things seemed to be holding up reasonably well. She tried to sleep on the cabin floor to avoid being thrown from her bunk.

'The crests of the waves were a beautiful sight, but a worrying one,' she said. 'Around noon the wind eased slightly and it was time to put up the storm jib.'

But she was concerned about her small makeshift mast. Before she put the sail up she wanted to finish a small repair job in the yacht's aft compartment. It was a decision that probably saved her life. The wind was gusting and had changed direction as the storm system moved on, causing the swells to combine into monstrous seas. She was at the back of the yacht in the narrow tunnel-like passage that linked the main cabin and the watertight aft compartment containing the yacht's steering systems.

'It was then that I heard it coming ... like a powerful locomotive. I instinctively crouched down. I knew it was going to flatten the boat.' A rogue monster wave crashed over the yacht, launching it through a semipitchpole, end-over-end. At the same time the yacht did a corkscrew rollover through 360°. She was thrown onto the roof, choked by a rush of ice cold water. 'I could feel it rolling. I fell on the bulkhead, then on the ceiling, then on the other bulkhead. When I opened my eyes the boat was full of water. If I had been on deck I would have been washed away. It was very great for me that I was not there.'

The whole incident had lasted not more than 20 seconds. Isabelle crawled out of the tunnel and was speechless at what she saw. The yacht's cabin roof above the navigation station and her living quarters had disappeared. There was a gaping hole of 5 sq m where the carbon fibre coachroof had exploded under the water pressure. All she could see was forbidding grey sky and the sea washing in as waves continued to sweep the deck. The air pressure had plucked a lot of loose items out of the yacht in the rollover. The devastation was as sure as it was complete.

'I was standing in water with equipment floating around me. The batteries and generator and other electrical equipment were submerged. I was lucky. Everything that was at the navigation station was sucked out of the boat. If I had been sleeping or at the chart table, I would have been washed away ...'

On deck, most of *EPC2*'s jury masts and rigging had been swept away by the ocean. Isabelle's world had literally turned upside down 920 miles south-south-east of Adelaide. The boat was very low in the water, almost half submerged. She had to act quickly.

'A second wave would definitely finish us,' she thought. For two hours she bailed out as much water as possible using a bucket and stretched a sail over the gaping hole in the cabin roof, using a salvaged spar as a ridgepole for her makeshift 'tent'.

'All the steering systems were gone. The tiller had come away under pressure, leaving a hole which was leaking water into the once watertight rear compartment.'

The water temperature was freezing and the current was taking Isabelle further south, away from the nearest land. The air temperature was only 5°C with the wind chill factor sending even that plunging to -15°C. At first she thought she might try to go on. Her defiant optimism told her she might somehow rebuild the jury rig. Slowly reality dawned as fatigue took over. The steering system was destroyed. She was exhausted from sailing for three weeks with a jury rig.

'With the state of my boat and my personal state I knew it would not be safe to try and get to Sydney. I had to save what could be saved.' Two hours after the rollover, and for the first time in her seafaring life, Isabelle took out her distress beacons, two Alden 406 EPIRBs, and as night began to fall she switched them on.

'The small lights began to flash and up there in the stars the satellite picked up my call,' she said.

Like all yachts in the BOC Challenge, Isabelle had two emergency beacons, a liferaft and survival gear in case she had to abandon her yacht in extreme conditions. 'When I switched on my EPIRBs I was quite confident of my rescue. I knew it was a good system … I had never used it before, but I have seen it working for other people. It is an incredible organisation,' she told reporters later.

Both EPIRBs were triggered just before six in the evening Sydney time. Ashore, BOC Challenge staff alerted by a satellite ground station immediately went into their well-rehearsed emergency procedures. An anxious message was relayed by Peter Dunning from Race HQ in Charleston: 'Isabelle, do you have problems? We have a 406 EPIRB alarm from you. Please let us know, Pete.'

Search and rescue operations were co-ordinated by Australia's MRCC in Canberra, while in France Isabelle's family were notified.

The BOC Challenge has a history of fellow racers coming to the aid of competitors in distress. In this instance, Nigel Rowe, more than 250 miles away on board *Sky Catcher*, received a message from Race HQ: 'Once more we need your help. Two EPIRB 406 alerts from Isabelle. Not responding to Standard-C polls or messages. Please be on standby. Please cease easterly progress until we sort this one out.'

Nigel, battling against survival conditions himself in the same low pressure system, was hove-to in 50–60 knots of wind with huge breaking seas and damaged self-steering.

At Royal Australian Air Force bases near Sydney and Adelaide, flight crews were scrambled on long-range aircraft. A military search plane was on standby to fly to the yacht's last known position at first light next day.

As darkness fell on that first long night at sea, Isabelle, realising how far from land she was, knew that no rescue bid would be attempted until the next day. The forward watertight compartment, where her sails were stowed, was the only area on her stricken yacht not submerged in water and not structurally compromised. It was there that she sought refuge.

Lots of things had disappeared in the waves. The aft compartment was full of water and she didn't know if the rudders had gone because she had to shut the watertight doors to keep the boat afloat. She gathered clothes, food and survival gear, including a hand-operated desalinator for making drinking water, and moved into the forward compartment. After the rollover this was to be her home for the next three days. She changed into her one-piece survival suit to try to conserve body warmth in the chilling conditions and wrapped a reflective foil space blanket around her.

It was a sleepless night for BOC race officials, as well as those on duty at Race HQ. All efforts to contact Isabelle by satellite messaging and long range radio had been in vain. From the slow drift of the EPIRB signals they knew something was badly wrong. Was Isabelle still with the yacht or in her liferaft? Or had the yacht sunk, leaving only the beacons afloat to transmit their bleak alarm?

Early next day a C-130 Hercules aircraft left Adelaide at 0400 on a mercy mission to find Isabelle and her yacht. The plane carried an extra passenger, Serge Viviand, head of Isabelle's shore support crew. The plane, equipped to drop liferafts, hand-held VHF radios and other survival gear, took four hours to reach the search area after a refuelling stop in Tasmania.

By dawn, Isabelle was already awake with the cold and had started work to clear the deck of broken rigging and spars ready for any rescue operation. She was tired and staggered around as the mastless yacht pitched and rolled in the heavy Southern Ocean swell. Suddenly she heard a distant rumble and looked up to see a plane flying overhead.

SEA DARK, SKY CRYING ••• 59

At around 0900 the plane had reached the search area. But sighting Isabelle was not easy. The positions given by the two distress beacons on board *EPC2* were sometimes as much as 9 miles apart. And to make things even harder, from the skies above, the white deck of the stricken yacht was invisible against the backdrop of breaking wave crests. It took an agonising two hours and 50 minutes before the Hercules confirmed a visual sighting of the yacht. Isabelle on deck jumped up and down and waved to the search plane to show that she was uninjured. She was reported to be 'fit and well' and 'very near the location that her distress signal had begun transmitting.'

It had been an anxious 18-hour wait before the world knew that Isabelle Autissier was alive and still aboard her yacht.

'When I heard the plane it was a great moment for me,' said Isabelle. 'Communication was impossible because my radio was out of action. I sobbed with emotion.'

From the time they arrived, the Royal Australian Airforce never left Isabelle. Having found their needle in a haystack, they didn't want to risk losing her again. Military aircraft relayed every few hours and remained on station, like guardian angels, keeping a watch over her and monitoring the yacht's drift. The Hercules took some three hours to fly to her position and was able to stay four hours before flying back to refuel. An Orion PC3 antisubmarine aircraft also remained on vigil during daylight hours.

The rescue planes tried to establish voice contact to get details of her physical condition and the extent of onboard damage. But Isabelle's own emergency hand-held radio, even in its waterproof bag, had been flooded and rendered useless. At the same time the Australian Navy frigate, HMAS *Darwin*, was despatched from Fremantle, Western Australia. It was not expected to reach Isabelle's position for four days, on late Sunday afternoon. A Seahawk helicopter was despatched from Albany to rendezvous with the frigate and join the rescue mission.

With only visual contact possible with Isabelle, the Hercules plane, flying low over the water at 200km per hour, made precision drops of liferafts and supply canisters loaded with survival items, including flares, water and a hand-held VHF radio. Knowing that Isabelle was unable to manoeuvre the yacht, the pilots and crew invented a new system. They dropped two plastic canisters strung together with a

floating line. The plan was that the canisters, dropped upwind of
EPC2, would drift down towards the yacht and float either side of the
hull with the line snagging on the yacht's keel to stop them drifting
past. The first drop missed the yacht. On the second, the rope broke
and the canisters were lost in the heavy swell and gusting winds. Eventually, Serge Viviand, on the same Hercules that had spotted *EPC2*,
reported back to the BOC Challenge that an 11-person liferaft
containing a hand-held VHF radio had been successfully dropped in
the 50-knot winds and gigantic seas. Isabelle had managed to secure it
alongside the yacht. The liferaft was inflated and 'the yacht was bobbing
around like cork,' said Viviand. 'Both *EPC2*'s masts were down,
though a portion of the main spar was secured on deck.'

'The pilots' skills were amazing,' said Isabelle. 'What they could do
dropping me things at high speeds just above me was incredible ...
through a large hole at the rear of the plane I could see small figures
moving.'

Frustratingly for the rescue crew, Isabelle did not realise that the
liferaft contained a radio for her to make contact with the plane's
crew.

By now the rescuers and Isabelle had worked out a kind of system
for communicating. If they wanted her to come on deck they would
pass over very low 'making one hell of a noise!' If they wanted to drop
equipment they would first drop smoke markers to calculate the drift
and wind direction. The crew of the Orion aircraft tried signalling by
Morse and hand to tell Isabelle that the liferaft contained a radio. The
second afternoon after being sighted, Isabelle located the radio and
made voice contact with the crew of the Orion.

For the first time she learned that HMAS *Darwin* was en route to
her position, having recalled its sailors from their Christmas holidays.
She was also told of plans to lift her off her yacht by *Darwin*'s on-board
helicopter in two days' time.

She told the rescue plane that the rear compartment of *EPC2* was
flooded and she had lost all steering capability. She added that she had
plenty of food and water in her stores. The RAAF Orion PC3 aircraft
crew arranged a regular radio schedule with Isabelle.

While Isabelle faced a wait of some 40 hours, she also started to
come to terms with the impending separation from her yacht, which

had become such a part of her life after three years of work and thousands of miles.

December 31 brought mixed emotions. Relief that rescue was imminent, for she had been told that she would be lifted off her yacht by helicopter early that morning. Sadness that she was leaving her yacht. But she was overjoyed to hear that a salvage attempt was going to be made from Hobart to recover *EPC2*.

In one of the last drops from the plane there were two apples and a carefully packed beer for New Year's Eve 'celebration'. They also dropped two new EPIRB beacons so that before abandoning her yacht, she could activate them to assist the salvage ship in finding *EPC2*. The signals would last a maximum of 60 hours, probably less as the cold temperatures drained the lithium batteries. It had taken nearly three hours for search aircraft to find *EPC2*, so what chance did a salvage vessel have, with its much more limited field of vision at sea level?

Isabelle's last night on board was strange, damp and cold. 'A New Year's Eve in the darkness of the sail locker, wrapped in a rescue blanket.' She took photographs of herself and the damaged yacht as a final remembrance.

As dawn lit up her dark world, another low, noisy fly-past brought her up on deck. The wind was blowing 20–25 knots. A new noise filled the sky. 'At sunrise I heard it coming. It happened very quickly.' A Sea Hawk helicopter was hovering over the area which she had cleared on deck at the front of the yacht. She activated the EPIRBs.

'An incredible acrobat was hanging from a rope. He made it onto the deck and put a harness around me and we were winched back up together.'

It was 0659 Sydney time on New Year's Eve. Three days after the rogue wave had overwhelmed her yacht, Autissier suddenly felt a great pang of sadness as she looked down on the heaving deck of *EPC2*.

'This is the first time I had to leave my boat. It was very difficult. The yacht represents three years of my life, thinking about and preparing for the BOC. After the first leg everything was so wonderful for me. I had a big lead. But I have done a BOC before. I know what can happen. But this time the Indian Ocean was very tough for me ...'

Within 30 minutes the helicopter had landed on HMAS *Darwin*, which turned towards Adelaide with an ETA of midday 2 January.

In a ship to shore call to the BOC Race office in Sydney, Isabelle said she was feeling good. 'I am dressed like a sailor in the Australian Navy,' she said. 'The colours are good for me.' The colour of her fleet air arm jump suit was grey. She was not quite in mourning.

On board she showered, ate and slept deeply. Some 24 hours after she had been airlifted aboard, she boarded the helicopter again as the warship approached the Australian coast and was flown to Edinburgh Air Force Base near Adelaide, where she stepped on to dry land for the first time in 37 days. Her smile and expression of relief said it all.

'I am here because of you and I will never forget that,' she told her rescuers. She was reunited with her shore crew, wearing a T-shirt that bore the legend: 'I spent New Year's Eve with 200 Aussie sailors.' She had finished the race with only 'my wet passport and my wet credit cards'.

So ended one of the most dramatic rescues in the history of ocean yacht racing as the courageous Frenchwoman twice lost the rig from her yacht in one leg and then found her life in deadly jeopardy. The incident graphically demonstrated how fate and fortune could single out even the best prepared yacht in the race while others less well prepared survived to sail on.

■ LESSONS LEARNED

- Many lessons would be learned from Isabelle's rescue. Most important was the question of making a yacht more visible to searchers. The white deck of *EPC2* proved almost invisible against the breaking waves. Having a yacht's deck painted in a bright, visible colour, or having a sheet of fluorescent material that could be tied to the deck to make sighting easier, would be a necessity in future.

- As Isabelle observed of her first dismasting 'a mast can become a horrific hammer of carbon fibre threatening to puncture the hull of a yacht'. She was quick to cut away the rig, using a hacksaw, pliers and a knife. A good hacksaw and spare blades as an essential safety item aboard an offshore yacht. Many skippers carry strong bolt-croppers.

- It's also essential in a dismasting not to ditch the entire to rig overboard. Try and save what you can to set up a jury rig of some sort to sail to safety. Isabelle tried her best to save the boom, but in this instance it was not possible. A spinnaker pole was eventually used to fashion a jury rig to sail to the Kerguelen islands.

- Days later, when her world turned upside down again as the yacht was rolled, it was Isabelle's two 406 EPIRB distress beacons that were her saviour. Other essential life-and-death equipment aboard the yacht included a forward watertight compartment, plus survival gear. Shutting the watertight doors to keep the boat afloat, Isabelle gathered clothes and food. Her survival gear, included a hand-operated desalinator to make drinking water. She also had an emergency hand-held radio, but even in its waterproof bag, it had been flooded and rendered useless.

- To conserve body warmth in the chilling conditions she wore a one-piece survival suit and wrapped a reflective foil space blanket around her. Isabelle's own Hercules plane, flying low over the water at 200km per hour, made precision drops of liferafts and supply canisters loaded with survival items, including flares, water and a handheld VHF radio.

THE CAT THAT CAPSIZED

Yacht	*Lazy Daisy* (29ft 6in Catalac catamaran)
Skipper	Lionel Miller
Crew	Bruce Rankin, Bill Tulloch, Charlie Tulloch
Bound from	Inverness to Kinghorn, Scotland
Date of loss	24 October 1980
Position	off Rattray Head, Scotland

Lazy Daisy had left Inverness at 1345 in good weather on a day in late October 1980, bound for Kinghorn on the north bank of the Forth, some 250 miles away. Lionel Miller tells the story.

WE QUICKLY SETTLED INTO A three-hour watchkeeping routine. The weather remained fine and the wind gradually strengthened until we decided to put in a reef just before sunset. The sea was steadily becoming lumpier and all except Bruce began to suffer seasickness from time to time, but without too serious an effect on performance. The boat was making excellent progress and we were in good spirits. Mine were improved still more when I caught Bruce retching and attempting to spit to windward (ex marine engineers are not used to being sick, unlike us family sailors).

Bill and I left Charlie and Bruce in charge at 0200 and got our heads down for a highly appreciated rest in warm sleeping bags. The noise below was continuous and the boat felt like an old car being driven fast on a rough track but we were tired and pleased to pass the responsibility to the other watch for a bit.

We were roused from our wet sleeping bags by a shout from Bruce:

'Your watch.' As we came on deck we could see that we were rounding the corner at Kinnards Head and the NE Force 6 was giving us a broad reach as we turned south. Big rolling seas were swept with silver grey spume under a brilliant cold full moon. Unfortunately, our stomachs were unaffected by the beautiful scene and we both moved quickly across to the leeside to be sick. That chore completed, we all got busy to dowse the reefed main and open out the roller jib. Bruce, off watch after three hours on the helm, disappeared below to make himself a thick cheese butty and Charlie fastidiously removed his boots and jacket and climbed in the still-warm quarter berth. My watchmate, Bill, decided to call the Coastguard on VHF to report all's well (a task which my stomach would not allow) and then came back on deck. The boat was handling well as the wind came aft and we had obviously seen the last of beating for a bit as we turned ever further towards the south.

We were making great time and had actually caught the last of the south-going tide round Buchan Ness over six hours ahead of our planned time. Bruce and Charlie had debated whether to go into Fraserburgh, but the look of the harbour entrance in the offshore seas, plus the excellent chance of getting round on the favourable tide, persuaded them to press on. I was well pleased with the way things were going and handed the helm to Bill for a spell. Lying in the cabin out of the wind I was reasonably warm and comfortable and I wondered whether to get my exposure suit and wellies on, but the thought of going and searching in the forward cabin hanging locker was not appealing. After ten minutes or so, the motion altered and I suspected an increase in wind. Out on deck again Bill suggested reducing sail, but I wanted to keep the speed up so as to get well clear of the strong tidal area before the tide turned north. I therefore took the helm to assess the situation. We were doing 6–8 knots SE with an apparent wind speed of 25 knots from the north under full jib. The boat was certainly flying along but the heel was not excessive and with the wind so far abaft the beam I felt quite content. The waves were now giving us some fast sleigh rides as we boiled along and, despite the darkness and cold, at 0530 we were having a great sail.

Suddenly I found the boat going downhill at an alarming angle, the high flared bows were almost under water despite their enormous reserves of buoyancy, and the hulls vibrated with a deep humming sound as we tore through the water at 12 knots plus. This was unexpected and rather frightening. Bill again looked at me to see if we should reduce sail, but I felt the problem was the size and steepness of the wave rather than the wind forces, so I turned the boat so as to present her port quarter to the seas, which did not look any bigger than previously. Down below, Bruce lay awake listening to the crashing and banging of the waves against the hulls. He did not like the sound of our speed as we tore down the waves, and his cheese sandwich was not helping either. Charlie on the other hand was sleeping the sleep of the just – just off watch.

Bill suddenly noticed that the inflatable dinghy, which we carry hooked to the aft rail, had come untied at one end. He knelt on the seats and leaned over the rail as he struggled to bring it inboard. I hoped that he could manage to tie it on again successfully, as it would be far too cumbersome to have lying around in the cockpit. It was difficult to concentrate on the problem while steering because of the need to keep a watch on the waves coming up astern.

Looking round now, all thoughts of the dinghy problem vanished. The wave coming up now was very big, perhaps 30ft, but the threat of destruction was in the 5ft-high breaking crest which was commencing its avalanche down the long slope towards us.

This was obviously a 'survival wave' for our boat with its large open cockpit and lovely big windows. I shouted a warning, and then concentrated on holding the boat on course to take the sea on the quarter, but it was impossible. The stern was smashed round and we were hit almost broadside by many tons of water travelling at 20–30mph. The enormous thrust of the impact lifted the boat into a vertical position and the press of water under the bridgedeck completed the capsize in a matter of 2–3 seconds.

Below, Charlie awoke in mid-air as he flew towards the ceiling. Hitting it, he expected to fall on the floor, but instead the floor fell on him, followed shortly by a lot of ice-cold sea!

Meanwhile, in the other hull, Bruce felt a mighty lurch and heard the loudest cacophony it is possible to imagine, as bottles, pans, plates, tools flew across the boat and smashed into the windows over his head. Tonic and lemonade bottles exploded and several knives and forks stuck into the hull after falling the full width of the boat. Bruce thought, 'He's been and gone and done it' as the cabin rotated around and things crashed down towards him.

Outside, Bill was flung across the cockpit as the boat accelerated sideways and lifted. He distinctly remembers the blue flash as the batteries shorted out, and then we were both in the water under the boat. I thought 'when the boat sinks, we will all drown', and reckoned we had about 15 minutes left. Bill swam under the cockpit seats to the outside but my brain had begun to work again and I realised that the boat might not sink after all.

Inside the boat, Charlie picked himself up off the ceiling and made his way forward through the waist-high water and debris while his mind grappled with the problem of finding the way out. 'Up' was now down and 'right' had become left. The normal route out to the cockpit was turn right, up steps on to the bridgedeck and right again. The new route in the cold wet darkness was left, downwards and left again. Pursuing this course, he came across Bruce who was attempting to find the door catch. Eventually, Bruce found the knob, opened the door an inch or two then pushed it wide as the pressure equalised.

On the other side of the door I had heard Bruce and Charlie talking and swam over to help open the door and to advise them that we might be better off inside the boat rather than outside. They came out and we started to discuss whether to go outside or not, when suddenly the air under the cockpit disappeared into the hull via the open door and the floor of the cockpit came down to push our heads under water. That curtailed the discussion and we all dived towards the outside.

Bill, of course, had been outside for some minutes and, ever litter conscious, had tidily collected a floating fender and lifebelt and put them into the dinghy, which had luckily come unhitched from all its fastenings, except the painter, and lay bobbing happily at the stern. He had just climbed in when our three heads popped up and we realised that we had all come through the first test.

Once we had all got in the dinghy and saw that the boat was not going to sink immediately we decided to climb onto the bridgedeck and take the dinghy with us. Unfortunately, the dinghy was impossible to untie and none of us had a knife. Luck was on our side again, however, because the painter broke as we climbed out and we soon gathered on the bridgedeck with it. The waves occasionally washed through between the hulls but although we had no way of tying on, it was quite easy to stay put and the upturned hulls broke the force of the wind.

Exposure was now the problem, particularly for Charlie who had taken off his windproof jacket and boots when he went to bed. We all huddled together against the windward hull, which made a good windbreak.

Ashore we could see the lights of civilisation, but we knew that it could be a long time before we were spotted or even missed after our reassuring radio check. Time passed rapidly, although we began to ache from standing in one spot and to shiver from the cold. A grey dawn broke and we could see that though the tide was carrying us north, the wind was pushing us inshore slightly. Another hour and we could see that we were drifting towards a long shallow bay fringed by sand dunes. We decided to beach through the surf in the dinghy as the big waves could have easily rolled and smashed the cat on top of us.

About half a mile off the beach the wreckage began to drag on the bottom and our drift slowed. We launched the dinghy and began paddling with our hands downwind towards the breakers. The waves were piling into magnificent combers as they swept in and at first we dreaded the thought of eventually entering them. After almost half an hour of exhausting paddling, however, we were disappointed every time one missed us and we had to paddle some more.

We developed a technique to prevent capsize in the breaking crests. We all threw ourselves sideways towards the breaker as it struck and after a while we were able to judge quite well just how hard we needed to thrust to remain on an even keel. Obviously our second moment of serious danger was imminent and we all wished each other luck every time 'the' big one bore down on us. After a while we began to feel a bit stupid at this abortive ritual and so we yelled at the waves to come and get us. Eventually, one heard and it impressed us considerably as it mounted and surged towards us. It broke and swept down on us head high in a mass of frothing foam. Bruce and Bill were pushed forward by the impact and the rope Bill was holding broke. Charlie and myself at the front were thrown back by the acceleration and then we were off. The dinghy (just 9ft long, completely full of water and four grown men) picked up to full speed to match the wave and wriggled like a live thing beneath us. Our heads and shoulders emerged from the foam and we shouted with the exhilaration of surfing at 20 knots in towards deliverance. The surge carried us as though we were an underwater bobsleigh and we covered the 200 yards into the beach in less than half a minute.

Will we buy another multihull? Most definitely – a monohull would certainly have been rolled 360° and might have sunk with the loss of all hands.

■ LESSONS LEARNED

- *Lazy Daisy* was a Catalac catamaran, modified by having 7ft by 12in keels fitted to her hulls. It is very tempting to say that, in this case, the catamaran was capsized because of her excessive speed. But no one can be sure what would have happened had she lain a-hull.
- Lionel Miller seems to have been unaware of any risks and remembers that 'the waves were giving us some fast sleigh rides as we boiled along; despite the darkness and cold, we were having a great sail'. Then the warning came: 'Suddenly the boat was going downhill at an alarming angle, the high flared bows were almost under water, despite their enormous reserves of buoyancy. The hulls vibrated with a deep humming sound as we tore through the water at 12 knots plus.'
- Miller also recalls lying in the cabin out of the wind. 'I was reasonably warm and comfortable and I wondered whether to get my exposure suit and wellies on, but the thought of going and searching in the forward cabin hanging locker was not appealing.' Perhaps, like the rule of thumb on reefing, the time to act in such circumstances is when you first think of it. Exposure to the elements became a problem later on.
- For *Lazy Daisy*, with her large open cockpit and big windows, the avalanching wave that capsized her in a matter of seconds

was not survivable. But for offshore passage-making, when extreme conditions can catch you out, a surveyor would undoubtedly look closely at the method and speed of draining the cockpit, as well as recommend carrying plywood storm shutters, with an internal strongback, to bolt over the biggest ports. Having secure lockers to stop galley knives becoming deadly projectiles in a capsize is another consideration.

- The importance of always carrying a sailor's knife was highlighted when Miller and his crew took to their dinghy and couldn't untie the painter. Fortunately, luck was on their side when it broke.

seven

THE GRANITE GRAVEYARD

Yacht	*Quiver* (21ft 6in gaff cutter)
Skipper	Michael D Millar
Crew	Richard Penn
Bound from	St Peter Port, Guernsey to Lannion Bay, North Brittany
Date of loss	4 June 1971
Position	NE side of Les Triagoz Rocks

Michael Miller, a past President of the Old Gaffers' Association, accompanied by his grandson as crew, left Chichester Harbour on Saturday 29 May 1971, with the intention of attending an Old Gaffers' Rally in Braye Harbour, Alderney, later that weekend. Millar had owned Quiver *for 16 years, and Richard Penn had sailed with him for almost as long.*

QUIVER WAS THOUGHT TO HAVE been built in Cowes in 1895 and was probably converted from an open boat around 1920. Late in her life she was fitted with a small inboard petrol engine. Because of contrary winds, they did not cross to France directly, but called first at Yarmouth, Isle of Wight, Poole, and Lulworth Cove, where they spent the Sunday night. After setting out on Monday morning to sail to some Devon port, the wind became favourable for a Channel crossing and they set course for Alderney, arriving in Braye Harbour early on Tuesday morning (too late for the Old Gaffers). They moved on to Guernsey after hearing a forecast that it would soon blow from the north-east. Two frustrating days were spent in St Peter Port, which they left on Friday morning.

'We decided to head for Lannion Bay in the eastern end of Morlaix Bay; it appeared to have easy access by day or night (we should probably arrive in the dark, and those French leading lights are terrific), and was reputed to be good holding in firm sand. It promised a cosy anchorage on a weather shore. Furthermore, it was downhill all the way. We did not then realise how steep that hill was to be.

The direct route from St Martin's Point (SE corner of Guernsey) took us between Les Sept Iles and Les Triagoz, two of the reefs lying off the Brittany coast, then between Les Triagoz and Ile Grande, the latter being on the 'corner' of Morlaix Bay, there being a safe gap of over 3 miles between the two. However, this course (240°M so far as I can remember) was dead downwind, and as the wind was a bit fresh for spinnaker work for a crew of two, it would have meant a very tiring day at the tiller. So we decided to make a dogleg of it, and steer due west until the DR put us north of Les Sept Iles, then due south until we found them. This worked very well, enabling us to keep the head-sails drawing all the time, especially when the wind fell light during the afternoon, when we shook out the reefs and changed up from No 2 to No 1 jib.

During the afternoon we saw a French fishing boat executing some alarming manoeuvres, and stood by to take evasive action in view of the stories one has heard of yachts being 'attacked' by such vessels; however, it seemed that she was only locating and picking up her pots on the Banc des Langoustiers, and we were able to exchange cheery greetings as we passed them.

Soon after dark, we picked up the Les Sept Iles light where expected, and, crossing this with a radio bearing on Les Roches Douvres, got a satisfactory fix which showed we were back on our rhumb line.

Being quite happy with the fix, we altered back to the original course of 240°M, and in due time picked up the light on Les Triagoz, where expected, fine on the starboard bow. We were now sailing on a dead run, boom to port and staysail goose-winged to starboard. The log was giving us 5 knots, the fixes indicated that we were making a good 3½ knots, which confirmed the rather meagre information gleaned from the charts and tidal stream atlas that there was an 1½ knot head tide. This tide was supposed to run till about 0400, dropping to about 1 knot in the last hour.

Until about 0130 the sky was clear though the visibility was still apparently poor, and a brilliant moon, three-quarters full, moved steadily round until it was right in our track. If only it had stayed there … but it was not to be. Some heavy cloud came up from the south, across the wind, and blotted everything out, leaving us with nothing but the two lighthouses.

By 0200 we had drawn abreast of Les Sept Iles, and I had a feeling that we were being set somewhat to the SE towards the outlying dangers at the western end of that reef. I therefore altered course more westerly, until the Les Triagoz light was just open to port, for about half an hour, and until I was satisfied that we were well clear of Les Sept Iles. I then altered back about double the amount until Les Triagoz was well open in the starboard rigging; a quick check on the chart confirmed that at 31 knots we made good 2 (and nothing had changed to alter this), we would clear the eastern tip of the Les Triagoz reef by about 1¼ miles, a comfortable margin. At about 0300, I was just contemplating resuming the compass course when *Quiver*, with a resounding crash, stopped dead.

There is, of course, no excuse for wrecking one's ship on a well-charted reef, especially when one can see two lighthouses and one has a commanding wind. But there are, perhaps, reasons. I will suggest three. The first is that during that last hour we had done the full 5 miles over the ground; in other words we had lost the 1½ knots head tide which we had been experiencing, and which we should have had for another hour at least. One can only assume that it was masked by the reef into whose shadow we had sailed; there may even have been a counter-eddy: at any rate we were undoubtedly 1½ miles further on than I thought we were. The second reason may have been that I made my detour by eye on the lighthouse, rather than on compass courses – not very seamanlike. The third reason was undoubtedly because it was 3 o'clock in the morning. We both felt wide awake, and were thoroughly enjoying the ride. I was (thank God) at the helm myself, while Richard was below planning the next move. But at that hour one is not at one's brightest, we may have been taking careless bearings, plotting carelessly, or simply doing our sums wrong; we shall never know, as the deck log and chart went down with everything else.

After the initial impact, which probably broke the stem and

certainly opened up the hood ends, *Quiver* shook herself free of the half-tide rock she had struck, luffed a bit, and went charging off again into the dark. She took a great tombstone square on the bowsprit end, and again stopped dead; in the dim light from the cabin one had the feeling of being in a flooded graveyard, with great slabs of granite sticking up all round, and the water boiling on unseen tombs beneath. She swung round, hinging on the bowsprit, until the port bilges found some of these on which she then pounded for several minutes. We let go all sheets to try to take some of the weight out of it, but the swell kept her pounding until she finally slid clear in a northerly direction. To keep her quiet (and reduce the frightful din of flogging sails), we furled the jib and backed the staysail, leaving the main sheet free. Thus hove-to, she fore-reached at about a knot in water which within a few yards gave a depth of 35 fathoms. We had hit the top of a 200ft cliff.

A quick look below revealed a hopeless situation; Richard was already on the pump, but the water in the cabin was rising at an alarming speed. Water was gushing in both sides of the stem forward, under the port bunk, and again under the cockpit. It would not have been easy to try to deal with one puncture in Force 5 on a pitch black night in a fair old seaway; four or more holes were out of the question – we had to abandon.

While Richard set about releasing the dinghy (9ft Nautisport, fully inflated, upside down on the coachroof), I started in on the flares. My main armament was some seven or eight of the 'Roman Candle' type; they burn a steady red flare in your hand, while throwing up a succession of red balls to a very satisfactory height. They all went off beautifully, and the display must have lasted at least four minutes, possibly longer; the only snag was that there was no audience. The mainland coast was a good 3 miles off, but the visibility was much less than that; I felt sure that the lighthouse should be keeping a watch, but at 0300 … ?

We started loading up the dinghy: oars, rowlocks, pump and bailer. Food? We found a big plastic gash-bag, shoved in cakes, biscuits, tarts, and tied a knot in it. Water? It was all in the tank, with a tiny galley pump and no container to hand. At that moment, six long-life milk cartons conveniently floated out of their locker; in they went. What next? I grabbed my wallet and travellers' cheques; personal kit

– one large travel bag each. Next? My second bag, with all the ship's and personal papers – in it went (it wasn't until two hours later that I realised that it was the wrong second bag; all I saved was a lot of useless hardware).

By this time the water was over the cabin bunks, slowing down a bit as it had more room to spread out, and the relative buoyancy increased, but still rising visibly. We grabbed a few more bits and pieces, but then decided we had better get out in case she took a wave into the cockpit and plunged suddenly. We had been something over ten minutes, probably about quarter of an hour, from the first impact. After we let go, *Quiver* went on fore-reaching in a northerly direction, while we started drifting rapidly WSW. The direct cabin light disappeared quite quickly over our limited horizon, but the glow from it on the sails could be seen for another five minutes or so as she sailed sluggishly into the darkness. Then she just disappeared.

I won't go into all the sordid details of the next ten hours. It was a hell of a long time. Every quarter of an hour or so a wave would sweep right over us, to make sure we were kept as cold and wet as possible. We bailed it all out again, though there was not really much point. We never saw a suspicion of land or vessel the whole time. Cramp was rather trying.

I found that I had in my pocket my plastic hand-bearing compass. It was comforting to confirm, by sighting up wind, that we were being blown WSW, and that therefore France lay somewhere to leeward. I tried rowing, but found that I could not do anything very effective, except in short bursts which were very tiring. I felt however that I had to try to do something useful, so kept gently paddling across the wind in a generally southerly direction, thereby reducing the possibility of missing France altogether. We decided that we really did not know what the tide might be doing to us. Even if we had managed to grab any charts or pilot books which were floating around in the cabin, they would have dissolved before we could have made any use of them.

Sometime about midday, Richard declared that he had been watching for a timed quarter of an hour the same two slag heaps directly to leeward. Unlike all the other land we had been imagining, they were still there. They could only be Ile de Batz. Soon they joined up and became a proper island, with the cliffs above Roscoff appearing opposite. Then a buoy went past, obviously the landfall for the Roscoff channel. Things were looking up … or were they?

As the actual coast became visible, it was increasingly apparent that it was very knobbly; the lighthouse in the channel had spray bursting 20 to 30ft up it; what would happen when we got in among that lot? I decided to try to row across our track sufficiently to guide the dinghy into the Roscoff channel, in the hope that we might be able to pop into the harbour as we went past, or at least find a lee behind it.

Just as I started the lighthouse-dodging operation, I saw the bows of a vessel pointing at me from windward. Digging in my bag, I found a large yellow towel which we hastily lashed to an oar, and which Richard waved vigorously aloft, while I resumed rowing, trying to dodge being flogged in the face by the wet towel. The langoustier, for such it was, altered course away from us to keep to his channel, and we quite decided that he had not seen us. Then figures appeared on deck; the ship stopped, turned, and slowly took up station to windward of us; a rope was thrown, we were hauled alongside. The rolling of the ship made getting aboard relatively easy; you step on the rubbing strake as it rolls down, then you are catapulted over the bulwarks as she goes back. They gaffed our gear with an outsize boathook, then hauled up the dinghy as well.

After that, life became somewhat more civilised. The crew took us down to the aft cabin, stripped us off, and delving into their own bags, found enough spare clothing to kit us out warm and dry. They brewed coffee and laced it with rum; they found some hard tack and butter, chocolate and fags; they did it all with great good humour; one can ask no more of any man.

We were not, as we thought, bound for Roscoff, but for Mogueriec, some 5 miles further west. *Le Rayon de Soleil* (she was the only sunshine we saw that day) was heading for home and Sunday dinner, and the tide being right, was taking the short cut inside Ile de Batz; otherwise …

On arrival at Mogueriec, we met our host for the first time; he had been at the helm hitherto. M Jean Baptiste Le Bihan is a great powerful jolly man, patron-pêcheur, a man of substance, and with a great heart. Initial difficulties over language soon became easier, as he has acquired some English from frequently marketing his catches in Cornish ports.

Our first visitor was the douanier who took one look and decided he was not interested in us. Then came a gentleman who introduced himself as of the French Navy. He was subsequently described in the local newspapers as 'Syndic des Gens de Mer à Roscoff' and 'l'Administrateur de l'Inscription Maritime de Morlaix'. We never did discover which hat this M Balcon was wearing that day, but he made the civilised suggestion that it would be more comfortable if he were to interview us with a glass in our hands, so we adjourned to the local café. Having satisfied him that *Quiver* was not a danger to shipping (he must have been Receiver of Wrecks as well), he undertook, after making his report to his own authorities, to notify the British Embassy in Paris; they in turn reported to the Foreign Office, who telephoned Richard's parents with the true story of what had happened, thus forestalling the inevitable inaccurate, press reports.

Meanwhile, Mme Le Bihan had gathered up all our wet garments, plus our saturated baggage, shoved them into the boot of her car, and taken all home. There she rounded up some neighbours, and they spent the whole of Saturday afternoon and evening feeding it all through the washing machine, hosing out our bags, spreading out all our other bits and pieces to dry. Sunday she spent drying and ironing, so that by Sunday afternoon we had the whole lot back, ready to pack.

Now came the embarrassing bit. We had no passports, therefore my travellers' cheques were useless. We were rapidly eating our way through the few francs I had forearmed myself with at the local hotel. I could not get any more money till I had a passport; I could only get a passport in Paris; how to get the fare? I offered Baptiste (as our host is known to his friends, among whom I now count myself lucky to be numbered) some English money, knowing that he frequently visits British ports, but he would have none of it; we might well need that before we got home. He would buy our rail tickets; and he did just that at 6 o'clock on the Monday morning, after driving us 20 miles into Morlaix to save a taxi fare.

After sorting ourselves out in Paris, we duly obtained temporary passports; then, liberty at last, some money! An evening in Montmartre was indicated, and enjoyed.

We caught the night ferry back from Dunkerque to Dover, where, just to rub things in, the ship went aground while turning to back into her berth. We were rather glad to get home.'

■ LESSONS LEARNED

Quiver was lost because of erroneous estimates of tidal currents. Such mistakes are much more likely to be made at night than during the day when, except in fog, there will be so much more visible evidence by which to assess drift or leeway.

Michael Millar talks about a clear sky with a brilliant moon, three-quarters full, which helped. Until heavy cloud came up from the south and blotted everything out, leaving them with nothing but the two lighthouses.

He was happy with the fix he obtained from Les Sept Iles light and the one on Les Roches Douvres, and altered *Quiver*'s course. But later he had a 'feeling' that they were being set to the south-east and altered course again. 'At about 0300, I was just contemplating resuming the compass course, when *Quiver*, with a resounding crash, stopped dead.'

Millar suggests three reasons for this. The first is that he had lost the 1½ knot head tide which he should have had for another hour at least. He wonders whether it was masked by the reef into whose shadow they had sailed; 'there may even have been a counter-eddy'. At any rate they were 1½ miles further on than he thought. The second reason 'may have been that I made my detour by eye on the lighthouse, rather than on compass courses – not very seamanlike'. The final reason is that at 0300, even though they both felt wide awake, 'one is not at one's brightest, we may have been taking careless bearings, plotting carelessly, or simply doing our sums wrong; we shall never know, as the deck log and chart went down with everything else...'

When they had to abandon *Quiver* in the middle of the night, Millar and his grandson were not well prepared, but then *Quiver* was only sailing between Guernsey and Brittany and they were no more than 3 or 4 miles offshore. But the importance of a well-prepared 'grab bag' or 'panic bag' is demonstrated.

The water was all in the tank, with a tiny galley pump and no container to hand. Fortunately, 'six long-life milk cartons conveniently floated out of their locker'. Into a second bag, Millar put all the ship's and personal papers. Two hours later he discovered it 'was the wrong second bag; all I saved was a lot of useless hardware'.

After deciding to abandon ship, Millar's immediate concern was to get out of *Quiver* and into the 9ft Nautisport dinghy, which, fortunately, had been stowed fully inflated upside down on the cabin top. He also had to signal their distress. He had some seven or eight hand flares. They all went off beautifully and the display lasted at least four minutes, but there was no audience. The importance of keeping in hand a flare for 'a last chance' cannot be underestimated. Flares are one of the many ways in which distress can be signalled, but they cannot always be relied upon, even when in date.

eight

PUMPING FOR THEIR LIVES...

Yacht   *Mariah* (86ft staysail schooner)
Skipper   Ed Clark
Crew   Bruce Paulsen, Chip Williams, Beth Brodie, Jimmy Joner,
            Jay Linsay, Elisabeth Storm
Bound   south from City Island, New York State, USA
Date of loss 26 October 1980
Position   approx. 200 miles SE of Cape May, New Jersey

Mariah, an Alden-designed staysail schooner, was built in 1931, and her owner, Ed Clark, wanted her down south for the winter of 1980–81. They left City Island, New York, at 0100 on the morning of Thursday 23 October, having 'flushed out the bilges, using every pump on board – to see that each was functioning properly'. Bruce Paulsen relates the subsequent events:

THE NIGHT WAS COLD, but crystal clear. The huge clock at the Watchtower Building read 44°F at 0600; a beautiful day, with crisp Canadian air and north-west breezes. Both Bendix and NOAA predicted good weather with a slight trough developing over the middle Atlantic region which could produce some storm activity, but nothing serious. We were not worried since we knew we would be well east of any trouble.

At 0900 we left Ambrose Tower to starboard and were joined by a family of sparrows. The wind was north-west at 15 knots as we broad-reached under full sail. Beth set our course at 140°M, which would take us out across the Gulf Stream. We had a beautiful day of sailing, but by evening clouds began to roll in, and the wind picked up. It was time to shorten sail, so Jimmy and I furled the flying jib, while Ed and Chip double-reefed the main. This left us a bit under-powered but made for a manageable, balanced rig. After a chicken dinner and a brief sip of Jay's renowned homemade wine, we broke into watches.

Jay and I were on deck as the day came to an end. The clouds continued to build as we looked to the west. 'There'll be no sunset tonight,' I told Jay. By 1900 the wind began to veer and increase. At 2000 we dropped the main staysail. The wind, now 25 to 30 knots, swung around to the north-east. We had trouble holding course at 140° and headed down to 160°M. At 0400, we spotted a school of porpoises which lifted our spirits on a cold, grey night.

The wind increased as daylight approached, and continued to shift to the right; by 0600 it was straight out of the east at about 35 knots. The sunrise was a brilliant red; the sparrows had disappeared. Friday was cold and unpleasant, as the wind kicked up to 40 knots, and veered south of east. *Mariah* was working hard and began to leak, which was hardly unusual for a boat of her age. By afternoon our small 7 gallons-per-minute electric pump had trouble keeping up.

Mariah had four bilge pumps aboard; besides the electric pump there was a Whale Gusher on the deck. Its capacity, however, was only about a quarter of a gallon per stroke. Then, there were our big guns: a 50-plus gallons-per-minute Jabsco that ran off the Lehman diesel, and a 75-plus gallons-per-minute firehose/bilge pump that ran off its own one-cylinder diesel mounted in the lazarette. Either could handle any kind of problem. Both had functioned properly ashore. I had said with pride to visitors, 'If we have anything aboard *Mariah*, it's bilge pumps.'

By 1900 Friday we were leaking badly enough to engage the Jabsco. Ed turned over the diesel, and flipped the pump. It worked for a minute or two, but then grew hot and stopped pumping altogether. He took the pump apart and discovered the impeller had been completely destroyed. We inspected the intake for pieces of debris, but the fine screen was still intact. Confused but undaunted, we scraped out all the remnants of the old neoprene impeller, making sure to leave the cylinder perfectly clean. Ed then installed a spare impeller and reassembled the unit. By the time the pump was back together, however, the water in the bilge was over the level of the belt that drives the pump, causing it to slip around its pulley whenever the pump was engaged. Before we could operate the pump, the water level had to be reduced. We then began the gruelling process of bucket-passing which was to last for the next 30 hours.

Beth, Jay and I bailed for about half an hour before the water level was low enough to try the pump again. Ed cleaned the belt with degreaser and once again cranked over the diesel. As before, it functioned for a minute or so before growing hot and stopping completely. Jimmy began pumping the deck pump, but its small capacity made it relatively useless. The rest of us kept bailing with the buckets.

Still not overly worried, we had yet to engage the automatic-priming, one-cylinder diesel, our USCG-approved monster pump. However, once turned on, it would not prime, perhaps because of the 10ft waves. Jay, who knew pumps, assisted Ed, but after repeated attempts, it still would not hold a prime.

By 2400 the decision was made to head for New Jersey and safety. We could still keep up with the incoming water, but we had no pumps. We were 300 or more miles from Bermuda with the wind south-east at 40 knots and increasing. Beating and bailing for three or four days did not seem particularly inviting. Cape May, however, was about 200 miles to the north-west. We could perhaps pick up some gas-driven pumps there and then continue. At 0100, Saturday, we gybed and began to run with the seas at 290°M. We kept bailing.

The wind increased to 50 knots, and squalls were frequent through the night. Seas grew to 20ft or better, leaving both Jimmy and Elisabeth incapacitated by seasickness. Bailing was constant and unbearable, thanks to a break in the main fuel line leaking diesel into the bilge. There was no time for rest, and daybreak brought no relief.

By 0600 the water was a foot over the floorboards. Something had sprung, and it was getting difficult to keep up. At this point, the first of a long series of Maydays was sent, and the tanker *Navios Crusader* relayed our message to the Cape May Coastguard. At 0830 the Coastguard informed us that an aircraft was on the way to drop a 140-gallons-per-minute bilge pump. The news gave the whole crew an emotional lift – the cavalry was coming over the hill. At 1030, Beth, manning the radio, told us that an aircraft was near.

We expected a helicopter, but a huge C-130 transport plane appeared instead. Slightly taken aback, we hoped they were good at high-speed air drops. Our only sail was the double-reefed main staysail, which gave just enough steerage to manoeuvre in the mounting seas. I tried to keep *Mariah* heading 300°; the plane would make its final approach on the reciprocal course. After several practice runs, the pilot approached with amazing speed; we watched anxiously for the drop, but nothing happened. Then Ed spotted a bright orange parachute about 200 yards behind us, to weather. Recovery was impossible, since we could not head upwind. The C-130 headed back to Elizabeth City, NC, for more pumps and would not return for four hours. For the first time, we realised we were in danger of losing the schooner and possibly our lives.

Shortly, the Coastguard informed us they had despatched the 210ft cutter *Alert* to our position. The 30ft seas, however, were keeping her under 10 knots, and she was over 100 miles – 10 hours – away. At noon, two of the main staysail seams blew out, and within minutes the sail was in ribbons. Now running under bare poles, we were pushed by waves as big as houses. Steering was difficult and tiring as the waves continued to mount, yet it provided the only relief from bailing.

At 1430, the C-130 reappeared. This time the orange drum containing the pump was dropped about 300 yards ahead of *Mariah*. I steered toward the drum, visible only every two or three waves, and finally it appeared on the crest of the wave ahead of us. Ed gaffed the parachute which immediately began to tear. The drum submerged as the pressure on it increased, and finally broke away. Strike two.

Another pump was dropped well ahead of us, and once again I pointed *Mariah* toward it. The trail line was difficult to spot in the foamy sea, and once we saw and gaffed it, it was too late. There was no loop in the end of the line; it slipped off into the sea. Strike three.

At 1600 the C-130 departed, telling us an H-3 helicopter was on the way with more pumps, and that another C-130 would circle us until he arrived. *Alert* was getting closer, and the merchant vessel *Dorsetshire* was standing by. By now, however, we had bailed for about 20 hours, and the diesel fumes had formed a thick haze over the knee-deep water in the bilge. Diesel coated everything in the cabin, and the floorboards on the leeward side were floating. Exhaustion was setting in. We were losing ground quickly.

The radio chattered again; it was the Coastguard telling us that the helicopter had been delayed and would not arrive until 2200, four hours away, and we received a message from *Alert* that due to our rapid forward progress, even under bare poles, she would rendezvous with us around the same time. Perhaps our long-awaited pump would finally make it. Meanwhile, we kept working. Ed stopped to rest for a while, knowing that one of us would need to be fresh when the pumps arrived. With Beth on the radio and Jimmy doubled over with pain, that left three of us to bail and steer. Seasickness could not hold us back; Jay vomited into the buckets as he dumped them overboard.

At 2145 the helicopter arrived. The winds were up over hurricane force with waves well over 40ft. I brought the boat up as close to the wind as possible, about abeam to the seas. The water in the saloon was chest high, and the heavy maple floorboards began to slam around, tearing apart the interior. The lee rail was down, with only 3 feet of freeboard on the cabin port and side. In the pitch dark, the helicopter had trouble manoeuvring around our 86ft mainmast, and after half an hour backed off and radioed that instead of lowering a pump, he would begin evacuation procedures. We still wanted a pump more than anything else, but were obviously in no position to disagree.

We were told to inflate our Avon liferaft, which Chip had readied, to place two people at a time into it, and trail it aft. Elisabeth, not a sailor, was overcome with fright, so the captain decided to put her and Jimmy into the liferaft first. Ed streamed the raft out behind *Mariah*. The helicopter's huge floodlights illuminated the monstrous waves as the basket bounced across the water and the liferaft. Jimmy strained to grab the basket, but half an hour passed before he got a good grip and helped Elisabeth into it. Overall, it took nearly 40 minutes for both to reach the helicopter.

As Ed hauled the raft back into the boat, a gust of wind flipped it over, partially filling it with water. He brought the raft upright and alongside, however, and Jay and Beth prepared to jump in. Before they could do so, a huge wave broke over the boat, knocking both of them over the lifelines. Ed hung onto Beth and hauled her aboard, and, Jay, thanks to his safety harness, was brought back aboard. Once the wave had passed, we saw that the top ring of the liferaft had deflated. Beth, back on the radio, told the pilot of the fate of our liferaft. We were then told that the operation had to be abandoned, but that the cutter *Alert* was standing by to complete the evacuation.

Our batteries were long since dead, and the wave had drowned the generator that had been running a single light bulb that was our sole means of being identified. As *Alert* steamed straight for us in the darkness, Ed searched the wreckage below for *Mariah*'s flaregun. He found it and fired when the cutter was about 150 yards away.

Below, I grabbed my wallet and car keys. The cabin was a mess. No one had bailed since the helicopter arrived, and all the floorboards were floating; they had destroyed most of the interior. Diesel fumes filled the air; I got out as quickly as I could.

Meanwhile, *Alert* launched a 19ft, hard-keel Avon inflatable with two frogmen aboard. They brought it quickly alongside *Mariah*, and we all jumped on as quickly as possible – Jay head first. *Mariah* had only 3ft of freeboard on the windward side, and the leeward rail was awash. We hoped she could make it through the night.

By 0030 we were safe and sound aboard *Alert*. The captain, Commander Armand Chapeau, informed us that we were to stand by the schooner through the night, and perhaps, if she was still afloat at daylight, a pump could be taken aboard and we could take her in tow. But around 0130 *Alert* received orders to hurry to another distress call to the south-east. *Reliance*, another 210ft cutter, would proceed to *Mariah*'s last known position to search and perhaps take her in tow. But 24 hours of searching proved futile. *Mariah* surely went down during the night.

The schooner was lost but we still didn't know how lucky we were. Later we learned that the storm of the weekend of 25 October claimed many boats and many lives; it was vicious, unpredicted, and caused extensive damage and losses all along the north-east seaboard. *Mariah* was not her only victim; another was the 33ft *Demon of Hamble* with her owner, Angus Primrose, the noted English ocean racer and designer of *Gipsy Moth IV*, in which Sir Francis Chichester had sailed alone around the world.

Every time a storm of such intensity strikes, all of us on the water learn many lessons, most of them the hard way. Questions are raised about sailors and their equipment. Why is it, then, that a main chapter in almost every sailing disaster story is pump failure?

No doubt Bruce Paulsen considered he had done his homework so far as the bilge pumps aboard *Mariah* were concerned, since before setting out to sail her south from City Island, New York, he had 'flushed out the bilges to see that each was functioning properly'. *Mariah* had no less than four pumps on board. 'Besides the 7 gallons-per-minute electric pump there was a Whale Gusher on the deck ... Then there were our big guns: a 50-plus gallons-per-minute Jabsco that ran off the diesel engine and a 75-plus gallons-per minute firehose/bilge pump that ran off its own one-cylinder diesel mounted in the lazarette.'

Despite all this, the 50-year-old *Mariah* was soon in difficulties, because when she began to work and leak in a 40-knot wind, the 7 gallons-per minute electric pump could not keep up, and when they 'turned to the engine-driven Jabsco, it worked for a minute or two, but then grew hot and stopped pumping altogether'. It was discovered that the impeller had been completely destroyed. By the time they had installed a spare impeller and reassembled the unit, the water in the bilge was over the level of the belt that drives the pump, causing it to slip around its pulley whenever the pump was engaged. To reduce the water level so they could operate the Jabsco pump, they began to bail with buckets – and continued to do so for the next 30 hours. But the Jabsco impeller once more burnt out. The monster firehose pump was supposed to be self-priming, but 'perhaps because of the 10ft waves', it never did, so they kept on bailing. All of which lends support to the saying that 'no bilge pump is as effective as a frightened man with a bucket'.

It has been estimated that a two- or three-man team working flat-out can take some 200 gallons an hour out of a boat by bailing with buckets. This rate of transfer could not be matched by a relay of people working a single pump. Des Sleightholme, former editor of *Yachting Monthly*, once carried out a 'live' experiment by opening a 2½in skin fitting in a 24-footer, and found that she took in 40 gallons in 2½ minutes – just about matching the capacity of most large diaphragm pumps.

The planes attempted to drop pumps to them by parachute but they could not head upwind to the first. The second orange drum containing the pump appeared on the crest of the wave ahead but when they gaffed the parachute it immediately began to tear and the drum submerged and finally broke away. The third pump was dropped successfully well ahead of them but the trail line was difficult to spot in the foamy sea as there was no loop in the end of the line; it slipped off into the sea.

By the time the helicopter arrived, the winds were up over hurricane force with waves well over 40ft and the water in the saloon was chest high, with heavy maple floorboards slamming around, tearing apart the interior. The conditions even caused the top ring of their liferaft to deflate.

PLUNGED TO HER DOOM

Vessel	*Martinet* (99 ton ketch-rigged 'boomie' barge)
Skipper	AW ('Bob') Roberts
Crew	Jerry Thomason (mate), Freddie (third hand)
Bound from	Swanscombe, Kent to Norwich, Norfolk
Date of loss	February 1941
Position	in Hollesey Bay, off Aldeburgh, Suffolk

Many sailing barges were lost during World War II, most of them by hitting mines laid in the Thames Estuary; but one barge, the Martinet, *foundered in rough seas off Aldeburgh in the winter of 1941. Bob Roberts was skipper at the time, and they were bound for Norwich with a cargo of cement intended for use at one or other of the airfields then being hurriedly built in East Anglia. The trouble really sprang from the fact that sailing craft were not, at that time, permitted to proceed after dark – which in February meant a short sailing day. Consequently, instead of reaching Yarmouth by midnight on the second day out, Roberts had to anchor the already leaking barge off Orfordness in rising wind and sea. Bob Roberts takes up the story:*

HAVING GOT THE *MARTINET* OFF to her anchor in the morning I hastened ashore to Gravesend, where I had to clear out of Customs and get my secret documents from the Admiralty office. The mate and third hand were left to batten down the hatches, scrub round and get the barge ready for sea.

We had a new third hand with us this time, a young barge-mate out of the river craft who was waiting to take a berth in a motor ship. He was a good seaman and did his job without having to be told what to do. That is a great thing about men in sail who are any good – they don't need telling when there is a job which obviously wants doing. They just go and do it.

We sailed out of Sea Reach at the crack of dawn and made a splendid run down-Swin and over the Spitway, coming abreast of the Naze in the late afternoon. By this time our lovely west wind had all but disappeared and in its place came a doubtful breeze from further south. There were threatening clouds driving over us and the mate and I discussed the advisability of going into Harwich for the night.

The *Redoubtable*, a big Mistley-owned barge – one of the finest wooden sailing vessels on the coast – went scooting over the Stone Banks under our lee and I had a good mind to follow her. But the tides were such that we should not be able to get out of harbour in the early morning and therefore should fail to make Yarmouth before the next night.

After we had weighed up all the possibilities, I let the *Martinet* run on down to Hollesley Bay and anchored under the highest part of the Whiting Sand. That was about five o'clock. I did not like the way the wind was freshening, but it was just one of those chances forced upon us by the wartime anchor-at-night regulation. We could have been in Yarmouth by midnight under pre-war conditions.

I was somewhat alarmed when we came to pump her out before going below for our evening meal. There was a lot of water in her, much more than I had expected. But we sucked her out and then fell-to round the cabin table. While we thus gorged upon the mighty mound of hash the cook had prepared, the mate, who sat next to the bulkhead dividing the cabin from the hold, said that he thought he could hear a lot of water slopping about. We removed a piece of the bulkhead under the mate's bunk and looked into the well. The water was almost on the floor of the hold – and we had sucked the pumps only ten minutes before!

We left the meal half-eaten and hurried up on deck. We got both the big pumps aft working and the three of us settled down to regular spells, two pumping while one rested. After half an hour of this I went below to see how much was left in her. To my horror there was no difference – if anything, she had more water in her than when we had abandoned our meal and restarted pumping.

It was pitch dark now and there was not much hope of finding where the leak was, especially as the barge was deeply laden. I had a look round with a torch, but apart from an old leak in the counter (on which a shipwright had spent an entire day recently without making the slightest improvement) I could not find any place bad enough to warrant all this pumping.

There was only one thing left to do – pump all night and get her into some sort of harbour – anywhere – as soon as it was light. In these ominous times all the beaches were mined as a defence against the probable invader and it was not possible to save a vessel in distress by beaching her. She would only be blown to bits if not first sunk by a salvo from the shore batteries. And all the harbours were bolted and barred at night by defence booms and nets. So there was nothing to be done except try and keep her afloat with the pumps until daylight allowed us to make a move.

Eleven o'clock. The pumps were just about holding their own. Then the starboard one choked. Frantically we took it to pieces and lay flat on the deck, the seas breaking over us and washing through our clothes, to reach down the pipe in a desperate attempt to clear it. Each of us had a try in turn but the stoppage was down in the very bowels of the ship. In the end we had to resort to a small pump in the hope of our being able to stick to the ship until daybreak. I was becoming doubtful. In fact, it was not very pleasant blundering about below decks up to my knees in water and knowing that, being cement loaded, the ship might take a sudden plunge to her doom.

Each in turn went below and put his personal belongings into kit bags, finally bringing up a stock of hard biscuits, condensed milk, corned beef and the usual items that shipwrecked mariners endeavour to have beside them. It was no good taking any chances. She might not last until morning.

She sank so low in the water that eventually the tops of the pumps were submerged. It was half-past two. We were wet through and the wind seemed very cold. We could feel sleet driving above the spray. Pumping was no longer of any use – or even possible. A gloomy trio, we mustered aft under the lee of the wheelhouse. Our prospects were dark indeed. If we took to the lifeboat and lived through the breakers in the bay we were faced with the risk of landing on a steep shingle bank down which the pebbles and stones rushed at amazing speed with each recoiling wave. It was a bad place to try and beach a small boat. And even if we succeeded in getting ashore we should almost certainly be either shot by the soldiers on guard or blown to smithereens by a land mine.

For two hours we hung on to the side of the wheelhouse, cold, tired and hungry, wondering how long she would last. One more inspection below brought me to a decision. There was so much water in her that she might sink at any moment, though she might wallow in a half-sunken state for many hours, as wooden vessels often do.

We lit a rocket but it misfired, hit the mizzenmast and went straight down into the sea. We tried another and were more successful. It soared skywards in a graceful arc, leaving a trail of sparks behind it. Immediately afterwards we lit a flare so that if anyone on shore had seen our rocket they would be able to determine the position of our vessel by bearings.

It was half-past four. I hoped that the coastguards at Orfordness would see our signals. At least we were advertising the fact that we were in trouble. I felt bound to do that as the lives of the crew depended on my action. Whatever risks I take myself, I was in no way entitled to gamble with other people's lives.

Our supply of signals was limited, so we waited 20 minutes before we again sent up a rocket and a flare. This we continued to do until about eight o'clock, when the dim streaks of dawn could be seen over the North Sea.

The *Martinet* was practically awash. Only her proud head and shapely counter were above sea level. I estimated, although I could not be certain, that since she had not already gone down she would last several hours more.

It was the third hand who first saw that our salvation was at hand. His keen young eyes spotted something bobbing up and down in the white capped seas to the eastward. It was the Aldeburgh lifeboat coming to our assistance.

Now that help was near I felt a grim reluctance to leave the ship. I imagined that the old devil in her was laughing at me. Apart from that, the *Martinet* had been my home for practically two years, and I had grown fond of the old vessel in spite of her bad reputation. And although I had decided that the time had come to abandon her, there lingered within me a dim spark of hope that perhaps she might be saved. Commonsense told me that her days were about to end, but I could not bring myself to realise it. But there was no holding back now. The lifeboatmen were shouting to us to get ready to jump as they manoeuvred to bring their craft alongside.

It was not an easy matter for the coxswain to take us off the *Martinet*, half-submerged as she was, rolling heavily and with the seas breaking right over her. He brought his boat round in a wide sweep under our port quarter, but at that moment the barge took a wild sheer away from him and the gulf between us was too far to jump.

We hung on while the lifeboat motored down to leeward again and at the second attempt she rose on a sea and almost landed on our deck. As she crashed into our bulwarks Jerry and the third hand slung their kitbags into her and jumped. As she descended into the hollow of the sea I followed them and we all landed in a heap in her cockpit.

The coxswain had come alongside on the tideward side of the barge to make sure of getting us off and he had some difficulty in getting away from the stricken vessel. With three sickening jolts the lifeboat struck the *Martinet* and the seas descended mercilessly on both the rescuers and the rescued. At last the little boat's head was pushed clear and she plunged out to windward.

'Which of you be the captain?' shouted the burly, red-faced coxswain, shrouded in dripping yellow oilskins.

When he had identified me we had a brief conference on the fate of the *Martinet*.

'You 'adn't reckoned on tryin' to save 'er?' asked the coxswain with a forlorn hope of profitable salvage.

I looked over at the *Martinet* and shook my head. Her midship decks were no longer visible above water, even when she rose on a crest, and she had that unnatural, out-of-time motion which spells the doom of a vessel in distress.

'She won't last long now,' agreed the coxswain. 'She's too far gone. We'd better leave 'er and get you chaps ashore. Go t'hell if you don't look some'ut wet and cold. This 'ere sleet don't 'elp, neither. Where's that there bottle of rum, Horace? Open 'er up. Them biscuits, too.'

As we chugged northwards to Aldeburgh, running before the

wind and careering giddily down the steep-sided seas, the crew told me their story.

The coastguards at Orfordness had seen our rockets and had telephoned to Aldeburgh. The lifeboat crew were called from their beds at five o'clock in the morning and they hurried down to the beach. There was a heavy sea breaking onshore and there was no hope of getting the biggest lifeboat afloat because an enemy air attack had damaged the slipway the day before.

The only thing they could do was to try and haul off the little 'summer' boat, as they called her. This boat was designed for minor rescue operations in fine weather and was hardly fit to be launched in a winter's gale. But these Suffolk men are a hard lot, and although there is no harbour at Aldeburgh to shelter them from onshore winds, they have never failed to go out in answer to a call for help. Waist-deep in the icy water, with the blinding sleet driving almost horizontally, they struggled to get the little cockleshell afloat. Three times men and boat were flung back on to the shingle beach but at the fourth attempt they got her off and drove her out through the breakers.

They deserved that rum.

'Go steady with that bottle, me lads,' laughed the coxswain. 'Don't forget the shipwrecked mariners.'

By the time everyone had had his turn with the bottle it was empty. By a nice piece of judgement there was just enough left in the bottom for the last man, the entire operation taking not more than three or four minutes.

When we arrived off Aldeburgh beach the coxswain told me that there was a boom defence and minefield between us and the shore. He would not be able to beach his boat as he would in the ordinary way. She would have to be brought broadside to the breakers to get in through the narrow gap and round the inner shoal.

'You'll get a wet shirt when she hits,' he warned us.

As she struck the beach the seas broke right over our heads and the boat all but capsized. I found myself sprawling in the backwash and some soldiers ran down into the water and dragged me up. Jerry and the third hand were wading ashore, hauling their sodden kitbags after them.

Ten minutes later we were having a hot bath in a waterfront hotel.

The people on shore had everything ready for us – dry clothes, hot food, hot whisky and cigarettes. They are accustomed to playing host to shipwrecked mariners in Aldeburgh.

After we had eaten I telephoned the Orfordness coastguards and they told me that the *Martinet* was still visible, wallowing half-submerged in a heavy sea. The wind was of gale force and they did not think she would last much longer.

A few hours later she sank. That was the end of the wicked old *Martinet*, last of the 'boomie' barges.

■ LESSONS LEARNED

- The nightmare scenario of blocked bilge pumps is graphically described by Bob Roberts. When the starboard pump choked, they 'frantically took it to pieces and lay flat on the deck, the seas breaking over us and washing through our clothes, to reach down the pipe in a desperate attempt to clear it. Each of us had a try in turn but the stoppage was down in the very bowels of the ship.' Many boats have sunk because the pumps got blocked by floating debris – sometimes it's due to labels washing off cans of food or charts and books turning to pulp.

- When it came to firing distress flares, there were also lessons to be learned. They lit a rocket but it misfired, hit the mizzenmast and went straight down into the sea. The next was more successful and soared skywards. Sensibly, immediately afterwards, they lit a flare so that if anyone on shore had seen their rocket they could determine the position of their vessel by bearings. And since the supply of signals was limited, they waited 20 minutes before again sending up a rocket and a flare. They continued to do this until dawn, when the lifeboat appeared. Conserving your flares for a second or indeed last chance is a vital consideration in these circumstances.

THE MAST THAT MOVED...

Yacht	*Banba IV* (38ft gaff-rigged cutter)
Skipper	Malcolm Robson
Crew	Merrill Robson, Tex, Hank and John
Bound from	Cape May, USA, to Sark, Channel Islands
Date of loss	6 July 1969
Position	approx. 1,200 miles E of New York

This laconic account by Malcolm Robson, and the one that follows by his wife Merrill, tell how they lost first Banba IV *and then the* Maid of Malham.

BANBA IV WAS A 20 TON CUTTER designed by Fred Shepherd and built by the Whitstable Shipping Company in 1911. Malcolm Robson and his wife Merrill had left Annapolis, Maryland, towards the end of June, after giving *Banba* a very thorough refit, including 'new rigging, all running gear replaced, sheets turned end-for-end, new bowsprit rigging, new parts for the vane steering, scrubbed and painted and sails strengthened. Fuelled up to the eyebrows, watered and victualled for five men for eight weeks, for the non-stop voyage to Guernsey, about 3,500 miles.'

At midday our new crew arrived, three husky American yachting types between 17 and 24, and an hour later off we went, through the Chesapeake and Delaware Canal to Cape May, our jumping-off point.

Armed with a five-day forecast of Atlantic weather from the US Navy, it was unfair of the gods to send us east winds for three days. What could we do except battle on, southward? Runs of 20, 50, 70 miles a day weren't going to take us home at record speed! The next

••• 95

day it blew. Not the ocean winds we had had on the southern route westward, but good old North Sea wet'n-windy Force 7-plus and 10ft swells into the bargain. Then it stopped. Yes, dead calm and poor old *Banba* stumbled down holes in the ocean, crashed into solid walls and skidded into mountains. And all with sails lowered and the engine using precious fuel just to keep her head to the seas. When eventually the winds came they were Force 1, but from the north. On for an hour, Force 8 from the west, then another day of dead calm. This continued for five days and we gloomily watched our fuel dwindling until in the end we stopped the motor and drifted.

It was about here that we knew that the bread was mouldy, so every loaf was unwrapped and dried in the fitful sun. It wasn't serious though, as we had plenty of nosh aboard and water for 75 days. About here, too, the port fore-brace parted with chafe and the yard fell on deck. Again it wasn't serious as later that day we put her on a reach and were able to send a man up the mast for repairs.

So far, so good; and the crew were in good heart. By 5 July we had nearly 900 miles on the log and only a quarter of the fuel used. 'Pity about the fuel,' I thought, as after the 23rd sail change, the squaresail tore from yardarm to yardarm. Heigh, ho, we have plenty of spare canvas aboard, though stitching would be impossible until the weather moderated a bit. It was reefed, too.

It was that evening that we first noticed that something not altogether right was happening to the mast. We could hardly set up the starboard runner lever, the backstay was too tight. Too tight? Now I know *Banba* would much prefer a docile cruise around Brittany than these antics in mid-Atlantic, but I thought of her wrought iron framing straps, the 4in by 5in frames, the oak planking and more. Besides, she wasn't making any water, except through the decks above our bunks, so I puffed away the cloud no bigger than a man's hand. But when, the following day, the mast must have been a foot out and it took two men to flip the runner lever over, I thought again (strumming a top E from the backstay) and decided that either the mast step had moved or the tongue at the foot had broken off. *Banba*'s mast of solid pine is 52ft long, and weighs half a ton and is held up with massive ⅝in shrouds, forestay and topmast shrouds, but the thought of this stick waving about in a Force 9 breeze was a cloud a bit bigger than a man's hand.

So we hove-to under tiny staysail immediately and considered the situation. Newfoundland was 450 miles and against the prevailing winds, and on the starboard tack, dangerous for us. The Azores were some 1,100 miles away and very far south of the sailing ship-recommended track, and against the prevailing wind for the last part. Bermuda was 700 miles upwind. Total fuel was about 90 hours in calm, and say 270 miles at half speed. Total Trinidad rum: about three cases. Say your prayers, lads, and away with prohibition!

We had seen several ships along this Atlantic highway, though by now we were a little to the south of the main steamship tracks, and I had a small secret thought that ... well. But what a decision! To carry on. IF the wind didn't exceed, say, Force 7? We read the US pilot chart for this July and it showed us 1.5 gales above Force 8. IF the swell-after-gale wasn't as bad as we had already had? IF we could hoist sail properly ... so many ifs. Or to abandon *Banba*. With the round trip almost complete? With our home for a year to go to the bottom? Six hundred charts, instruments, clothes, tools, nautical books, everything?

All day I turned over the problem, sitting mostly in the cockpit being rained upon, until about teatime I spied a large freighter a mile away to windward in the grey murk. The problem solved itself. I called the crew aft, read them chapter 23 of *Hornblower*, put on lifejackets and sent up a red flare.

'Passports and money only,' I said, starting the engine. For nobody would have a second chance once near the freighter, it would be 'Jump' and then would come the crashing of rigging, splintering of planks, etc.

With the exception that my trousers fell down at the critical moment, all went well: the ship made a lee and I brought *Banba* alongside the scrambling nets. The yacht alternately smashed into the vertical walls or rose and fell crazily 10 feet or so. But we all made the deck and willing hands rolled us over her rails. I staggered to my feet and counted the heads, five, and looked back to see *Banba* rolling her decks under 50 yards away. Her engine was still running in astern gear and within a few minutes she was lost in the driving rain.

■ **LESSONS LEARNED**

Perhaps the best lesson to be gleaned from the late Malcolm Robson is his ability to retain a sense of humour and perspective faced with so many insurmountable problems.

He seemed to have done everything he could. Fifty-eight year old *Banba IV* was given a thorough refit for the non-stop voyage to Guernsey of about 3,500 miles. But the five-day forecast was a work of fiction. They had a bit of everything thrown at them: east winds for three days, a North Sea wet'n-windy Force 7-plus, 10ft swells, dead calms, a Force 8 from the west … 'Poor old *Banba* stumbled down holes in the ocean, crashed into solid walls and skidded into mountains. And all with sails lowered and the engine using precious fuel just to keep her head to the seas.'

It was thought that either the step of *Banba*'s 52ft-long mast of solid pine had moved or the tongue at the foot had broken off. But still Robson described half a ton of mast waving about in a Force 9 breeze as 'a cloud a bit bigger than a man's hand' and he hove-to under staysail to consider the situation.

With 'so many ifs' over whether to abandon *Banba*, Robson spent all day turning over the problem, until he spied a large freighter a mile away to windward and took the seamanlike decision.

eleven

SLOWLY SINKING...

Yacht	*Maid of Malham* (48ft Bermudian sloop)
Skipper	Malcolm Robson
Crew	Merrill Robson
Bound from	Galapagos Islands to Marquesas Islands
Date of loss	1973
Position	7° 48' S, 110° 57' W (about halfway between Panama and Tahiti)

Maid of Malham *was designed by Laurent Giles as an ocean racer for John Illingworth and was built by King & Sons at Burnham-on-Crouch in 1936. She was very different from* Banba IV, *but her fate was the same.*

LET ME GIVE YOU THE FACTS. Halfway between Panama and Tahiti *Maid of Malham*'s rudder came adrift at the foot, and, though we could steer, the Pacific came in through the trunk, with only Merrill and me to pump it back again every hour or two. We bore away under a small jib only in the rumbustious SE trades for two days, and discussed survival with more than just academic interest. Our landfall in the Marquesas was 20 days away; the Galapagos Islands were 1,000 miles back, upwind, upswell, upcurrent; the Pacific Routings showed shipping to be as good as non-existent. Thinking about the inflatable liferaft made morale, if possible, lower. At this point – over to Merrill:

I was baking bread. Malcolm was working out his morning sight. Finished, he went on deck, gave a roar: 'a ship'. I thought he was joking, there never was a ship. Then I looked at his face, near tears of relief. Hurrying below. 'The flares.' 'I've been dreaming about this, the million to one chance.' Bang. Bang. Two red Very lights soar up. 'Are they slowing down?' 'Can't tell.' 'What nationality?' 'Port something … London.' 'Yes, they're turning. Thank God.' 'Down with the jib, ready with the sheet?' The engine starts but oh dear … 'Don't forget the wheel's disconnected.' 'It's the tiller – you work the controls.'

'Get some stuff together, there may not be much time. Where's that sail bag?' 'In the booze locker stopping the rattle.' Now then. Passports, ship's papers, money in that box. Into the bag with it. Oh, there's that photo. Tear it off the bulkhead – the lovely one of the children. Now the small clothes locker. Thank goodness I had put shore things in a plastic bag for dryness. 'Malcolm, put some shoes on. Have you got your specs?' 'I'll bring lifejackets.' In the flag locker. Put mine on then help Malcolm with his. Nearly alongside. Lovely big ship, grey and red. Rails lined with people. They've thrown down a warp. Round the anchor winch and make fast. What's that fellow with the walkie-talkie saying?

Near enough now. Malcolm bawling: 'We're making water. Can you take us two on board?' Talk. Shout. Crash against ship. 'What's your weight?' '15 tons.' 'We have a crane to lift 25 tons.' 'Malcolm, he says they might lift us on board.' 'Our draught is 8ft and the mast 65ft. It's going to be a job, but we'll help.' Down snakes a pilot ladder. 'Can you let down a line for this bag?' Catch it now. No panic, it's over. Tie it firmly, proper hitch. Over the side, no matter if it trails in the water. 'Up the ladder, Merrill.' Slow now. Wait until the *Maid* is at her highest point. Then up, no hesitating. Nearly there. My leg hurts, must have scraped it. The top. Willing hands, jump down on solid ground. Steel. Malcolm next. 'Come this way to the Captain.' Walk. People. Grim faces. Cameras. 'Welcome on board!' 'Lord, how we feel for you.' 'Are you all right?' Four long flights to the bridge. Out of breath. Shake hands. Malcolm talking … four, five officers. Captain and Chief Engineer having second thoughts of lifting operation. Crew might get bashed about. Must take out mast first. Operation scrubbed. Malcolm going down ladder for more salvage. Sack on heaving line. Water sloshing in cabin. There he is in cockpit, jolly good. Sextant, chronometer. Wonder if he has remembered second sextant we bought from Canal pilot? What's he holding? Hand-bearing compass. Come up. Don't wait too long, they're casting off the *Maid*. Long warp trailing astern, that's bad, could get in ship's propeller. Our *Maid* won't leave, she hugs the ship. That crosstree is going to spike a porthole in a minute. Lord, how it's scraping. What a noise, scattering paint. Now both spreaders broken, poor *Maid*, what an awful end. Doesn't she look long and slim from so high up, never seen her from here before. There's the jibstay gone, still she won't leave the ship. Seems to be sucked in close, though the ship is going slowly ahead. Right under the stern, can't bear to look at her.

'No, we don't carry a transmitter, what's the point? The range is so small when you are on the oceans.' 'Our guardian angels certainly were hovering when this ship chose to be in the same spot of water at the same time.' I can't see our boat any more; oh yes I can. There she is rocking about, getting smaller. She's low in the water. Poor, lovely, *Maid of Malham*.

■ **LESSONS LEARNED**

- Halfway between Panama and Tahiti with *Maid of Malham*'s rudder broken at the foot and the Pacific coming in through the trunk, the Robsons were fortunate to find a rescue ship in an area where shipping was rare.
- Looking back to nearly 40 years ago, we can appreciate how vastly different our sailing now is from the tough game it was then – satellite and radio communication, EPIRBs and many other facilities have vastly improved our chances of survival in cases of emergency. But none of these things has altered the fact that skippers face the same difficult decisions today as they did when sailing began.

twelve

THE BOAT THAT BROKE UP

Yacht	*Triventure* (29ft Islander trimaran)
Skipper	John Nicholls
Crew	Malcolm Beilby
Bound from	Aldabra Island, Indian Ocean to Lourenço Marques, Mozambique
Date of loss	11 November 1969
Position	Mozambique Channel, Indian Ocean

Malcolm Beilby tells the story of the loss of the trimaran Triventure, *which John Nicholls built in a backyard in Sydney in the early 1960s. For a year after launching her, he sailed around Sydney Harbour and the nearby coasts and then in 1968 he planned to sail the trimaran back to his native England.*

The first leg, 'with three friends on board, was a leisurely voyage up the resort-studded Queensland coast and across the Coral Sea to Port Moresby', where Nicholls met Beilby, who agreed to join Triventure *as crew as far as Durban.*

From Port Moresby the voyage continued via Timor, the Christmas and Cocos Islands, the Seychelles, Aldabra Island and then south into the Mozambique Channel, where their troubles really started:

THE OPENING ACT OF *TRIVENTURE'S* tragedy began on John's 29th birthday, Friday 31 October. We'd hand-steered through a quiet night and in the morning a southerly breeze began to pick up. We set Angus up and went below to sleep.

Just before midday, *Triventure*'s motion and the wind noise awoke us to freshening conditions with black clouds and rain ahead. By 1400 the wind working against the current had whipped up a nasty, steep sea and we were slogging into it under reefed main and working jib.

At 2000 John had just relieved me on watch when we heard a loud, sharp crack. A torch search failed to reveal anything wrong in the main hull or the wing decks, and we tried to convince ourselves that it must have been caused by some small floating object that had been thrown against the hull. But ominous creakings became apparent and persistent and John took a torch into the port float to investigate. Watching from the cockpit it seemed an eternity before he emerged and when he did his words dropped the bottom from my stomach.

'Get the sails off her!' he shouted. 'The float's coming off!'

Together we had the canvas down in seconds and *Triventure* lay beam-on to the seas and rode them like a raft while John, with characteristic calm, prepared a cup of tea. The plywood main spar in the forward edge of the wing deck, he explained, had broken inside the float where it butted against one of the major bulkheads. The bulkhead also was broken, and water resistance against the fin was flexing the float outwards away from the main hull. With the sails off, the stress would be minimised and he proposed G-clamping the broken frames to hold them overnight until repairs could be made in daylight.

We fished four clamps from the tool box and John took them into the float, while I packed a haversack with tinned fruit and prepared some water bottles in case we had to take to the raft.

John was amused by my dire interpretation of the situation and assured me that leaving the boat was the last thing in his mind. Then he climbed into his bunk and went to sleep. Lucky him. I lay awake for hours listening to the creaking of the fractured plywood.

In the morning the wind had dropped a little, but the sea was still steep. Seasickness repeatedly forced John from the cramped confines of the float, but he bolted strutting either side of the broken spar and bulkhead and we set about getting *Triventure* under way again. The outer shrouds, from the float gunwales to the masthead, were disconcertingly slack, a sign that the mainspar was no longer straight, but there was nothing we could do but take them up and hope for the best.

Under sail the severity of the damage was more obvious. With the port float to windward we could see the gunwale rising and falling as the float flexed in and out on the edge of the wing deck.

The first night after the break was spent hove-to under reefed main, but the next day, Sunday, the weather eased and on Monday we were becalmed again. We awoke after an afternoon sleep to find half a dozen large dorado and twice that number of sharks circling the boat. The dorado refused to take a hook and John spent a futile half-hour hanging over the side trying to shoot one with his speargun. When an evening breeze got the boat moving again the sharks lost interest, but the dorado stayed with us and through the night they cut phosphorescent streams through the dark water as they paced *Triventure* towards the African coast.

We decided to abandon plans of making Lourenço Marques and to head instead for Inhambane, a Portuguese port several hundred miles north and correspondingly closer to us. Inhambane is situated 8 miles up a wide tidal estuary, which we reached late on Tuesday afternoon and anchored about 6 miles from the town. Not knowing what to expect, we sat on deck that night and speculated on the significance of the distant lights, and John, an unseamanly teetotaller, dreamt of Coca-Cola. In the morning we battled up to the town against a very strong tide and anchored about midday off a long wharf.

Remembering our difficulties in Portuguese Timor, we were surprised by the affability of the Inhambane harbour authorities who quickly cleared us to go ashore. The harbourmaster himself drove us to a timber yard and advised us where to get supplies.

Inhambane was quite a surprise. We expected a dusty, one-horse, one street town and found instead an extensive, substantial town with lawns, trees and sidewalk cafés along the main thoroughfare. My chief recollection, however, is of alarmingly high prices. In the five days we were there we spent more than 60 US dollars on a minimum of timber, glue and a modest amount of supplies.

Through the days John laboured in the oven-like confines of the damaged float, reinforcing the broken bulkhead and mainspar and securing the inside planking of the float hull back to the stringers and frames from which it had pulled away.

I attended to minor jobs about the boat and got the stores and water aboard. In the evenings we'd go ashore and join the citizens at the cafés or stroll along the front. In this fashion the days slipped quickly by and though we did not realise it, the good weather was passing with them.

On Monday morning, 10 November, we went ashore early to clear our papers and get a weather report before sailing but the harbourmaster, who had agreed to translate the previous night's forecast for us, was not in his office. His deputy handled the paperwork but when the harbourmaster had not returned more than an hour later we decided to snatch what was left of the ebb tide and take a chance on the weather. As it was the tide turned before we were halfway down the estuary and as *Triventure* battled against it, it became sickeningly apparent that the float was still flexing badly.

We reached the open sea in the late afternoon and John entered the float but could see nothing working there. Evidently the main spar break had been the primary trouble but fixing it had done nothing for the weakness that had developed inside the wing deck itself between the float and the main hull. John accepted the fact with fatalistic resignation and decided to press on for Durban, 400 miles south. But his plans, shaken by the first troubles, had now come crashing down around him. Ahead had been another year of cruising and the hope that successful completion of his voyage might help him win sponsorship for an attempt in the Single-handed Transatlantic race. In Inhambane he thought his repairs had removed the threat to his boat and future but now he was faced with the certainty that *Triventure* could not be taken past Durban.

Meals at sea are usually looked forward to as highlights of the day but tea that night was a bleak affair.

Overnight our luck finally ran out. The wind picked up steadily from the south and the reaction on the current quickly resulted in a steep sea. By dawn we were hove-to in a 40-knot gale and it was worsening.

At 0700 the rending sound of tearing wood told us the end had come. We scrambled from our bunks and into the cockpit to see the port float, fortunately to windward, swinging up and down through almost 60° as though on a huge hinge along the edge of the wing deck.

John put up the jib, and I eased her away in an attempt to run west for the coast which we knew could not be far away; but it was apparent as we gathered forward speed that the float was tearing off even more quickly. In no time the arching stanchions crushed and flung the glassfibre dinghy overboard from its chocks on the wing deck, and as we put *Triventure* back on to the wind, the float came away completely. While I held the boat into the wind John cut the guardrail wires between the cockpit pushpit and the float stanchions. But he could make no impression on the port outer shroud, the only thing now keeping the float beside us. Tethered by that, the float plunged wildly up and down, smashing into the remains of the wing deck, and we feared it would push a stanchion through the main hull.

Luckily the chain plate pulled out first, and the float swirled away astern as I put the helm over to head for the coast again. Now all the strain was on the port inner shrouds, and as John ran forward to attend to the jib they gave way. The mast and sails came down on him and he disappeared beneath them.

One moment *Triventure* had been gathering speed and the next she was lifeless and wallowing with her spars and canvas half overboard.

For an instant I thought my companion was overboard too. I think I stood frozen until he freed himself from under the mainsail. Most other things of that morning I can remember with crystal clarity but actually seeing him emerge from the tangle on deck, I cannot. Certainly he was on his feet before I had moved from the cockpit.

Amazingly, he was unhurt. The mast had actually hit his back, throwing him to the deck, but the starboard stanchions and guardrails had checked its fall and prevented it from pinning and crushing him.

Now things were right out of our hands. Together we attempted to drag the mast back on board, calculating that its weight lashed down on the starboard float top would hold the float down and prevent the boat from flipping over to port on the backs of the waves. But in the pitching seas the mast's weight was too much for us. We could not get it fully on board, and instead lashed it as best as possible diagonally over the cabin top with the end hanging over the starboard side.

Below, the cabin was a shambles and every violent lurch made it worse. The wind was already easing and few of the waves were now breaking, but every so often a white top would slam into the port beam and push *Triventure* violently to starboard. Then she would lurch alarmingly to port as the crest passed beneath.

John was thinking as clearly as ever though when he suggested breakfast and, on the understanding that he wouldn't be too demanding, I put the kettle on and buttered some bread. I was passing him his second slice when he looked around the crushed weathershield and spotted *Slavisa Vajner* looming past not 400 yards away.

Breakfast was forgotten as we waved from the cockpit but it seemed the tanker had not seen us as she steamed majestically past. The first flare was blown into the water, the second was a dud and John was preparing the third when we saw the ship turning slowly to starboard. Back she came, this time so far upwind that only her superstructure was visible. As she went by, two smaller ships came into sight and away to the west the coast was visible.

John considered taking a gamble on being washed ashore, but we decided against it when we found the radio, with its aerial down, could not contact the tanker which was obviously making rescue preparations. The 70,000-ton ship was manoeuvring to be directly upwind of us when she lost forward motion. The 40 minutes that preceded our pick-up was necessary to switch the single big diesel engine from the crude oil used at sea to the fuel oil used in manoeuvring.

A couple of hundred yards away two rope ladders dropped down her towering side, and as we bumped alongside down came throwing lines and a hawser. John made it fast, then followed me up the ladder clutching his typewriter and precious *Times Atlas* under one arm. Then, barefooted on the slowly rolling steel deck, we found ourselves skating helplessly to either side as we attempted to follow a crewman to the bridge where Captain Uros Lombardic was waiting. In good English he offered to hoist *Triventure* on to his deck but explained that 15 minutes would be needed before auxiliary steam could be raised to power the winches. John, considering the risk to crewmen, decided against it. Instead, he asked for time to go back aboard and get off what he could. The Captain agreed, and we returned to the rail where John donned a safety harness and went down the ladder.

I took pictures from the rail, then followed him down. He was at work in the cabin when I reached the deck and noticed the float bow cracking under the pounding against the steel plates alongside.

'Hurry it up! She's breaking up!' I yelled in alarm, and panicked us both. We grabbed the bare essentials, bagged and sent them up on the heaving lines, and cast *Triventure* off.

Then, as the tanker slowly gathered way, we paced *Triventure* along its deck and she fell astern looking like a crippled seabird exhausted and helpless on the water.

'I can always build another,' said John as we stood at the rail watching and filming until his yacht was lost to sight among the swells.

■ LESSONS LEARNED

As Rob James pointed out in his book *Multihulls Offshore*, written just before his death, multihulls gained a bad reputation, in the 1960s in particular, because a lot of amateur-designed and amateur-built craft foundered, causing unwanted and unwarranted adverse publicity for multihulls in general.

Nicholls built his *Triventure* in a backyard in Sydney in the early 1960s and planned to sail her home to England. When the plywood main spar in the forward edge of the wing deck broke inside the float, together with a bulkhead, Nicholls tried G-clamping the broken frames to hold them overnight until repairs could be made in daylight. Further repairs were made ashore, but they left without a forecast – 'to snatch what was left of the ebb tide and take a chance on the weather.' As it happened, the tide turned before they were halfway down the estuary and, as *Triventure* battled the tide, it became apparent that the float was still flexing badly. The decision to press on for Durban, 400 miles south, proved unwise. Overnight, their luck ran out. The wind picked up steadily from the south and the current resulted in a steep sea. By dawn they were hove-to in a 40-knot gale listening to the rending sound of tearing wood.

thirteen

RESCUED IN PYJAMAS

Yacht	*Maaslust* (45ft yawl-rigged boeier)
Skipper	John P Wells
Crew	Margaret Wells, Frank Philips, Freda Philips; children on board: Peter Wells (22 months), Nichola Philips (12 years)
Bound from	Deauville, Normandy, to Langstone Harbour, Hampshire
Date of loss	29 July 1956
Position	off Selsey Bill

This account of the loss of Maaslust, *one of the Dunkirk Little Ships, is by Margaret Wells, whose 22-month-old son Peter was on board at the time. Maaslust, a boeier, was built of steel in Holland in 1923. Having left her mooring in Langstone Harbour on 20 July 1956, she made an uneventful night passage to Cherbourg. Visits to St Vaast, Isigny and Ouistreham followed, and by the end of the week she was in Deauville:*

IT IS VERY DIFFICULT FOR ME to write of preceding events when my mind's eye can see nothing but the picture of a gallant Dutchman, *Maaslust*, abandoned to fight a losing battle against fantastic seas; but this is to be an account of the happiness she gave us during her last weeks and a requiem for her brave spirit.

Neither John nor I had been very keen on the idea of Deauville and Trouville, knowing that all 'the best people' go there and feeling that it would not be our 'cup of tea' at all. However, we were favourably impressed and unhappily allowed ourselves to be talked out of our plan to make Fecamp on Saturday and to return to Shoreham on Sunday. Had we not succumbed to the fleshpots, how different would be the ending of this story! However, it must be admitted that we thoroughly enjoyed ourselves, meeting by chance old friends from Le Havre and being hospitably entertained by them and by the Monks. We visited the casino, where we gained entrance to the Inner Room without even our passports! We basked and bathed to the music of the orchestra at the swimming pool, we shopped in the market and bought presents in the sloping streets. On the first evening I had surpassed myself by producing a dish of *moules* which were voted nearly as good as those in Cherbourg.

Having been lured to remain in Deauville, neither John nor I was anxious to move, and so we did not entirely regret the falling barometer, suspecting that our departure would be delayed by weather conditions. However, by Friday the glass had steadied, the thundery atmosphere had passed and we decided that, subject to a satisfactory weather report, we would set sail for England on Saturday afternoon.

On Friday evening John radioed Niton, requesting a report from Dunstable for 1100 next day, together with a long-range forecast for the Channel area. The message came through at 0900: southerly wind, Force 1–2 veering westerly, and increasing to 4–6 on Sunday evening. This obviously gave us no excuse to tarry, and Saturday morning was spent on a provisioning orgy in the market.

We had arranged to refuel at 1400, and were more than annoyed to find the fuelling wharf abandoned and no one at all interested in telling us where to find the attendant. It was here that a factor arose that was for us to have fateful consequences. The skipper believed in having ample reserves of fuel at all times, and this rule will never again be relaxed. But time was passing and, having waited for the attendant for over an hour, there was no immediate prospect of receiving our expected replenishment. We had on board fuel for four to six hours' running in case the wind failed. So, impatient to be on our way, we cast off from the wharf and made sail. But had it not been for intransigence at the fuel depot we should, no doubt, have brought the ship safely to port at the end of our journey.

We eventually left Deauville-Trouville at 1500 on 28 July, immediately meeting a lumpy sea. The weather was fine and the wind free, but the sea, meeting *Maaslust*'s plum bows, knocked her way off. John had to be talked out of a farewell visit to Le Havre. We blamed our late visit to the casino the previous night for our unwonted lack of enthusiasm for the homeward journey, and turned our eyes resolutely from the coast of France – more's the pity.

Being a great believer in the nourishment of the inner man, I made a gargantuan stew on the way out and Freda was the only one who did not partake to capacity. She, perhaps wisely, preferred Dramamine. I took the first watch from 2100 to 2300 and did not enjoy it. It rained, and the seas made the old girl extremely heavy on the wheel – one moment's lapse of concentration and she would do her best to gybe. The breeze was not excessive, however, and there was nothing to indicate that we should turn back. We had a little trouble with the diesel's water pump, and the man off watch had to keep an eye on the gauge in case the filter clogged again – we motor-sailed to help her through the waves. At 0100 on Sunday 29 July, we took the staysail off her because it was doing no good and at 0400 the first reef was taken in. From then on conditions deteriorated rapidly.

The increasing SW gale brought squall after squall and the seas rose higher. We had long abandoned the idea of making Shoreham, since the entrance is a nasty one in any weather, so we headed for the lee of Bembridge Ledge. It was soon necessary to take in the second reef, and she still made 7 knots, with seas 12–14ft high to surmount. We watched the two 12ft dinghies with anxiety as comber after comber crashed down upon them, but their gripings held them firmly against the davits. Twice seas filled the mainsail and *Maaslust* lay right over, but up she came again like the gallant fighter she was. The scene below decks was indescribable: the stove jumped its gimbals; the cutlery broke out of its locker, crashing to the ground with devastating noise; the saloon table lifted itself bodily, abandoned its weights and came to rest, none too gently, upon my recumbent form; the combined radio and television set took charge; in fact everything that was not screwed or bolted down became a potential menace.

Small Peter slept peacefully enough until the vessel first lay over, when he became a little frightened and, once awake, very seasick. He needed a prolonged cuddle to calm him but eventually resigned himself to the double-cabin berth with Freda and Nicky, where the three of them shared their misery with mute stoicism. Poor Freda, who feels sick at the suggestion of a ripple on the water, was heroic, for when the whole mattress rose up and landed half on the floor, she wedged herself against the bulkhead to hold the children in. It was indeed hellish down there, but, even so, those below had little idea of the seriousness of the situation with which we were faced.

After settling Peter and stowing and wedging all that I could in the saloon, and having parted company with the stew, I went up into the wheel house to survey the scene. One has read of the icy hand which grips one's vitals in moments of dread, but although I have had several hazardous occasions at sea I had never felt it before. The sight of the waves, 30ft from base to crest, green-grey and streaked with spume and sand, was for the first moment truly petrifying. Later there was no room for fear, although one accepted the fact that survival was unlikely. I remember a feeling of thankfulness that the three of us would be going together, regret that Peter had seen so little of life, sorrow for our parents, and regret about our dogs and our lovely home, but no fear of the end. Perhaps our sensibilities were numbed by the physical battle in which we were involved, for, discussing it later, we found that we had all reacted the same way.

By 0900 it was evident that our hopes of finding a lee under the Isle of Wight were groundless; in fact we were now in a far worse situation, for the seas were steeper and closer together. Before we reached the forts the tide turned to the eastward against us and, despite all that Frank could do at the wheel, we had soon driven past the Nab towards the lee shore of Hayling.

It was impossible to keep the vessel head to the seas, for they came so rapidly that she could only take every third one, the others breaking over her with 6ft of solid water upon the decks. She could not free herself of the weight of the first before the second was upon her, and the side decks were perpetually awash, but still she rose. The backlash of the wheel was so great that Frank refractured an old wrist injury (we knew nothing of this until later) and it was physically impossible to stand on deck against either the wind or the sea. I doubt that the three of us would have survived had it not been for the high bulwarks and stout handrail, for in such weather lifelines were quite ineffective. Near the Nab the parrels of the double-reefed mainsail began to go, and a rent started in the leach, so we decided to take it off her. To do so I had to let go the lee signal halyards against which the gaff had fouled, and they blew out of my hand to stream away like wire at 60 degrees from the mast. Shortly after this the mizzen blew out – the heavy canvas tearing down a cloth like calico. We now depended for our lives upon the gallant Porbeagle engine with its limited fuel supply.

When we were a few hundred yards off Hayling shore we let go both our anchors, one a 2-cwt CQR, the other a 2-cwt fisherman. As the fisherman bit in, the chain vibrated so violently that the whole forepart of the ship trembled and in a few minutes the claw stopper jerked off and the whole chain went over the side, leaving the CQR to take the strain alone, until its chain also parted under water with a crack like a whiplash. At this moment I yelled to John to hold on as an enormous comber came crashing down on us on the foredeck; I was to leeward and clung to the binnacle bolted through to the deckbeams below. It came away in my hand as the sea hit us; and it, the kedges on deck and John came down upon me. We can only ascribe it to a miracle that I ended up under the dinghy, which must have risen to receive me, surrounded by clutter, but unhurt with the dinghy's keel pressing the back of my thigh. But with its weight supported by the combing I was extricated from this uncomfortable situation before the next ton of water descended.

By now Frank had won sufficient offing to pass the Chichester Bar buoy and there was a rapid consultation as to the advisability of trying to make the harbour. Seas mountains high were breaking upon the Winner Bank and we realised that one touch and the children at least would be doomed, our chances of getting through were to say the least remote, even at full throttle. So we decided not to risk it. John and I turned our attention to the engine bilge, which had taken a lot of water through the wheel-house doors and a loose skin fitting. The bilge pump was not man enough for the job and priming it was virtually impossible with the motion of the ship, so we set to with a bucket and basin, bailing alternately. The engine was partially submerged by now, the water slimy with diesel oil and green paint from a tin which had burst asunder, and as it surged from side to side great spurts flew up into our eyes from the belt pulley driving the dynamo.

By the time we had bailed out the engine bilge and repaired the skin fitting, Frank had got us past the Mixon Rocks. At odd moments we had been sending up rockets and handflares with little hope of attracting attention – visibility was less than 100 yards because of the height of the seas, the tops of which were broken into a welter of flying spume – and we sent one up for luck to a vessel to seaward of us. At this moment the after end of the rudder parted, the vast iron girth snapping off like tin. We realised that there was little now to do but to keep the water out and hope as the beach at Selsey drew nearer. I went below to look at the main bilge, which needed attention but was not alarmingly flooded. As it was of steel, we had always kept it bone dry and had omitted to test the pump, which not unnaturally refused to function now. Accordingly I spent an unhappy time bailing into the galley sink and being sick!

Freda and the kids looked as if they were past caring, until an enormous jolt shook them to life. My immediate reaction was that we had hit a buoy (of all things, in those waters!) and I prepared to bail harder in case we had sprung a leak. I could hardly accept the fact that it was actually the lifeboat.

My only recollection of the next few minutes is of the sight of Peter, suspended in nothing but his pyjama top over the seething water, as John handed him across to our rescuers. My bare feet were slippery with paint and oil so that I came a cropper on the lifeboat deck, knocking myself out momentarily on a cowl, and the next thing was the incredible sight, which I shall never, never forget, of our beloved vessel battling there alone. I could not believe that we had actually left her, and even now, in spite of everything, I wish we hadn't. It was desertion of a faithful friend, and, though human life is infinitely valuable, we shall always feel remorse, knowing as we do now that the wonderful old lady did not give herself over to the whim of the seas, but fought on for many hours after we left her.

Who knows to how many anxious hearts she brought relief and joy, at the darkest period of the last war, bearing home husband, son or loved one. One of the 'little ships,' she bore the proud battle-honour, 'Dunkirk, 1940'.

The rescued crew of *Bloodhound* were already aboard the Selsey lifeboat, so that by the time a third rescue had been made and the crew from the yacht *Coima* had been taken on board, the small hold was crammed with seasick bodies for the four long hours it took to reach and enter Portsmouth Harbour.

That same night, John and Margaret Wells went to Shoreham to contact their insurance broker, feeling sure that *Maaslust* would already be ashore and might be salvaged, even though her engine had been left running to keep her head to the seas when they had abandoned. On the Monday, hoping against hope, they scoured the coast between Selsey and Newhaven and found nothing, but at Littlehampton they learned that the Dutchman had been seen lying off at 1000hrs on the Sunday and had looked as though she was waiting for the tide, to come in! She was seen again, 'clawing out to sea'. *Lloyd's List* gave her as being afloat on Monday morning – but after that – silence.

■ LESSONS LEARNED

Maaslust was not a motor-sailer in the modern sense, but even devoted owners of such traditional Dutchmen would not claim that these picturesque flat-bottomed craft sail well to windward. So, when a sequence of gear failures occurred while they were near the Nab Tower, Margaret Wells knew that they then depended for their lives on 'the gallant Porbeagle engine, with its limited fuel supply' – partially submerged though it was.

Having arranged to refuel before they left Deauville, they found the fuelling wharf unattended, leaving them with fuel for just four to six hours motoring, a factor that was thought to have fateful consequences. The skipper believed in having ample reserves of fuel at all times; 'a rule which will never again be relaxed'.

On Day 2 conditions deteriorated rapidly with a SW gale and squall after squall. Wisely, they abandoned making Shoreham, since the entrance is a nasty one in any weather. Soon it was evident that hopes of finding a lee under the Isle of Wight were groundless. Here, the seas were steeper and closer together and before they reached the forts the tide turned eastward, against them, and they were driven past the Nab towards the lee shore of Hayling Island. Below decks the stove jumped its gimbals, the saloon table lifted itself bodily – a graphic example of how every-thing that is not screwed or bolted down can be a deadly menace.

A few hundred yards off Hayling shore they let go both anchors, one a 2-cwt CQR, the other a 2-cwt fisherman. As the fisherman bit in, the chain vibrated so violently that the claw stopper jerked off and the whole chain went over the side, leaving the CQR to take the strain alone, until its chain, too, parted under water with 'a crack like a whiplash'.

When the engine bilge took a lot of water through the wheel-house doors and a loose skin fitting, the bilge pump failed, proving impossible to prime with the motion of the ship, so they had to bail with bucket and basin. Have you checked your bilge pumps lately?

Almost invariably, the violent motion of the bilge water had swilled matchsticks, bits of rubbish or labels from food cans into the valves of those earlier bilge pumps.

fourteen

DEADLY CHAIN REACTION

Yacht	*Thelma* (27ft gaff-rigged cutter)
Skipper	AW 'Bob' Roberts
Crew	AF 'Bully' Bull
Bound	round the world from England, westabout
Date of loss	1 March 1935
Position	Chatham Bay, Cocos Island

Long before he won fame as a skipper of Thames spritsail barges, Bob Roberts and his mate 'Bully' had sailed the little gaff cutter, Thelma, *from England to Cocos Island in the Pacific, where she was lost when her anchor cable parted. The voyage is described in his entertaining book* Rough and Tumble. *Roberts had felt uneasy about the anchorage in Chatham Bay, but put his doubts behind him when Bully asked why he was worried. He takes up the story:*

IT WAS AN OPEN ANCHORAGE and no place for rough weather, but being so calm it did not seem that there could be the slightest danger in lying there for a few days. It would not take us long to top up our water tanks and get away for the Galapagos. It was only those queer fancies of mine that made me dislike the place, and I even went so far as to reveal my thoughts to Bully as he stirred the porridge in the galley with a sweaty hand.

'I don't like this place much.'

'Want to move further out?'

'No, she's as safe here as anywhere with the hook in this patch of sand.'

'Well, what don't you like about the place?'

'Dunno. Just a hunch.'

In the meantime I altered my ideas about a kedge anchor. We were not so lavishly equipped as to have two anchor chains, and our custom was to lay out a kedge on a stout manilla warp. As our 2-inch tripping line had already chafed through on the jagged bottom in only two hours, I felt it would be useless to use a kedge on a warp.

After solemn deliberations we decided that if the anchor chain did not hold her it was quite certain a chafing warp would not. Likewise, it was impossible for our main anchor to drag. It could not drag from that patch of sand because it was surrounded by mushroom coral. This mushroom coral grows some little way off the bottom and spreads out according to its name. Thus if the anchor dragged, the lower flukes would go under the coral and hold there so fast that it would be unlikely that we should ever get it up again.

So there did not seem to be much danger of *Thelma* dragging her anchor, especially as the weather was dead calm and there was no current to speak of in the bay itself.'

Roberts and Bully spent three days watering ship by ferrying a cask to and fro between *Thelma* and the shore; and then, having met a man named Cooknell, they were persuaded to join in a search for the 'Cocos' treasure. The search was unsuccessful and throughout the five days Roberts remained uneasy and depressed. The return to Chatham Bay was in a ship's lifeboat.

'I was glad to be on my way back. A cloud of depression seemed to be hanging over me all the time at Wafer Bay. While the others scampered in and out of the water and played golf on the beach with a round stone and a crooked branch, I could only sit around and mope. I must have been dull company.

I thought it was sheer tiredness after our efforts in the jungle, but as things turned out it was that vague mental warning to which the human mind is sometimes subjected when something dreadful is going to happen. At last, in the ship's lifeboat, we bore away to cross Chatham Bay; I felt no qualms at not sighting *Thelma*'s stumpy stick straight away. But as we grew closer I stood up in the prow and scanned the bay. *Thelma* was not there!

Wild thoughts ran through my head. Then, far away in a corner of the bay, I caught sight of her. She was but a few yards from the rocks.

Even as I watched, a huge wave lifted her up and carried her in. We rowed like fiends, but the tide and current were against us. I stood there and saw her rise again and disappear. When the next breaker came she did not come up. She was down on her beam ends with the surf pounding over her.

There was very little wind but it was impossible to get the lifeboat alongside in the breakers. We anchored a little way off and veered down as near as possible. The sight before us almost broke my heart. There was the gallant little vessel, which I had loved and cared for all these years, which had brought us safely through fair weather and foul for nearly 7,000 miles on this cruise alone, in her death throes on that lonely shore.

All our worldly belongings danced and swirled among the rocks. A bunch of dollar notes disappeared in the foam. Pieces of timber floated everywhere. It was enough to chill the heart of the bravest soul. To complete the mournful scene, Jimmy the ship's cat, drenched and scared, meowed pitifully from the masthead. I took one look at the way she lay and knew that the vessel was doomed. She hardly rose an inch to a breaking wave, and there was a sickening grinding and snapping of timbers with each cruel blow. Every wave broke clean over her and forced us to cling on for our lives.

We fought our way down into the tiny cabin. Each wave filled her up and we were imprisoned like rats until it subsided. We choked and gasped as we grabbed such things as were within reach and passed them out on deck. It was impossible to stay below for long at a time, and as I struggled in the cabin I could feel the rocks under my feet. The whole of her starboard side was ripped out. Something was sticking up through the cabin floor. There was nothing to be done except to try to save everything possible.

At low water *Thelma* was almost high and dry and I was able to discover the cause of the wreck. Trailing from her bow were many fathoms of anchor chain but no anchor. One of the links had been sawn clean through as if with a file. It was the work of the mushroom coral. So sharp was the edge of it that in five days it had cut through a heavy chain link as the vessel swung gently to her hawser. I should never have believed that coral could cut through solid iron so efficiently. Later we found pieces on the beach which would file through any iron or steel we possessed. But the knowledge came too late. The worst was done. Some time after the wreck we found that anchor still firmly embedded in the sand and it took four of us to weigh it from the lifeboat.

■ LESSONS LEARNED

Even 'heavy three-eighths-of-an-inch chain from a big Whitstable smack' could not prevent *Thelma* from blowing ashore when coral cut through the iron chain 'as if with a file'. Bob Roberts had felt uneasy about anchoring in Chatham Bay: 'An open anchorage and no place for rough weather. It was one of those queer fancies of mine that made me dislike the place.'

Roberts considered laying out a kedge as well as the bower anchor, but decided that since 'our 2-inch tripping line had already chafed through on the jagged bottom in the matter of two hours, it would be useless to use a kedge on a warp'. That was the danger signal he ignored. For if a warp could be chafed through in hours, even a chain might go the same way if left for days. In fact, they left *Thelma* for five days before returning to find her among the rocks.

Anchoring in coral without careful checks can also run the risk of chain wrapping itself around a coral head, which can cause inextricable problems. Apart from the risk of being 'trapped', shortening the scope increases the shock loading, which can cause chain to snap, or put a fatal strain on deck gear.

WHEN FEAR CAME IN WAVES

Yacht	*Gartmore Investment Managers*
Skipper	Josh Hall
Bound from	Charleston, South Carolina, to Cape Town
Date of loss	18 October 1994
Position	500 miles off the coast of Brazil

While taking part in the first leg of the 1994–95 BOC Challenge Around Alone single-handed race, Josh Hall's 60ft racing yacht, Gartmore Investment Managers, *sank in cold, four-mile-deep South Atlantic water 500 miles off the Brazilian coast after colliding with a submerged object – probably a ship's container – at over 10 knots in rough seas.*

AS THE BOC AROUND ALONE fleet settled into the start of its fifth week at sea, Josh Hall, some 700 miles south of the Equator, had been in the south-east trades for about five days and was going great guns under full sail. The seas off this section of Brazil's coast had been unsettled, with bands of current kicking up some nasty, confused seas. Josh was hand-steering to stop the boat slamming over the backs of the waves.

Dusk was coming up with the wind blowing mostly over 22 knots true as *Gartmore* powered upwind at 10 knots. She came off the back of a wave, much like many others that threatened to loosen the fillings in the skipper's teeth. Josh nudged the wheel, expecting a soft landing, but was thrown up against it as the boat staggered to a standstill.

'It was the most horrendous landing you could imagine. The boat reared up and there was the most incredible rending sound as the bow came down. I realised something really bad had happened. It was almost as if we'd run aground,' he said.

As the yacht picked herself up again and started sailing, Josh rushed below, punching the Autohelm 7000 self-steering into action as he went.

BOC yachts have exceptional safety features, including a forward collision bulkhead designed to cope with just this sort of emergency. Already a huge amount of water had flooded the yacht through a 10ft-long gash. Water was halfway up the inspection and access hatch of the forward watertight bulkhead. Worse than that, the bulkhead itself had been fractured by the impact, allowing water to pour into the main part of the hull through a crack.

'My heart went to my stomach. It seemed as though it was happening to somebody else ... as if I was watching a bad movie. I had never felt so panicked or scared in all my time at sea. The fear came in waves. I didn't know what to do first. The real danger is a kind of paralysis from fear, not fear itself. In my mind I just knew I had to prioritise things. In a panic situation you try to quell the panic. I thought, "Is this it?"

'My adventure aboard this superb racing machine had turned into a nightmare. To get hold of myself, I was walking up and down very quickly in the cabin thinking "What do I do first? What do I do?" Suddenly there was so much to do that a full crew would be stretched to its limits.'

Josh's first priority was to get off a Mayday signal. He rushed to the chart table and hit the two red distress buttons on the Trimble Galaxy INMARSAT-C telex modem. He had to stop for a few seconds and read the instructions.

Within minutes UK Coastguard officials in Falmouth, Cornwall, alerted Charleston Race HQ that Josh was in trouble. It was 1950 GMT. At the same time Josh threw the switch on the INMARSAT-M satellite telephone, which would take about ten minutes to warm up. *Gartmore* was one of only three yachts in the race that were equipped to telephone direct to anywhere in the world.

Next, as water gushed in, he did his best to shore up the damaged area with floorboards and sailbags. Because she was holed in such a structurally strong area, Josh felt that *Gartmore* had struck the corner of something hard, like a shipping container. He switched on the big electric bilge pump forward of the watertight bulkhead and led another hose into the damaged area from a take-off on his water ballast pump. With all his pumps going he was shifting the best part of 5,000 gallons (19,000 litres) of water an hour. Despite this, there were 2 or 3 feet of water throughout the yacht and it was rising.

He picked up the telephone to call Race HQ and let them know what was happening. Peter Dunning, an old friend, was on duty. As the co-ordinator of every BOC Challenge, Dunning has been through every crisis in the race and was typically calm and reassuring.

He agreed that Alan Nebauer on *Newcastle Australia*, 90 miles to the north-west, was Josh's nearest competitor. Charleston would try and raise Alan by radio or Standard-C to divert him to the rescue.

It was agreed that Josh would leave his SSB radio on the 4MHz frequency on which skippers chatted each night and he would wait for Alan to call. As a back-up rescue aid, Josh activated his 406MHz EPIRB (satellite distress beacon). Finally, he would talk to Race HQ on INMARSAT-M every hour to update the situation.

Outside, it was getting dark and Josh needed to get the mainsail down to stop *Gartmore* burying her bow under water. He also needed to turn around and start heading towards Alan, instead of away from him.

With half the staysail up, *Gartmore* was jogging along at some 3 knots with the whole foredeck awash. Josh hoped that slowing her down would stem the flood of water inside. The fact that the bows were down with the weight of water up forward helped to keep the batteries and engine dry at the back of the boat. Josh desperately needed them to maintain power to his bilge pumps and communications. He used pieces of floorboard to make a dam at the main bulkhead around the galley to stop water flooding the batteries.

'Once I got started, the effort and involvement removed the panic. What stood me in good stead was having dealt with other situations. I've been involved with dismastings, broken booms and personal injury. But my biggest asset, communications-wise, was the COMSAT satellite telephone.'

Some 20 minutes after Josh's Mayday, Charleston made contact with Alan Nebauer, who responded to their urgency message. At first Alan wondered if something had happened back home. Then, when he heard Josh was in trouble, he worked with communications co-ordinator Larry Brumbach to plot an intercept point for the two yachts. Newcastle proceeded on a southerly heading at 7 knots, while *Gartmore* set a course to the west at 4 knots. This gave an average combined closing speed of 11 knots and put Alan some seven hours away.

By now Josh was coming to terms with the fact that *Gartmore* was fatally stricken. For a time he had thought he might be able to shore up the damage, stem the influx of water and limp somewhere. But the nearest land was more than 250 miles away. He accepted that his yacht was just going to be a floating island for him before rescue came. He would be lucky if she remained afloat. The creaking and groaning of the watertight bulkhead was frightening. If it burst open, the flow of water into the yacht would be doubled. *Gartmore*'s satellite phone was ringing every half-hour as Josh dealt with 15–20 calls over the next few hours before Alan's arrival.

Falmouth Coastguard, officially co-ordinating the rescue, called every hour and the Brazilian Coastguard on standby called four or five times. They were searching for ships nearby to divert to *Gartmore*'s aid, but were unable to locate any.

The Brazilian's English was undoubtedly better than Josh's Portuguese, but the language problems prompted some bizarre exchanges. As Josh failed in his polite attempts to explain that he didn't have time to answer bureaucratic inquiries about the yacht's registration papers, he was forced to hang up on them saying: 'Sorry, I'm too busy!'

He also wanted to speak to Laura, his wife, back home in Ipswich. He didn't want to scare her, but was concerned that she might have been alarmed to receive a call from the authorities about his EPIRB distress signal. He wanted to reassure her. He also needed to hear her voice.

A few days earlier she had called him to say that she was expecting their second child. Now it was his turn to break the news that their yacht and life-savings were sinking under his feet.

Back home in Suffolk it was 10 o'clock in the evening when Laura picked up the phone. She had already spoken to Peter Dunning, who had spelled things out very well, so Josh didn't have to go through it all. But it was an emotional phone call.

'I broke down a bit at that point,' said Josh. 'We were a bit teary. I remember saying, "I just want to be at home." Laura was very good.

She's very solid and strong and I guess she'd had time to deal with the situation. Peter had assured her help was on its way to me. I phoned three times throughout the whole night's drama to let her know how it was going and also just to hear her voice. My parents drove over and spent the night with Laura. When my younger brother rang me a few minutes later for a chat I don't think he believed me when I told him the yacht was sinking and I was about to get into the liferaft.'

Time ceased to have much meaning for Josh as he pumped and prayed. He had first made radio contact with Alan some two hours after the fatal collision.

'I can remember the relief that he was on his way. He asked me if it was bad and I said, "Yes, get here as soon as you can." But I didn't want to panic him because I knew he'd be sailing as fast as he could. At the same time, I wanted to impress on him the urgency of my situation. We agreed to speak on the radio every half-hour.'

In an attempt to defuse the tension in the midst of Josh's crisis, Alan Nebauer tried cracking a joke over the radio.

'What?' said Josh, failing to see the humour.

'Don't worry, it's just my Aussie humour trying to cheer you up,' said Alan.

A few hours later, Alan had his own sense of humour failure when he 'lost contact' with Josh for more than an hour ... Josh was busy trying to shore up the damaged hull and Alan's call was drowned out by the noise of the bilge pumps and engine running. Ninety minutes passed by before Josh remembered his radio schedule. Alan, meanwhile, had been 'freaking out', having called constantly and received no reply.

Down below on *Gartmore* it was a depressing scene with water still rising.

Josh, up to his hips in water, put on his survival suit. By now his concerns were concentrated on the integrity of his watertight bulkhead. If it gave way, or the pumps packed up, things would escalate rapidly. He decided to put his liferaft over the side, as an insurance.

'It was a six-man liferaft and I remember how heavy it was. I could only just pick it up ashore. But a frightened man has the strength of ten ... it went over easily and I tethered it alongside inflated so it was ready if I needed it. I was sponsored for all my safety equipment by a local company back home – Suffolk Sailing. When I left Shotley Marina to head to the start of the race, the boss, Graham Gardiner, came down to wish me well and I'll always remember him saying: "Unlike all your all other sponsors, I hope you never have to use what I've given you!" I was going to seriously disappoint him. There I was using everything he'd given me.'

Earlier, Josh had received a message from Peter Dunning asking him to hoist his SART (Search and Rescue Transponder) up the mast so that Alan could home in on it to find him.

In one of their radio calls Alan encouraged Josh 'to try and save as much kit as you can'. In the drama and panic it was something that hadn't even occurred to Josh. Each hour from then on he spent about ten minutes between pumping, trying to grab bags that were already packed and throw them into the liferaft.

'I'd borrowed a couple of laptop computers and put them in the liferaft, but they got swamped. I grabbed family photos of Laura and Sam (his son aged two-and-a-half) which were stuck above the chart table. What do you take? My whole world was in that boat. You look at all the bits and pieces of gear that you accumulate over the years … I felt we were one of the best equipped and prepared boats. I had to abandon all my navigation books and the sight reduction tables given to me by Robin Knox-Johnston. But I managed to grab my sextant. If I'd only managed to grab one thing it would have been the sextant.

'Alan was being updated on my position constantly by Race HQ, who were polling my GPS by the INMARSAT-C satellite. Ten miles away he also picked up the signal from my transponder on his radar. We agreed that to confirm my position I'd send up a red parachute flare, so I went on deck and fired one off. My masthead lights operated on a 24-volt system and were very powerful. He'd seen us!

'We were also fortunate that when Alan closed on my position there was almost a full moon at 0300 in the morning. Eventually Alan came up on the radio and said "Can you see me?"'

'I went up on deck and there he was in the moonlight, 200 yards away. He rolled up his headsail and we went over to talking on our waterproof handheld VHFs.'

As Alan Nebauer looked across to *Gartmore*, illuminated by her cabin and deck lights, he realised she was going down. She was a sad sight. 'If you love boats you just hate seeing them in those situations. I'd hoped maybe we could put a collision mat under the hole and sail to Brazil, but it was obviously not possible. *Gartmore* was very low in the water.' The Brazilian coast was also 500 miles away.

Conditions had improved as far as the sea state was concerned, but it was still too dangerous for Alan to come alongside. The pitching in the swell could have damaged *Newcastle*'s hull. It was agreed that Josh would transfer to *Newcastle* in the liferaft. His final act before he abandoned *Gartmore* and his dreams was to turn off the bilge pumps and open up all her seacocks, thus ensuring that his prized yacht sank and did not pose a threat to any of the following yachts in the BOC fleet.

He found his longest line to hand, the mainsheet, tied it to the liferaft and jumped in. 'I thought it was important to stay attached to something at all times. But as it turned out it was a mistake.' The liferaft drifted 60–70 yards downwind and as *Gartmore* surged on the 10ft waves the mainsheet snatched the liferaft, causing it to be swamped. Alan passed close by under reefed main and threw a line to Josh, but just as he went to grab it, the liferaft was violently jerked by its umbilical line to *Gartmore*. Letting go of Alan's line, Josh grabbed his knife and cut the line to *Gartmore*. Severing this last link to cut himself adrift seemed a final symbolic gesture.

'I was on my own for the next ten minutes as Alan did another circuit round the liferaft. It was the loneliest I've felt at sea. Sad and scared, even though he was close by, these were all fairly alien emotions to me. It felt strange to be bobbing around not tied to anything. *Gartmore* was such a tragic sight in the moonlight. The number of times I've pulled away from the yacht in the dinghy leaving it on a mooring ... but from the liferaft it was awful to see her as she laboured hull-down.

'Alan's seamanship was superb as her rounded up on the raft for a second time. I tied on his line and he dragged the liferaft up to *Newcastle*'s wide open transom. I scrambled on board, safe at last.'

'Welcome aboard mate,' said Alan.

'Thank you!' said Josh, in the understatement of the race.

'We were both very emotional,' said Josh. 'I stood for about an hour at the back of Alan's boat totally stunned by it all while he got organised to get under way.'

Josh's sudden sense of isolation set against the speed of modern day satellite communications was paradoxical enough to bewilder anyone, let alone a shipwrecked sailor.

As Alan stowed his bags down below, *Newcastle* jogged around under mainsail. It must have been over an hour before Josh got his survival suit off. They had to get rid of the liferaft and since it was impractical to bring it aboard they cut it up with a knife and let it sink.

'Neither of us wanted to stay around to see *Gartmore* sink. When we left, the light on the SART was still flashing just under the spreader. Despite the seas running the light wasn't rolling because the decks were awash.'

Twenty-two days later Alan and Josh crossed the Cape Town finish line.

The media were eager to quiz them about the mid-ocean rescue drama at a packed press conference. Josh was surprised at how emotional he was.

'I'd had three weeks to deal with it mentally and I thought I'd pretty much come to terms with it all. I started to give an account of what happened and just broke down in tears. I hadn't actually cried about the loss of the boat until then. It suddenly all came home to me.'

The Cape Town Harbour Master informed Josh Hall of the thought-provoking fact that in recent years over 40,000 containers had been officially reported as lost from the decks of Atlantic container ships.

'How many remain semi-submerged, suspended, waiting, is anyone's guess. I was lucky – I had superb communications on board, including a satellite phone. The skilled experience of the guys at BOC race HQ in Charleston coupled with the seamanship of Alan Nebauer meant I was plucked from the nose-diving *Gartmore* just eight hours after the collision.

Josh used pieces of floorboard to make a dam at the main bulkhead around the galley to stop water flooding the batteries that he desperately needed in order to maintain power supply to his bilge pumps and communications.

In an emergency situation it's easy to panic and forget something essential. Immediately after the collision, Josh's priority was to send a Mayday signal and even he, a highly professional sailor, admits he had to stop for a few seconds to read the instructions before hitting the two red buttons on the satellite system. Many yacht skippers have a copy of the Mayday instructions (for VHF radio) pinned by the chart table – if only to aid novice crew.

Josh had a spare hose, linked to his water ballast pump, which he could lead to the damaged area. The flooding was too catastrophic to save the yacht, but it was a good idea.

The satellite phone, common on cruising yachts these days, proved a vital link to the race HQ where the rescue was co-ordinated. These days, yachtsmen have even been known to call their insurance company by satphone, to get permission to abandon ship and sink her as a danger to navigation.

Another invaluable piece of safety kit which is more common on yachts these days was the SART (Search and Rescue Transponder) which Josh hoisted up the mast so that Alan Nebauer's could home in on the yacht more easily by radar. Alan picked up the signal from 10 miles away.

Parachute flares are also essential in this situation – to pinpoint the position of the yacht in peril to the rescue vessel. Josh also had a powerful masthead light operating on a 24-volt system. Some yachtsmen have been known to fit a masthead strobe light for emergencies – like collision avoidance – though the legality may be in doubt.

Once again, handheld VHF radios, waterproof in this case, proved vital for inter-ship communication.

The essential knife, without which no yachtsman should go to sea, also came into play when Josh abandoned ship, only to find the liferaft tied by its 'umbilical' line to *Gartmore* at the critical moment. Cutting the line, as Josh said, seemed a final symbolic gesture.

sixteen

MYSTERY COLLISION, MIRACULOUS SURVIVAL

Yacht	*Dorothea* (Harrison Butler-designed 32ft Bermudian cutter)
Skipper	Peter Tangvald
Bound from	Cayenne, French Guyana to Fort Lauderdale, Florida, USA
Date of loss	12 March 1967
Position	approx. 40 miles S of Barbados

Dorothea, a Harrison Butler-designed wooden cutter, was built in Whitstable in 1935. Peter Tangvald bought her in 1959 and during the next five years sailed her round the world before writing his book Sea Gypsy. *After he and his faithful crew Simone were married, they decided to build a larger boat and to sell* Dorothea *in America, where she could be expected to fetch a higher price. Tangvald left Cayenne on 7 March, sailing single-handed, with the intention of making a stop on the way at Charlotte Amalie in the Virgin Islands, where he hoped to meet old friends. He takes up the story.*

MY WIFE STAYED BEHIND IN our newly leased house to watch over the huge pile of lumber and all the machine tools already purchased for the new ship. She told me later it had been a beautiful sight to see the ship tack down river towards the sea. Had she seen me when I crossed the bar, however, she would not have said the same thing, as one huge breaker swept the ship from end to end, soaking me to the skin in the process, while I wondered how strange it was that man is able to shoot rockets to the moon, yet be incapable of making oilskin which is truly watertight. Being wet and cold I decided to anchor for the night in the lee of the Iles du Salut about 30 miles from Cayenne.

Next morning, without having gone ashore, I set sail again, this time in much improved weather, well rested and cheerful. The wind was right on the beam and very fresh and gave *Dorothea* her maximum speed. In fact, from us leaving these islands till the moment of the accident, she made the greatest average speed of her life, covering 170 miles a day from noon to noon; but I must add that the speed over 40 of these miles was probably due to the strong South Equatorial Current helping us along.

Then on the night of 12 March it happened. The weather had covered up with black clouds and rain squalls. The night promised to be dark as there was no moon. Although the ship steered herself with her self-steering gear, I sat by the tiller, breathing in the last rays of daylight. The evening meal was on the stove down below and would soon be ready. Then when the new night was complete and I had just decided to go down below for dinner, the ship struck.

She struck so hard that she shuddered. But then she kept on going as before. I knew that I was many miles from the closest land and had about 1,000 fathoms of water below me, and thus could not have bounced on a reef. For an instant I thought that I had collided with a native fishing boat, as they often don't bother to use any lights, but dismissed the thought immediately, as I knew that I would have heard not a little swearing. Indeed, shining my electric torch all around the horizon revealed nothing but water. Thus I can only presume that what I had hit was possibly a large tree trunk or some wreckage which had been floating on, or just below, the surface of the sea.

Down in the saloon I was horrified to see the water already washing above the floorboards. The collision had sprung a very serious leak in the ship which until then had never leaked more than a bucket of water a year. I immediately realised that at the rate the water was coming in, the ship would soon sink unless I was able to localise the damage and make temporary repairs, but this proved an impossibility due to the inside ceiling which hid the planking with its damage. Thus water was leaking in between the outer and inner skin of the boat with no possibility of access for me to the damaged spot. To look for it from the outside would no doubt have been possible in a calm sea and in daylight, and I might then have been able to nail over it a piece of canvas; but as it was, with a rolling ship, in heavy seas and pitch darkness it was an impossibility, and perhaps even suicide as the copper sheeting had no doubt been torn and its sharp edges would soon have cut me to death.

To realise suddenly that one is on a sinking ship, far from land, outside of any shipping lane and with no lifesaving equipment on board is most depressing, and perhaps even more so on a pitch dark night, windy and with frequent rain squalls. But however unhappy I was, I never stopped trying to figure out how to save my own life.

The dinghy was just 7ft long and of flimsy plywood construction, while the seas were heavy and frequently breaking; but with luck even the smallest boat can survive quite rough conditions. Down in the chart room, with water swirling around my legs, I saw that the closest land was Barbados, about 40 miles away but dead to windward of me and thus out of the question for me to reach; but to leeward was the long chain of the Grenadine Islands about 55 miles away. Presuming that the dinghy would not be swamped before then, these should be easy to reach with a following wind, and the only navigational difficulty and danger would be to avoid letting the wind and current sweep me between two islands and into the Caribbean Sea where we would have no more land to our lee until the American mainland.

Thus with the greatest possible care, I launched the dinghy and was greatly relieved when I had been able to do so without damaging it or letting it be filled with water. To get a dinghy in the water singlehanded is not the easiest job in the world even in a calm harbour, but in a heavy sea and a rolling ship it is very awkward indeed. I let her drift off to leeward on a long painter so that she would not get damaged against the side of *Dorothea*, and then went below to assemble all the gear I considered desirable for increasing my chances of making land alive.

First of all I took the two plastic bottles, each containing 2½ gallons of fresh water which I always kept as emergency rations should *Dorothea*'s single tank have sprung a leak; then I half-filled a sailbag with food; then another sailbag with some clothes, then the chart and the compass; then an awning, a short gaff and some rope with the idea of a makeshift rig to cover the many miles to land; then the dinghy's folding anchor with a very long line, with the idea of having a last defence against being swept into the Caribbean Sea, should I miss the islands, hoping, of course, that I would get close enough to shallow water for it to be of any use. Then my two flashlights with spare batteries; then my lifejacket; and finally my papers and the cash I had in the boat, which I put in a watertight bag together with the spare batteries. I assembled all the gear by the cockpit, and as I walked up the companionway my eyes fell on the dinner-pot still on the stove. I had just been ready to eat when we struck, so not wanting to waste the work of cooking, took the pot along. When all was ready on deck, I pulled the dinghy alongside, quickly threw in all the gear, jumped in and pushed off.

I soon realised that I had grossly overloaded the little boat, as almost every wave shipped water into her, so I lost no time in throwing overboard part of the gear, as obviously even the most desirable piece of equipment would lose all its importance should the dinghy founder. The anchor with its line went over the side, then one of the two water bottles, then the life-jacket, as, come what may, I was not going to swim 55 miles. Then, thinking that I would either make land within a couple of days or not at all, I half-emptied the other water bottle.

This lightening made a tremendous difference, and if I now sat in the bottom of the boat instead of on the thwart, in order to lower her centre of gravity, the dinghy was both very stable and buoyant, lifting over every wave and hardly letting in any water at all. I let go the painter but held on the yacht's mainsheet for a while, looking at her with my torch, somehow reluctant to abandon her and to be on my own in that black night; but then a very strong squall came whistling down and I was unable to hold on any longer for fear of capsizing, even though *Dorothea* was hove-to. So I let go the sheet and drifted off to leeward. About 50 minutes had elapsed since the collision and *Dorothea* was lying very deep in the water. I saw her lights for a while and then suddenly they disappeared.

I felt utterly lonesome, wet, cold and rather worried about the future. I was, however, soon relieved to see how well that little dinghy managed in the heavy seas. She really floated like a cork and even when the top of a crest was breaking and overtaking us in a white foam, making me at first think that 'that one will swamp us', even then the little boat lifted bravely and the foam disappeared harmlessly below us.

I soon gained enough confidence to make the jury rig which I knew would be necessary if I did not want to spend days at sea before reaching the land. I then discovered that I had forgotten to bring the knife. I was extremely annoyed at myself for that, as I really had tried to do my best not to overlook anything. Fortunately I was able to tear the awning to the right size anyway by using my teeth to get the rip started. But I was entirely unable to cut the rope without a knife so I had to make the whole rig with one continuous length of rope, lashing one side of the 'squaresail' to the gaff which was to serve as square yard, then lashing the middle of that gaff to the end of one of the oars which was to serve as mast. From that same intersection I got out two lines to act as shrouds and then two more lines to the lower part of the sail as sheets.

When I had everything ready, I hoisted the 'mast'. The sail filled immediately but before losing control I was able to tighten the shrouds by taking up the turns around the thwart. I let the mast lean forward, thus not needing any forward stay which would have been very difficult to rig. Then by adjusting the sheets and steering with the remaining oar, the little boat scooted right along at a fair speed. Before I was able to rejoice much, however, I was suddenly dismayed by seeing the water rise in the bottom of the dinghy at a frightening rate. I then understood that it was the pressure of the sail which depressed the bow enough to let the water wash above it. The sail, hiding the bow from where I sat, had prevented me from seeing the danger. By moving quickly right aft and leaning over the stern thwart, then bailing out the dinghy, everything seemed under control.

At about 0130 I was startled and overjoyed to see a steamship coming toward me. This was almost unbelievable luck as these were little-frequented waters and this ship was, in fact, the first ship I had seen on the voyage since leaving Cayenne, not counting a few fishing boats along the coast of French Guyana. I flashed continuously the international distress signal, SOS, with my powerful long-range torch which I trained straight at her.

The ship came slowly closer and in my thoughts I prepared how I should board her. I presumed that the steamer would come alongside me at very slow speed and then throw me a rope for getting on board. I decided that I would make no attempt to save either the dinghy or anything in her except my papers and money. I would as quickly as possible tie the rope around my chest right under the armpits and make fast with a bowline. This knot never slips.

The ship was now very close and I could see her moving through the seas. I expected to see her slow down and set the course straight for me; but to my dismay the minutes passed without the ship altering course at all, then her bright red port light faded, as did her two masthead lights only to be replaced immediately by a single white light; her stern light. She had not seen me after all!

As the steamer's lights disappeared below the horizon, I stopped thinking about her and told myself that, after all, if the dinghy had managed these many hours, there was no reason why she should not continue doing so until I reached land. My thoughts wandered over to the new dreamship I was going to build and I decided that I would incorporate two strong, watertight bulkheads so that I would not again be put too easily in such an awkward situation. I also secretly thought that next time I would have a bigger dinghy and a real sailing dinghy at that, but I did not dare linger too long on any criticism of my present dinghy for fear it would bring me bad luck. After all, she was doing her best to save my life.

The night was long, sleep was impossible and I was shivering with cold, all my clothes being soaking wet. At last daylight came. And best of all, about an hour after daybreak, I saw land in the distance. It was a most comforting sight, but I soon realised that my makeshift sailing dinghy, which seemed only able to sail with the wind aft, could not point high enough to reach it.

An hour later two more spots of land appeared, so with three peaks from which to take cross-bearings with my compass I soon found on the chart the only three places it matched and could thus determine my own position. Then to my great joy I realised that the land I was seeing was not at all the closest land to me but that a lower land still below the horizon was much nearer and easier to reach as it was almost straight downwind. All I needed to do was to alter the course by a few degrees.

I became very cheerful, despite my tiredness from the lack of sleep, the cold, the uncomfortable position in the bottom of the dinghy, the strain of steering and having to counteract every wave, and now the glare and the heat of the tropical sun, not to speak of the emotional strain. After a few hours land did indeed appear dead ahead of us as expected and I could then steer straight for it, using the compass for checking crosscurrents which soon proved to be so strong that, had I not had the compass, I might not have realised their force until too late and then missed the island.

When I got close to the island and felt safe, I became careless and sat up on the middle thwart in order to get a better view to choose the best place to land. Immediately the bow plunged under the sea and the dinghy began to fill up. In a desperate move, I grabbed the 'mast', uprooting it and let it fall over the side. The dinghy was at once relieved but already so full of water as to have lost all stability and threatened to capsize or fill up completely. I was close to land but still much too far to swim for it. As quickly, but also as carefully as possible, I undid all the ropes holding the rig to the boat, then threw over the side the remaining bottle of water to give me more room for bailing and then bailed for dear life while all the time I kept shifting my weight to counteract the effect of the surging water. I breathed a sigh of relief when the dinghy was dry and had regained her stability. Without the rig I felt it was safe enough to sit up on the thwart and at long last stretch out my legs.

The island I had come to was called Canouan and was a small island in the Grenadines group. Its northern part was steep cliffs and impossible to land on, but its southern part seemed to be low sandy beaches. Unfortunately that part of the coast was bordered by a long reef on to which the whole Atlantic broke heavily. I was well aware of the danger of trying to land through such breakers and the sensible thing to do would, of course, have been to land on the island's lee side; but I was just too tired to even consider sculling all that way and I was also worried about the current perhaps being stronger than I and making me miss the lee side altogether. Thus I preferred to take the chance on shooting the reef.

As I came closer, an islander high on the cliff signalled to me not to come any closer but to go round the island; however as I disregarded his advice and he realised that I really intended to go through the surf, he directed me to the best place where the rollers were not too big. I tried to time it so that I would get over the critical spot between two rollers but my dinghy was not fast enough and a huge breaker came foaming against me. I expected to be capsized but hoped to have enough strength to swim the rest of the way.

Much to my surprise the brave little dinghy just popped up on top of the broiling mass of water and shot forward at great speed. When the wave died down I found myself in smooth water. In the meantime, the islander on the cliff had jumped into a rowboat and was now coming toward me. He then towed me into the bottom of a quiet bay and helped me up the beach to lie down as my legs were so weak as to hardly be able to carry me. I was so tired I felt sick, but I knew that once more the words of the fortune-teller who had told me at the age of fifteen that I was like the cat, born with nine lives, were still right. In fact, I should have two or three more to go!

■ LESSONS LEARNED

- It must be a terrifying conundrum for a single-handed sailor aboard a badly leaking monohull to choose between pumping, stopping to search for the cause of the leak, or abandoning ship while there is still time to launch the liferaft or dinghy and collect essentials.
- When Peter Tangvald's *Dorothea* collided with something at night SW of Barbados, he knew that the leak was serious because water was above the floorboards almost immediately. His heavily ballasted boat would soon sink unless he could quickly locate the damage and make temporary repairs; but 'this proved to be impossible because of the inside ceiling which hid the planking'. In such circumstances, some yachtsmen have been known to use a 'wrecking bar' (similar to a crowbar) to get past the obstruction.

- With no liferaft, Tangvald's remarkable 55-mile voyage to safety in his 7ft plywood dinghy is proof that a small wooden dinghy can, under favourable circumstances, serve as a lifesaving craft, giving the shipwrecked sailor a more active role in self-preservation. Fortunately, he had time to grab many essentials to construct his makeshift rig for the dinghy, but he forgot his knife. Once again, the importance of having a pre-prepared 'grab bag' of essentials for emergencies is demonstrated.

seventeen

SUNK BY A WHALE!

Yacht	*Guia III* (44ft ocean-racer)
Skipper	Jerome Poncet
Crew	George Marshall (navigator) Giorgio di Mola, Claudio Cuoghi, Giovanni Verbinni, Francesco Longanesi
Bound from	Rio de Janeiro, Brazil, to Portsmouth, England
Date of loss	9 March 1976
Position	approx. 500 miles SW of Cape Verde Islands

The Italian-owned Guia III *had sailed for Australia in their 1973 Admiral's Cup team under the name* Ginkgo, *but under her new ownership she had subsequently taken part in two of the three legs of the 1975–76 Atlantic Triangle races, the last one of which was between Rio de Janeiro and Portsmouth. The third leg started on 22 February 1976, and until 9 March the race continued without incident. Thereafter, George Marshall, navigator and sole Englishman on board, tells the story:*

WE STARTED FROM RIO DE JANEIRO with a very good chance of winning the Atlantic Triangle; everything required to make the boat a winner had been checked and replaced where necessary. One item that needed doing was the liferaft; its certificate was out of date and only the eagle-eyed scrutineers spotted this. Like most long-distance sailors we had only made sure that we had one. The raft arrived back only hours before the start and was placed in its customary position in the centre cockpit.

The race soon became the usual long-distance ocean racing routine. Up to the equator we averaged 150 miles a day, hit the doldrums on

6 March, but during the night 8/9 March the wind increased to 35 knots, moderating as the sun came up. At 2000 the watch changed and I, with the other two on watch, went below for what was normally the best sleeping time. After a very quick breakfast of hot chocolate, cookies and cheese, I wrapped a sheet around myself and was into the land of nod.

From the middle of a deep sleep I was awoken by a sudden crack and lurch upwards, and all the watch below sat up on their bunks. From the deck came the cry of 'Orca! Orca!' – even my limited Italian was enough to translate this as whales. The head of a crewman appeared in the hatch and pointing forward he shouted 'water in the boat'.

I put my feet onto the cabin sole and found that, indeed, there was water in the boat, over the tops of my ankles. Looking forward through the tunnel joining the forepeak to the main cabin I saw water rushing back. Diving forward into the forepeak I saw that the water was coming from the port side through the sail bins. I went back to the main cabin, got the knife that was always available on the galley, and went back to join Jerome our skipper and Giorgio from the deck watch. We cut the sail bins free and found what to us looked like an enormous hole. It was about 2ft below the waterline and just abaft the fore bulkhead. It was an egg-shaped hole 3ft long and 2ft deep. The planks had been forced from the bottom to the top and it was very obvious that whatever had done the damage had hit the boat with great force.

The water gushed in, and for a second or two we just gaped at the damage in disbelief. Jerome and I then tried to force the wood back into the hole but the strength of the remaining fibres of wood were too much for our combined weight. As we were doing this the remainder of the crew were handing the sails to take way off the yacht, the initial inrush of water making it impossible to tack or heave-to. As it became obvious that we were not going to get the damaged portion of the hull back over the hole, Jerome told Giorgio and me to go on deck and try to get a headsail over the hole. He continued to try and plug the hole from the inside with spinnakers and anything else to hand. The water was waist deep at this time and as fast as he pushed a sail in the gap it was forced back.

Giorgio and I went up on deck and freed the No. 2 genoa from the lifelines. I took the head of the sail and stepped over the lifelines with the idea of jumping down past the hole and carrying the sail with me under the hull so that the water pressure would suck the sail into the hole.

Looking down into the very clear water I could see the jagged hole with long cracks, fore and aft. Also lying alongside the yacht about 2 to 3ft down I could see a very big fish which was at least half the length of the yacht and appeared about 6ft wide. Giorgio also saw it and very emphatically told me to stay on deck. In truth, I had already changed my mind as I didn't fancy making a snack for whatever it was.

We then tried to take the sail around the bows, but by now the deck was awash and this proved impossible. Jerome appeared in the main hatch and said it was time to abandon ship. The rest of the crew had already started to get stores up from the cabin and I went down below to start my part of the abandon ship drill. As I waited for the hatch to clear I looked around *Guia* and saw on the port side a pod of killer whales circling around about 50ft from the beam. They are unmistakable with their white patches and tall fins, and for the first time I realised what had happened. On the starboard side a school of dolphins, fairly large and with a mottled green and black skin, were sounding.

Down below I found that the water was thigh deep and the boat rocking, swishing the water from beam to beam. The radio had been switched on and I soon had the first Mayday out on 2182 kHz. I knew that there was very little chance of it being picked up as we were by this time too far from land for the set to reach. A quick switch to the race control frequency of 4136.3 kHz and again a Mayday. The output meter on the set showed that the power was rapidly going as the seawater came over the tops of the battery. The water all this time was rising rapidly and soon Jerome and I were chest high. I continued sending Maydays on alternate frequencies until it was obvious that the set was only working on a bare minimum of power. As I was sending the signals I was helping Jerome by passing anything that floated past. All our kit that we kept for emergencies had already been passed up on deck and we knew that the liferaft had inflated and was being loaded.

Jerome then gave a very Gallic shrug and said to me that we must say au revoir to *Guia*, and told me to go on deck and get in the liferaft. I pushed the emergency signal button on the radio and noticed that it was transmitting, but at a very reduced output from normal. As we waded back to the hatch through the now neck-high water we managed to save a few more items – cans of fruit – a bag of mine that contained my camera and personal washing kit and a notebook and some cans of condensed milk.

A shout from outside said that *Guia* was going. This made us move up on deck just in time to see the bows dip and in about 10 seconds from a boat awash there was only the stern and the top of the mast out of the water.

I slid into the water and swam the short distance to the liferaft. As I clung to the side of the liferaft, *Guia* gave a very loud prolonged sigh as air trapped in the stern escaped and she disappeared entirely. I then attempted to board the dinghy and found to my alarm that something was holding me down in the water. Jerome tried to pull me in with help but couldn't. We soon found that the sea anchor had wrapped itself around me and that this was keeping me in the water. It then became a simple matter of hauling it and me into the raft.

On entering the raft I saw that it was just a heap of bodies, kit, food containers and clothing. Everyone just sat for the first few minutes and I am sure that they felt as I did. To see a fine yacht like *Guia* disappear so suddenly was a shock to us all. Also the realisation that we were many miles away from both land and frequented shipping lanes made us all a little unhappy about our chances of survival. Looking around there was no sign of anything; no boat wreckage, no whales; just the sea and sky. It was a very lonely feeling.

We started to organise the inside of the raft and take an inventory of what we had, and after we had inspected everything, decided that we were not too badly off. There was plenty of food, enough to last a month with care, a box of flares, Helly Hansen suits and waterproofs for us all. Three blankets, 800 cigarettes, matches, lighters, torches, lifejackets and three kit-bags with personal kit, including mine, with all my spare pullovers and some sailing trousers were on the raft.

All the food was in polythene casks and we were glad that we had decided that this system was used on *Guia*. We thought that if the liferaft was badly damaged then we might be able to make a float with the food containers.

Our only shortcoming was water. We only had 15 litres and we knew that we would be in trouble if we didn't get some rain or make some from a still. However, we were pretty sure that we could last until a rain cloud came along as the area we were in always produced some rain.

After sorting out the raft and the stores we all changed into the thermal underwear and on the advice of Giorgio rested and talked about our chances. After a long discussion we agreed that we were going to survive come what may, and that we had three chances of being picked up. It was clear that the only place that we could go was towards South America, with the odds of ending up somewhere in Venezuela. On the way we thought that within three days we should be somewhere near the mid-Atlantic route between the North American ports and Cape Town, then two weeks later on the shipping route between Panama and Cape Town and finally the inshore routes along the coast of South America.

After two hours, the sea anchor was hauled in and we set off from the scene at about 2 to 2½ knots. The sea anchor had made us decide to leave, as its violent snubbing was liable to damage the raft and we would sooner take our chance with a possible long trip than end up with a sinking liferaft.

A food container and two lifebelts on the end of a 20ft line kept the back of the liferaft to the wind and sea. It also broke up the worst of the waves so that only very occasionally did water come onto the canopy. The motion of the raft was fairly comfortable, the floating anchor keeping us from dropping too fast down the front of the waves. The only discomfort was from the damp on the bottom of the raft and from the conglomeration of legs in the centre. The oilskins and blankets made the floor comfortable but the only answer for the legs was to grin and bear it. Giorgio was told that he might be getting some practice in amputation if we had to spend too much time in the dinghy.

As night fell the watches were set for everyone to do one and a half hours in rotation. During the day only whoever was near the door had kept lookout as we knew that the best chance of seeing a boat was during the dark.

The lookout was stationed at the entrance with the torches, pumps and flares to hand. Each lookout was allowed two cigarettes and a cookie to keep him going during his watch.

As my turn was not until midnight I settled down to get what sleep I could. This proved easier than I thought but not until all the legs had been arranged to our mutual comfort.

At midnight Claudio Cuoghi, the youngest member of our crew, woke me and told me it was my turn for guardia. After a long complicated manoeuvre I extracted myself from the pile of bodies and sat at the entrance of the raft. A shared cigarette with Claudio and a chat about the sinking, then he wormed his way into the pile of bodies and I was left alone with the sea. The wind was still about 25 knots and the sea about 9 to 12ft high, but the raft was behaving perfectly well. Without moving I soon realised that I could cover 360° of the horizon every two to three minutes as the raft swung at the end of the floats.

I can't say that I thought any great thoughts during the time I was on watch except that I probably felt very much at rest. The sea is so huge that it is difficult to feel anger or sorrow at anything that it or its inhabitants may do to you. Like the jungle, the sea is neutral, and all that man can hope to do is live with it and accept all its moods.

After sitting for two hours, I gave one of the crew a shake and he took over the watch from me. It was more difficult to get a comfortable space on the floor and it took me a while to get into that half dozy state that precedes sleep. Just as I had got warm and comfortable someone leaned across me and shook Jerome. 'I think that I can see a light,' he said, 'but it could just be a star rising.'

I was at the entrance before he finished speaking, as I knew that there were clouds all around the horizon and it was almost certain that he had seen a ship. The three of us sat in the entrance staring out over our limited horizon. After what seemed an age we spotted a light dipping to windward. I wanted to put up a flare straight away (I had been delegated the job of igniting them as I had more practice than the others).

However, Jerome suggested we wait until we could see what it was and what course it was on. This seemed to me an even longer wait, but soon the second masthead light of a steamer showed itself. It became apparent that it would pass us about 3 miles downwind, and I put up the first parachute red flare. It went straight up and burst into a very satisfying red glow. After about 30 seconds it went out and we all stared at the lights of the ship willing it to alter course. We waited 10 minutes and then discharged two more para flares one after the other, aiming to send them across the bows of the ship. They both worked and as they drifted down, we saw the ship flash an Aldis lamp at us and the angle of her lights alter. Moments later all her deck lights came on and within minutes she went past us at a distance of 200 yards and stopped about a mile away. All our torches were lit, the buoy lights set flashing and I set to igniting the hand-held flares.

The next two hours were probably the most trying of my life. The ship made four passes at us but seemed to have great difficulty in seeing us. We only had ten hand-held flares, and some of those proved useless. My chief memory of those two hours is of violent curses against the people who sell such unseamanlike objects and gratitude to the sane ones who made the ones that worked.

Eventually the ship stopped downwind of us and we tried to paddle the liferaft to it, but as the ship was drifting faster than us we gave up and waited to see what they would do. From round the stern a ship's lifeboat appeared. It was only when we saw it that we realised what size sea was running. Most of the time it was out of sight and at first went away from our position. The last hand flare brought it back towards us, and soon we transferred to the lifeboat, taking all our kit from the liferaft with us.

The raft was secured alongside, and soon we found ourselves alongside the *Hellenic Ideal*. We still had to manage the ladder but the deck officer in charge made us all tie a lifeline around ourselves before allowing us to climb to the deck from the lifeboat; a very sensible precaution as it turned out. Not one of us after the climb was able to stand, and each of us collapsed against a bulkhead; I think it was more from relief than weakness. After a cigarette and a tot of something very strong we were led down below to the passengers' dining room. The captain then came down from the bridge, made sure that we were complete, and said that the ship was at our disposal until New York.

It is difficult to express your thanks to someone who saves your life, but to the seaman who spotted our flare, and the Captain, Dimitros Dimitri, and the crew of the *Hellenic Ideal,* thank you. Your skill, seamanship and hospitality will never be forgotten.

In 1972 and 1973 there were also high profile losses of yachts which sank after striking whales not far from the Galapagos Islands in the Pacific. The stories of the sinking of *Auralyn* and *Lucette* are told, respectively, in Maurice and Marilyn Bailey's best-seller, *119 Days Adrift* and Dougal Robertson's book, *Survive the Savage Seas*. In both cases, the survivors had a long time to reflect on their wisdom in deciding to take both a liferaft and an inflatable dinghy with them on their world voyaging.

Guia's skipper and crew were experienced ocean-racers, and it was expected they would be well organised so that even while some of them made last-minute attempts to keep *Guia III* afloat, others had already started to get stores up from the cabin. By the time their skipper made the decision to abandon, the emergency kit had been passed up on deck, and the liferaft was inflated and being loaded.

There was enough food, with care, to last a month; a box of flares (which were to prove their saviour); Helly Hansen suits and waterproofs for all; three blankets, torches, lifejackets and three kitbags with personal gear … All the food was in polythene containers. The only shortcoming was water. As it happened, they were rescued by a ship within 24 hours. But they were lucky.

Just as there are differences of opinion on the influence a sea anchor will have on the behaviour of a yacht in heavy weather, so there are uncertainties about the value of a sea anchor or drogue when attached to a liferaft. When it had been decided to try to reach land by drifting with the wind, *Guia III*'s sea anchor on the liferaft was hauled in, since it would slow progress. But George Marshall also pointed out: 'The sea anchor's violent snubbing was liable to damage the raft and we would sooner take our chance with a possible long trip than end up with a sinking liferaft.'

In recent years the design of liferaft sea anchors has improved, following tests which revealed that the snatch loads generated between a liferaft and its sea anchor in 20 knots of wind, with seas of 3 to 5ft, can increase to ten times the normal steady loading. The once commonly used 'handkerchief' type of drogue offered too much resistance and has since been replaced by a conical-shaped sea anchor made from porous material so as to reduce loading to a more tolerable level.

Five of the six-man crew of *Guia III* were trying to sleep during the first night in the liferaft, when the lookout said that he thought he could see a light. George Marshall wanted to put up a flare straight away, but the skipper insisted on waiting until they were certain. The experiences of others show that many flares have been fired, and 'wasted', because shipping was too far away to see them. On this occasion they waited until the rescue ship was about 3 miles downwind before firing the first parachute red flare and then waited ten more minutes and launched two more para flares, one after the other. The ship spotted them.

Getting aboard a rescue craft from a dinghy or liferaft is never easy in a rough sea if the rescue ship is a large freighter or tanker with decks high above the water. In such cases it may be safer to carry out the rescue in two stages, as the captain of the *Hellenic Ideal* decided to do when he stopped his ship downwind of the liferaft. George Marshall says: 'From round the stern a ship's lifeboat appeared; it was only when we saw it that we realised what size sea was running,' but they safely transferred to the lifeboat, taking all their kit with them, and soon they were alongside the *Hellenic Ideal* where 'we still had to manage the ladder, but the deck officer in charge made us all tie a lifeline around ourselves before allowing us to climb to the deck from the lifeboat. A very sensible precaution as it turned out. Not one of us after the climb was able to stand, and each of us collapsed against the bulkhead.'

eighteen

FIRE ABOARD

Yacht	*Strumpet* (28ft GRP replica of a Morecambe Bay prawner)
Skipper	Henry Irving
Crew	Barry Speakman, Jondo Irving, Joe Irving
Bound from	Wainfleet Haven, Lincolnshire, to Wells, Norfolk, UK
Date of loss	3 August 1980
Position	1 mile S of Gibraltar Point, approx. 6 miles S of Skegness

----

Henry Irving, author of the pilot guide Tidal Havens of the Wash and Humber, *had sailed those waters, summer and winter, for many years, usually in his own boat* Venture, *but this time in a friend's yacht,* Strumpet. *They had set sail from Wainfleet Creek at the northern corner of the Wash and were bound for Wells, some 30 miles away on the north Norfolk coast.* Strumpet *was a reinforced glassfibre replica of a Morecambe Bay prawner – a strong and sea-kindly vessel. Besides Barry, an old friend and experienced cruising companion, Irving had his two young sons, Jondo and Joe, on board. In company as they left the creek was another friend, Peter Tomlinson, in his steel yacht* Temptress, *with a crew of four. The mood was merry, Skegness had been enjoyable, the day promised to be good and Wells promised to be even better. Fifteen minutes later, all eight of them were aboard* Temptress, *and* Strumpet *was a blazing inferno. Henry Irving takes up the story.*

TIDE TIME ARRIVED THAT MORNING in the middle of ablutions, so it was necessary to postpone breakfast, start the engine and cast off lines. Wainfleet permits little dallying on the ebb. As I steered *Strumpet* down the tortuous creek between the withies, Barry prepared breakfast and served it up to Jondo and Joe. Since we were nearing the haven mouth, I suggested that he kept our breakfasts warm in the oven while raising sail. A leisurely breakfast under sail appealed to me much more than something crammed down astern of a noisy diesel engine. Jondo, fearing that he was missing something of interest, bolted his breakfast and rushed on to the foredeck to assist. Joe, unwilling to abandon his carefully prepared bread soldiers, stayed below to savour his food. Something, however, was spoiling his childish pleasure:

'Dad, there's an awful smell of fumes.'

'Oh, shut up. It's only the diesel. Eat your breakfast. I'll switch it off in a minute.'

The sails went up, I bore off, and switched off the engine.

'I can't stand these fumes. I'm going to eat my breakfast out there.'

By this time, I could smell something, so I summoned Jondo to the helm and scrambled below. A quick glance at the galley showed me that Barry had left no pans on the gas, and a peep into the oven revealed a reassuring pile of bacon, mushrooms and tomatoes, warmly awaiting the arrival of the as yet uncooked eggs. I looked at the engine temperature gauge. All fine. To check, I lifted the engine cover and smelled fumes, but the engine did not feel excessively warm. Thinking it must have been an oily rag on the exhaust, I climbed into the cockpit to check this, unhurried because the engine was now quiet and presumably cooling. Nothing amiss in that department so I looked at the sails and sea scene once more, assuming that the smell would soon go. Joe finished his breakfast so I asked him to go below and start cooking the eggs for Barry and myself. He disappeared, only to re-emerge immediately to say that black smoke was now pouring into the cabin from the fo'c's'le. I seized the large CO_2 extinguisher from the cockpit locker and scrambled below, but the dense black smoke prevented me from getting anywhere near the fo'c's'le.

I held what breath I had and directed the extinguisher into the smoke for a few futile seconds then rushed out on deck. The hatch boards were stowed in the aft locker so I could not quickly fit them. When I got my breath I realised that Peter, a friend in another yacht *Temptress*, had come close alongside and had hurled his extinguisher at Barry. We went on to the foredeck and I opened the hatch so that Barry could direct the extinguisher on to the source of the smoke.

Immediately, a roar of black smoke and flame shot out of the hatch, igniting the staysail and causing us both to stagger back with black faces and singed eyebrows.

My thoughts then turned to saving life rather than fighting fire. *Temptress* was still at hand so I called Peter to come alongside and take off crew. The sea was quite choppy, but the manoeuvre was well executed and the boys and Barry got safely on to *Temptress*. I attempted to unfasten the inflated dinghy from the cabin roof, but as I did so the forward section burst into flame so I abandoned the attempt. I called for a tow rope and managed to make it fast to the forestay, thinking that a sandbank was a better place to sink than a swatchway. By this time, the heat was becoming so intense that *Temptress*'s sails and rigging were endangered, and the boys were clearly in distress, so I jumped aboard. We towed *Strumpet* on a long line, which finally burned through while we were atop the Outer Dog's Head. The maelstrom that ensued was awesome to behold: sails burst into flame, the mast fell down, the Calor gas cylinder exploded in the aft locker and finally the hull slowly melted away till she sank. *Strumpet* was gone.

■ LESSONS LEARNED

Irving found he couldn't get through the cabin to the source of the fire in the fo'c's'le. He knew that he should close the companionway hatch to reduce air flow into the boat, but the washboards were stowed in the aft locker so he couldn't fit them quickly enough. A valuable lesson. Instead, he went forward on deck and opened the forehatch 'so Barry could direct the extinguisher onto the source of the fire. Immediately, a roar of black smoke and flame shot out of the hatch.' Always remember to seal up a boat on fire unless you can be sure a fire extinguisher will do its job.

Finally, when an attempt was made to unfasten the inflated dinghy from the coachroof, the forward section burst into flames, so they had to abandon the attempt. If *Temptress* had not been there to take them off, the crew of *Strumpet* would have been forced to jump into the sea.

As the nightmare subsided, the skipper spent hours sifting through the events to provide an explanation for the insurance company. He could only think of one possibility. There was no natural light in the fo'c's'le, so the boys, who were sleeping there, used a Camping Gaz lamp, which the owner had left hanging on a hook for this purpose. That morning, they used it to dress and then put it out. But it was only a matter of minutes before they were motoring down the creek in choppy water. The motion may have caused the lamp to jump off the hook and fall with a still hot glass on to one of the sleeping bags. This must have ignited the Dunlopillo mattress.

At the end of the day the lesson is that disaster can strike a small cruising yacht very quickly. 'If you can't cope with this, then don't go to sea. But don't get into a car either, and don't cross the road to get your morning paper!' said Irving afterwards.

nineteen

THE EXPLODING BOAT

Yacht	*Ladybee* (30ft gaff-rigged double-ender)
Skipper	James Houston
Crew	Margaret Houston
Bound from	Puilladobhrain, Argyll to Tobermory, Isle of Mull, Scotland
Date of loss	10 June 1972
Position	2 miles S of Duart Point, Sound of Mull

Ladybee was a double-ender of the Colin Archer type. She was originally called Lady Bridgella of Rhu *and was well known on the Clyde.* Ladybee *had served well as a slow but comfortable family cruiser for James and Margaret Houston and their children. The engine was a petrol/paraffin Kelvin, and in the spring of 1972 it was giving a lot of trouble.*

OUR CRUISE THIS YEAR BEGAN with the Lamlash Race when we took up our customary position of being last. Sunday was an absolutely perfect day for soaking up the sun, not to mention Jimmy Gillespie's cocktails before lunch. It came as quite a disappointment, however, to find that the absence of wind was soon to be joined by the absence of engine. It seemed that nothing short of oars would get us past the old wreck on Holy Isle until we secured a welcome hitch from one of these common white yachts.

Despite regular attention by notable engineers, our engine had given trouble all spring, and we were more than a little despondent to find that things were still not right and that the palliatives like stripping and cleaning the carburettors, renewing the plugs, etc, made little or no difference.

We thought it better to have the engine examined properly even at the expense of losing another precious day of our fortnight. We found that a manufacturer's engineer was coming down to Fairlie the following day, and so we were able to secure his services at short notice. We finally got away on Tuesday morning, and had a fine sail all the way to Ardrishaig. The engine started reassuringly as we approached the breakwater. But it packed up again as we circled around to await the opening of the sea lock gates. We ended up having to rush at the lock from some distance with plenty of impetus to carry us in. Help!

The next day, a very competent and helpful young man from the garage fitted a shining new starter switch, starter button and solenoid. He tested and realigned the starter motor and it was reassuring to see that everything at long last appeared to be functioning perfectly. One touch of the button – marvellous.

It was with confidence and perhaps a touch of bravado that we demonstrated our skill in gliding our 10ft beam serenely through what looked like a 9ft half-gate. At the sixth lock we found a small fishing boat having engine trouble and as the skipper was quick to notice our great power and manoeuvrability, he actually requested a tow! I really couldn't help laughing. Later on I felt quite superior by being able to diagnose the fault of his engine, and instantly produced a proper-sized jet-spanner to remedy it. I could see he was quite impressed by my knowledge of the engine and I secretly hoped that Margaret wouldn't spoil my act by revealing to him that his engine was exactly the same as ours.

The previous year, the first two weeks of June were sublime and we had fond memories of cloudless skies, sparkling water and warm southerly winds keeping the eternal swell crashing into the depths of Fingal's Cave. We drifted round the Mull in swimming costumes to arrive home the colour of Indians and stating knowledgeably that everyone should take their holidays in June, when the weather is always at its best.

This year the cold northerly wind blew through the buttonholes of our oilskins as we pounded our way with the tide up the Sound of Luing. Tacking back from the Mull shore found us near enough to Puilladobhrain to have us thinking of the warm pub over the hill at Clachan Bridge, so we fairly tore into that well-known sheltered lagoon. The cold wind dropped in the evening so that we could sit comfortably in the fading light and admire the nice new woodwork and homely interior of our saloon. But it rose again with us in the morning so the ham and egg breakfast was not to be enjoyed in the exposed cockpit.

We set off for Tobermory, choosing our time for wind and tide to be in the same direction, making for a flatter sea, but unfortunately these elements were coming almost exactly from the direction of our destination. Before leaving the shelter of Kerrera on our third tack, we brought the grey inflatable dinghy on board as it had been snatching at the painter while out in the Firth. Although it does spoil the view, we always like to keep it inflated, not so much for its immediate availability for use as a liferaft, but more because it is such a tiresome task having to inflate it each time. Anyway, the air valves had been leaking a bit in the spring, and although it had been serviced by the agents in Glasgow we noticed that sudden deflation was less frequent when the full pressure was maintained.

Several thoroughly secure lashings kept the dinghy a good 3 inches clear of the boom, and I managed to film some good shots as we left Bach Island rapidly to port, but it didn't look as though we had a hope in hell of leaving Duart Point to port. The best we made was a couple of miles south of that, and we felt rather tempted at the time to motorsail up the coast to save another tedious tack into the Firth.

But there was no particular hurry, so we went about as usual and turned our backs to the fresh wind and hauled the sheets in tight. Soon, however, a combination of good ideas like having coffee now, and perhaps reaching the Mishnish before closing time, prompted a reconsideration of the motor-sail idea. The coffee was therefore extracted from the cupboard on the uphill side of the boat and I reached forward from the cockpit for one touch of the button. The boat blew up.

Margaret was shouting something about her leg and I couldn't understand where she had disappeared to, or why I could now see the whole engine which had hitherto been concealed by the heavy plywood covers: or where all the flames suddenly appeared from; or where the companionway was that used to be bolted over the engine covers.

Ladybee must then have been given her head for I remember using both hands from a crouching position to tear, I think ineffectively, at a red jersey levering itself up into the cockpit. We were absolutely stunned. I remembered a fire extinguisher decorating a bulkhead at each end of our boat so here was the chance to try one out as I always wanted to. It wasn't necessary to open the forehatch because it had already disappeared and fragments of plastic could be seen clinging to the wet deck around the windlass, against which the hatch had undoubtedly smashed. The extinguisher had fallen from its bracket to the floor and in searching quickly for it I noticed the bulkhead was slightly deformed and the doorway which used to open into the saloon was now opening slightly into the fo'c's'le.

Anyway the extinguisher was a bit of a disappointment. The wind carried some of the white stuff into the sea and the remainder was soon to be exhausted. The jet seemed to choke a bit when directed towards the flames surrounding the engine and I wished that I had another extinguisher to try out because it looked like the petrol in the tanks would soon be on the boil. We forgot about coffee.

Meanwhile, we decided that it was now an appropriate time to secure a line of retreat. The lashings on the dinghy suddenly became fused to the rails and the fingers began to fumble frantically until we saw that the bow of the Avon had a great hole in it. The shock of this observation must have caused us to take stock, because we began to tackle the lashings in a more orderly manner; and perhaps we realised that despite the decompression of one half of the dinghy, the other half was miraculously staying fully inflated. We wasted no time in launching the dinghy that was tethered by Margaret while I collected oars and the pump. By this time we had agreed that it might be prudent to actually use the line of retreat before the petrol tanks blew up. As with fire extinguishers, we had also wondered about flares. A hasty return to the fo'c's'le confirmed that the flares along with the lifejackets were unobtainable in the saloon, but in any case there was as much smoke trailing across the Firth of Lorne as any flare would have made. I caught a glimpse of the fenders that we had been using to go through the canal and it occurred to me that they would have made quite good emergency floats when tied together.

I also hesitated to consider the new outboard motor but decided against that. We were getting a bit fed up with engine trouble anyway and surely nothing much could go wrong with a pair of oars. So we cast off at 1310 and *Ladybee* pulled rapidly away. Margaret gathered the deflated loose part of the dinghy around her waist to keep the water out as we began to row towards the Mull shore and we suddenly felt very sad indeed.

A second explosion perhaps ten minutes later confirmed that we were now in the safer vessel. While it had seemed that we were alone on the Firth of Lorne we suddenly noticed a steamer abeam of Lady Rock lighthouse, presumably on her way from Craignure to Oban, and we saw her alter course. Perched on each successive wave crest we could see *Ladybee* sailing now on a more southerly course back towards Puilladobhrain and away from the steamer. A flash of white light, followed a second or two later by a loud report, must have been the gas cylinders blowing up, and we wondered what the skipper of the steamer would be thinking. It looked as though he was getting quite close to *Ladybee* – if only we could let him know there was nobody on board. We did worry in case someone would get hurt trying to find out, but we were now miles away and a half-sized grey rubber dinghy is not the most conspicuous object on a dark grey sea.

We discovered later on that a report was issued at Southend (Argyll CRHQ) at 1331 hours from Oban radio to the effect that the car ferry *Columbia* was going alongside a yacht with a blue jib and white mainsail about 1 mile south-west of Kerrera Island. No one could be seen on board. It seems that Mr Devine, the Coastguard in charge at Oban, was immediately informed and within a few minutes he had put to sea in the *Callum Cille* and was making for the position.

We had, however, been spotted by someone on Mull, and it seems that Captain Leslie, the Coastguard Reporting Member at Grasspoint on Mull, was soon able to inform the *Columbia* that we were safely ashore. We didn't know this at the time, of course, but we did notice the arrival of other vessels in the area and saw with some relief that *Columbia* was able to depart.

I had been told as a child that if I ever fell out of a balloon (which I could never understand) I would be sure to land on a feather bed. It was only to be expected, therefore, that the rocky shore we suddenly gaped at as we made our diagonal journey should give way to the most beautiful sheltered sandy bay, precisely at the point where it seemed

we would fetch up. Margaret dissolved in tears as we walked up the
beach. She had left her make-up case behind!

Looking around the hillside revealed no immediate signs of life
until two figures appeared standing in the bracken some distance
away. I approached them to be informed (believe it or not) that 'some
boat was in trouble out there'. As I followed the sweep of the gentleman's arm I screwed up my eyes incredulously. Perhaps people had a
habit of coming ashore there with blackened faces and singed
eyebrows.

■ LESSONS LEARNED

- The two major causes of boat loss by fire or explosion – about
  equally responsible – are petrol and bottled gas. Petrol engines
  are something of a rarity in yachts these days now that small
  lightweight diesel units are available. *Ladybee*'s dual petrol/
  paraffin engine was designed to start on petrol and then to run
  on paraffin, which was cheaper than petrol. They tended to be
  troublesome, as James Houston found. His own explanation of
  the explosion that cost him his boat is given in a letter – 'After
  motoring out of Puilladobhrain and hoisting sail, we had a beat
  for a couple of hours towards Mull, during which time petrol
  from the carb, or somewhere, must have leaked into the bilge
  below the engine. The engine was enclosed in a watertight box
  in which the right mixture must have accumulated to be ignited
  by a spark from the new starter motor when we decided to
  restart it.'
- What happened immediately after *Ladybee* caught fire is
  instructive. With the engine surrounded by flames and the
  companion steps blown away, Houston's first concern was to
  help his injured wife out of the cabin and into the cockpit. He
  then remembered 'a fire extinguisher decorating a bulkhead at
  each end of our boat'. He discovered that the forehatch had
  been blown clean off and the forward extinguisher had fallen to
  the floor, whence he retrieved it, only to find that in use 'it was

a bit of a disappointment, because the wind carried some of the white stuff into the sea and the remainder was soon exhausted; the jet seemed to choke a bit when directed towards the flames'.

■ It would seem that Houston was using a foam-type extinguisher, and because he had no choice but to work from the deck its effectiveness was negligible. Extinguishers smother the fire by denying it oxygen and the blanketing substance, whether powder, foam or gas, must reach the root of the fire. But quite often when fire breaks out in a small yacht, it quickly becomes impossible to stay below, and the chances of aiming an extinguisher at the source of the fire are greatly reduced. The best compromise would seem to be to install at least two extinguishers; one of them just inside the main hatch and easily reachable from the cockpit, and the other accessible through the forehatch.

■ The flares, along with the lifejackets, were unobtainable in the saloon, but 'there was as much smoke trailing across the Firth of Lorne as any flare would have made'.

■ An inflatable dinghy, whether lashed on deck or stowed in a locker, becomes very vulnerable when a yacht catches fire. *Ladybee*'s dinghy, already inflated, was on deck, but 'the lashings suddenly became fused to the rails … and we saw that the bow of the Avon had a great hole in it'. Fortunately the stern half of the dinghy remained fully inflated, so Houston and his wife were able to get ashore safely in half a dinghy. Even when only half inflated, a rubber dinghy can serve as a small liferaft – provided there is no rough water to contend with. A liferaft, packed in a glassfibre canister, would not catch fire as quickly as an unprotected dinghy and there would, of course, be no delay involved while inflating it.

twenty

TRIMARAN FLIPPED AND SUNK

Yacht	*Boatfile* (Val Class 31ft trimaran)
Skipper	Nick Hallam
Crew	Nye Williams
Bound from	Newport, Rhode Island, to the Isle of Man
Time and date of loss	2300, 8 May 1981
Position	approx. 200 miles WSW of Mizen Head, Ireland

After sailing his 31ft trimaran, Boatfile, *to Newport, Rhode Island, USA, in the 1980 OSTAR, Rob James left her there until he had sold her to a new owner in the UK, who engaged Nick Hallam to sail her back. Twenty-one days out from Newport,* Boatfile *was lying ahull, riding out a Force 8 Atlantic gale in much the same way as she had done before. Nick Hallam writes:*

WE HAD BEEN LYING AHULL reasonably comfortably for 24 hours, the BBC Shipping Forecast at 0625 had talked of an improvement soon and the wind remained steady at Force 8 with regular seas of perhaps 20ft. Our drogue and warps were ready in the cockpit in case they should be needed, but the boat was lying quietly with the daggerboard fully retracted and the helm lashed down, drifting off to leeward leaving a conspicuous path of flat water upwind. Any wave crests that broke over the windward hull seemed to have little energy, while the boat's reduced lateral resistance, coupled with the high buoyancy of the amas (floats), allowed her to rise easily and keep out of trouble. We had ridden out previous gales in this fashion and didn't think this one would be any different. I was also not keen to run before the weather until it was strictly necessary, as that course would take us towards the centre of the low, rather than allowing the system to pass away from our area. It was Friday 8 May, and we were about 200 miles WSW of Mizen Head, keeping watch from below and waiting for the 1355 forecast.

We never heard it. At about 1300 we were picked up by something very big, and in a rush of broken water *Boatfile* was rolled rapidly over to starboard and settled into an irrevocably inverted position. The thing that had happened only to others had happened to us; we had been capsized.

The tiny, inverted cabin was a surging mess of loose gear, washing back and forth with every wave. The constant change of air pressure hurt our eardrums, but fortunately there was a surprising amount of light through the submerged windows, so we were able to get at our survival suits quickly and put them on, then secure our EPIRB (Emergency Position Indicating Radio Beacon) unit and switch that on. Looking at its tiny indicator light, I prayed that its signal was radiating out through the upturned hull.

We then jettisoned all superfluous gear and rescued anything remotely useful, planning to stay with the boat on the assumption that, like other capsized trimarans, she would stay afloat. To that end, we began laboriously to cut a hatch in the hull above our heads, to give us an escape to the open air and a safe lookout point from which to attract attention. It was a frustrating task: our collection of drills was wonderfully blunt and the GRP/Kevlar hull proved wonderfully tough, but we had to keep thinking and working. It was no use stopping to worry about the obviously worsening weather outside, nor to think of the 200 miles still separating us from south-west Ireland. Of course that's just what we did, but working helped ...

When the boat's stern was plunged into the trough of a wave, twice within 20 minutes, both times trapping us underwater in the cabin, we began reluctantly to suspect that the trimaran was starting to sink. We had difficulty accepting this. Still trying to convince ourselves that we could carry on cutting holes from outside, we gathered tools, flares, panic bag and the precious EPIRB and dived out via the main hatch to the world outside.

Conditions were appalling. There was no question of working, just hanging on desperately while steep, breaking seas repeatedly swept over us. The daggerboard had dropped out of its case and was lunging madly about, hitting the hulls. The impact of every sea was terrible, and Nye later reported seeing longitudinal cracks opening in the outer floats (amas). With no integral foam or other form of buoyancy, the little boat was clearly not going to remain tenable for long, even if she stayed awash, so we agreed to take to the liferaft. In the struggle to release it, I must have failed to cut one last lashing, because it had great difficulty in escaping from its valise, and when finally it did, it had lost so much CO_2 via the relief valve that it was perilously soft.

At this point, two things happened: Nye saw the Nimrod aeroplane, and *Boatfile* sank, tilting inexorably over and threatening to drag me down by my harness. I escaped and also cut the liferaft free. Our last sight of the trimaran was of the stern of the port ama pointing up at 45 degrees like a bright yellow finger, and the blurred, ghostly outline of the rest of the boat underwater. Within a few minutes, *Boatfile* had gone.

While Nye clung on outside, I scrambled in and tried to inflate the raft fully, but somehow was unable to make a proper connection between bellows and valve. Finally, in full view of the Nimrod, our raft was hit by yet another breaking sea and torn.

The Nimrod came in straight and level from dead downwind and dropped a pair of big liferafts joined by a long line. This we grabbed, but were unable to pull ourselves to the rafts because of the surge of the seas (by now between 35 and 40ft, with the wind at 60 knots, according to the Nimrod crew). The aircraft made another run. This time we made it to a raft, but it had a major leak in both chambers and after an hour of grim pumping to try and keep at least one chamber and the roof inflated it, too, was overwhelmed and torn apart by a succession of breaking seas.

We spent a dismal time, perhaps an hour, clinging to the bright orange remains of the raft, our Nimrod having disappeared. We felt utterly alone and very anxious. Had they lost contact? Had they waited until we seemed to be safe before leaving the scene to refuel? Our prayers were duly answered as the great white machine reappeared (a second aircraft, we later learned) and in an astonishing display of precision flying dropped two more rafts with such accuracy that the connecting line fell within arm's reach. We righted the nearest raft and clambered aboard, by now exhausted, as night fell.

A big Shell oil tanker had come on the scene and tried to come close enough to pick us up but her motion was too violent for a safe approach, so her captain moved away to keep station with us, while the Nimrod kept up a pattern of wide circles over us and the ship, marking us from time to time with blinding white floating flares.

Two more hours passed. We were both very tired, but tried to keep ourselves occupied by bailing and sponging out the ten-man raft and by keeping watch from the doorway. Finally, a new set of lights appeared downwind, quickly resolving itself into a big Sea King heli-copter. Flooding us with an array of mobile spotlights worthy of a scene from Star Wars, it manoeuvred overhead and lowered the winchman who scored a direct hit on the canopy, bounced into the doorway, said 'Hi!' and was immediately jerked into the air again as the raft sank 30ft into a trough. After a few more such violent jerks and heavy splashdowns (accompanied, I suspect, by some non-regulation verbal comments on the part of Bob Griffiths, the man on the wire), airman and raft successfully made contact, and in a very short time we were all safely aboard the Sea King, bound for Cork Airport for refu-elling, exhausted, bemused, but alive!

■ LESSONS LEARNED

One of the arguments in favour of multihulls is that they are unsinkable, as shown in other stories in this book. But this is not always true, as Nick Hallam found with *Boatfile*. Once capsized, they offer an upside-down refuge of sorts, but not always a safe or comfortable one. Nick and Nye were caught below when *Boatfile* capsized, with a 'surging mess of loose gear washing back and forth with every wave'. They 'started to cut a hatch in the hull, assuming she would stay afloat. But they soon realised the trimaran was starting to sink.

Nearly 30 years ago, the importance of having some assurance that an EPIRB is working was stressed by Nick Hallam, who checked its tiny indicator light and 'prayed that its signal was radiating through the upturned hull'. From subsequent reports it is clear that early signals were not picked up from inside he hull. Not until Nick and his crew had abandoned *Boatfile* for the liferaft. Then the EPIRB's distress signal, operating on 121.5 MHz, was picked up by a British Airways jumbo jet flying west across the Atlantic. A simultaneous signal from the EPIRB on 234 MHz was also received by an RAF Nimrod on exercise that day. Before the Nimrod could locate their liferaft, the plane ran low on fuel, and so another Nimrod was despatched from Kinloss in Scotland. Having found the liferaft, the crew of the Nimrod could see that it was only partly inflated, so they dropped a series of liferafts, on parachutes, before the yachtsmen could secure one and climb aboard. While all this was going on, an RAF Sea King helicopter of the 202 SAR Squadron based at Brawdy in Wales proceeded first to Southern Ireland and then, after refuelling, out over the Atlantic in total darkness to pick up Hallam and Williams with the aid of parachute flares – altogether a remarkable operation lasting some 8 to 10 hours.

The difficulties of launching a liferaft are illustrated in this incident, and others in this book. On *Boatfile*, Nick relates: 'In the struggle to release it, I must have failed to cut one lashing, because it had great difficulty in escaping from its valise, and when finally it did, it had lost so much CO_2 via the relief valve that it was perilously soft.'

Rushcutter's liferaft (see Chapter 3) was swept overboard when the yacht was rolled in the Tasman Sea, but fortunately, it was attached by its inflation line. A good start, but later Lealand tells of the troubles they experienced when the raft was capsized.

Liferafts are supplied either in a soft valise or in a rigid GRP container. A valise-packed raft must be stowed in a protected place, such as a cockpit locker, whereas a rigid canister-packed raft can, and should, be kept on deck at all times. There are pros and cons for both systems.

Multihulls caught out in heavy weather demand very different seamanship tactics from a monohull. Excessive speed when surfing downwind risks pitchpoling or capsize.

Nick reports that *Boatfile* was lying ahull in Force 8 winds, a procedure they had followed in other gales, and although they had a drogue and warps ready in the cockpit, they were not in use. The trimaran was lying quietly with the dagger board retracted and the helm lashed down so that she was drifting to leeward, leaving a well-defined slick upwind. They never heard the wave that caused their capsize, but they were 'picked up by something very big and rolled over'.

In the case of Lionel Miller's 29ft 6in Catalac catamaran, *Lazy Daisy* (see Chapter 6), he seems to have been unaware of any risks and remembers the waves giving some fast sleigh rides as they 'boiled along' having a great sail, despite the darkness and cold. Then the warning came: Suddenly he found the boat going downhill at an alarming angle, the high flared bows were almost underwater, despite their enormous reserves of buoyancy. The hulls vibrated with a deep humming sound as they tore through the water at 12 knots plus. The wave coming up was big, perhaps 30ft, but the threat of destruction was in the 5ft-high breaking crest which began its avalanche down the long slope towards them. *Lazy Daisy* was lifted into a vertical position and the press of water under the bridgedeck capsized her in a matter of 2–3 seconds.

It is very tempting to say that the catamaran was capsized because of her excessive speed. But who can be sure what would have happened had she lain ahull as did *Boatfile*?

twenty one

SUNK IN THE PACIFIC

Yacht	*Lucifero* (Oyster 37)
Skipper	Patricia Landamore
Crew	Will Flack
Bound for	Tonga in the South Pacific
Date of loss	24 May 1999
Position	approx. 100 miles from the Pacific island of Niue

Mike Smither was skippering his Amel Santorin 45 yacht, Akwaaba, on passage in the South Pacific with his wife and son, as part of the 1999–2001 Blue Water Round the World Rally, when he heard a Mayday call from fellow rally participant, 71-year-old Patricia Landamore. Her Oyster 37, Lucifero, had been holed and was taking on water some 100 miles from the Pacific island of Niue.

AS SOON AS MIKE REALISED that he was the nearest yacht to *Lucifero* he set off in a northerly direction as fast as he could in her direction. The time was around 1730 ship's time and the urgency was made all the greater knowing that Patricia was 71 years old and had only one crew, Canadian Will Flack (22).

'As we were sorting ourselves out, we got *Lucifero*'s last SSB broadcast giving her position and saying that they were taking to the liferaft,' Mike recalled.

'We calculated we were 60 miles away and it would take us some 10 hours to get there. We changed the watch system to ensure we all got some sleep because I knew we'd need our wits about us when we reached the search area,' said Mike.

Magic Dragon, the next nearest rally yacht, also headed north in case Mike needed to set up a search, which would be helped by the boats en route from Suvarov.

Patricia and Will had acted with incredible composure. As soon as they struck the unidentified object, the forward section of the hull had started filling and they hove-to. Night was falling, it was raining and the wind was gusting to 40 knots.

A Mayday was sent on shortwave 2182 kHz and VHF Ch 16 with no response. The 121.5 EPIRB was then activated. The yacht's distress call was eventually picked up by rally yachts when *Lucifero* interrupted their regular evening chat on HF radio.

Soon the boat had filled with water to the level of the cockpit. The pumps could not handle the flood and bailing made no impact. They grabbed a hand-held VHF, GPS, torch, food and clothes and took to the liferaft. At 1825 Mike had his last message from Patricia saying that they were abandoning the yacht. *Lucifero* sank within one minute of Patricia cutting the liferaft painter.

Mike, his wife, Chris, and their 22-year-old son, Jeremy, were sailing *Akwaaba* as fast as possible. Based on the two positions they had received, Mike worked out Patricia's probable position accounting for wind and current. 'Once we knew where we were going, we got the cabin ready for survivors with hot soup, space blankets and spare clothes,' said Mike.

'We contacted the rally organisers back in the UK via satcom to keep them informed about what was happening. Other rally boats were also converging on the search area and had alerted the authorities in New Zealand, some 1,500 miles away, via the SSB radio net. Soon the Maritime Rescue Coordination Centre (MRCC) in Wellington, New Zealand, was aware of the drama unfolding beyond its helicopter range and it scrambled an Orion aeroplane. Via the HAM radio net an SSB frequency and main calling channel were agreed so that as many boats as possible could listen in.

Meantime, Mike had been driving the boat as hard as possible, regularly surfing at 12 knots and blowing a panel in the genoa in the process. They arrived at *Lucifero*'s last known position in just under seven hours, at 0115, and set out along the drift path. The P3 Orion aeroplane arrived at the same time.

'We slowed down and set the boat up to go down the drift line, calling Patricia on the VHF radio at regular intervals. We talked to the plane pilot and they vectored us on a course and we continued to search. The plane couldn't pick up the 121.5 signal from the EPIRB and continued with its passes, dropping a green flare at the end of each leg.'

At 0300 Patricia heard the Orion overhead and fired a rocket flare which the Orion crew did not spot. But the Smithers picked it up 6 miles away and informed the Kiwi pilot. A second rocket went up which the aircraft located. It was now all up to the Smithers. The plane dropped a smoke flare and redirected *Akwaaba*.

'We were now in contact with Patricia via VHF radio and asked her to let off red flares. They tried two flares but neither worked.' Patricia was streaming a sea anchor from the liferaft and Mike asked her to pull it in.

'We went down to leeward and let them drift on to us. There were 12ft seas with regular 20ft waves and 40 knots of wind. It took 10 minutes before we managed to throw and catch lines. At 0400 we were alongside.

The P3 had offered to stay till first light, but Mike decided to get Patricia and Will aboard as soon as possible, as the wind, which had been 30–35 knots, got up to 40 knots. It subsequently dropped to 35!

The yacht was pitching and rolling, so timing was vital. As the boat rolled towards the liferaft, Patricia put a foot on the coaming and stepped up. Will followed after passing up the EPIRB, which was then switched off.

Mike checked with the Orion aeroplane before cutting the liferaft loose. Even with three of them they were unable to lift it aboard. Putting someone in the liferaft to puncture it was too dangerous. The air crew told them to let it go.

Patricia and Will were taken below, shaken but unhurt, and given that great universal comforter: Heinz tomato soup. Later, they were reunited with all the other rally yachts at the next stopover in Tonga.

■ LESSONS LEARNED

- *Lucifero* first sent a Mayday on 2182 kHz during the classic 'seelonce' period. There was no response to that, or a VHF call. There just aren't that many ships out there listening, especially now that DSC is standard, even in remote areas of the South Pacific. Mike felt the HAM radio nets were really helpful in a real emergency.
- The EPIRB was the first thing to alert the rescue centre. HAM radio nets, SatCom and shore calls followed. Two in-date flares had failed to work. Don't rely on any single option. The latest, more powerful 406 MHz EPIRB is the best option.
- You must keep EPIRBs upright. Having a pocket in the liferaft so that the aerial is vertical is a good idea. A detachable strobe would also be a bonus.
- *Lucifero*'s 121.5 MHz EPIRB had a flashing strobe which was so disorientating for Patricia and Will that they covered it up, which meant the aircraft could not pick up the signal until 200m away.
- Prepare your boat and crew, and rest while you've got the chance. Patricia and Will had not panicked. They were properly clothed and had taken a sleeping bag with them into the liferaft. They had even buoyed water bottles with fenders on long lines.
- Beware drogue lines from liferafts fouling the propeller of the rescue yacht.
- Contact via hand-held VHF radio had been very reassuring for Patricia. *Akwaaba* had done most of the broadcasting to comfort her and preserve her batteries. The hand-held GPS allowed them constantly to update their position.
- The HAM radio net was a key to the rescue, patching Mike through to the Maritime Rescue Coordination Centre. 'In a real emergency they came up trumps,' said Mike, who also praised the professionals of the air crew from 5 Squadron RNZAF.
- With the benefit of hindsight, Mike says he should have issued a Mayday relay via SatCom.

twenty two

DISASTER IN THE MOUTH OF THE ELBE

Yacht   *Pentina II* (33ft Bermudian cutter)
Skipper   Robin Gardiner-Hall
Bound from the German island of Borkum to Cuxhaven
Time and
date of loss 0600, 4 July 1979
Position   half a mile S of Scharnhorn Beacon

Robin Gardiner-Hall was sailing single-handed from Hellevoetsluis to the Baltic. His yacht, Pentina II, *was a 33ft Kings Amethyst with Bermudian cutter rig, slightly under-powered by a single-cylinder diesel engine capable of 4.5 knots in calm conditions. He left Borkum on 3 July and soon after midnight on 4 July, he was in the well-buoyed channel of the Elbe with a fair wind, Force 4–5 from the NW. Big ship traffic was busy, and to keep clear of it a course was maintained close to the line of starboard-hand buoys. The skipper takes up the story.*

AS THE CHANNEL TURNED MORE southerly, *Pentina II* came on a dead run and I decided to hand the main and proceed slowly under jib alone, since I preferred to reach Cuxhaven after dawn. I therefore rounded up to port to hand the main. However, the main was stuck – presumably because a screw had worked loose in the track, although I shall never know for sure. I could only lower the main about two-thirds of the way, and we were effectively hove-to on the starboard tack and slowly fore-reaching southwards. Realising this I gybed, made some offing from the side of the channel and rounded up to try again. I did not go as far as I should have done, because a nearby merchant ship was approaching. This time I made an error of judgement and struggled unsuccessfully with the stuck main too long. The result was that we drifted too far out of the channel and suddenly heeled over to an extreme angle, running well and truly aground on the edge of the Scharhorn Riff. The German chart showed just how steep the bank was very close to the buoyed channel. The area is marked *zahlreiche Wrackreste* and I regret that I have made the wrecks even more numerous.

I immediately laid out my 35lb CQR anchor and 20 fathoms of chain and handed the jib. I was still unable to lower the main completely, but lashed it to reduce the windage. I confess that I was not very worried: there were still five hours of tide to rise, the anchor was holding and I thought that I could wait for the tide to lift her off and then recover the anchor under engine. About an hour later the tide had risen enough to keep *Pentina II* afloat most of the time, but she was bumping and a heavy surge had built up over the bank. The engine was running full ahead and the chain was snatching violently. Suddenly, I heard a loud bang and found the chain had sheared the port samson post off at deck level. With some difficulty I re-secured the chain to the starboard samson post, having veered more chain to give a better catenary. Half an hour later we were again in heavy surf and pounding badly when the second samson post sheared in the same way as the first. The chain ran out and was lost; it parted the bitter-end lashing in the chain locker and the whipping end cut the lower starboard lifeline.

The situation was now serious: we were losing ground on to the bank, the engine was not really helping much – although I kept it running all the time – and the pounding was very bad indeed. As always on such occasions, the wind was increasing, or at least seemed to be (I doubt that it was ever really more than Force 6), and we were, of course, on a lee shore. Clearly the time had come to sink one's pride and let off distress flares.

Despite the heavy traffic in the estuary it was about an hour before I made contact with a ship. By now my distress signals were limited to mini-flares and flashing with a torch. I cannot really say that mini-flares are better than rockets and hand-held flares, but they produced results. My flashed SOS was finally acknowledged. Many ships had passed, and I think the problem was that in a busy channel like this they are far too busy looking for their marks and at other ships – to say nothing of the radar – to notice what is happening abeam, well out of the channel.

I now knew that rescue would be only a matter of time, but the incessant pounding made things very difficult. Fortunately, I had two very thick floating cockpit cushions filled with kapok, and most of the time managed to keep one of these underneath me; I think that this probably saved me from serious injury. I did, however, suffer two cracked ribs, and sitting down was uncomfortable for some weeks afterwards. My body was more black and blue than white below the waist. I was also soaked through but not really cold because there was always plenty to do. At one point I went below to make up an emergency bag containing ship's papers, passport, wallet, chequebook and so forth, but I was worried about doing this as several stainless steel bottlescrews had parted. The mast, which was deck-stepped, was rocking through quite an angle and I was afraid that it might fall on the cabin top and trap me below. The cabin was a sad sight with oily bilge water everywhere.

As dawn broke it was possible to see how far we had been carried down on to the shelf. We were now about half a mile south of Scharhorn Beacon, but at high water still about a mile from the Island of Scharhorn. At about 0600 there was the welcome sight of an approaching lifeboat, but it could not get within half a mile. They launched their *Tochterboot*, a shallow draft skimmer carried on the afterdeck, which appears to have a powerful engine and carried a crew of two. Shallow water prevented it from sailing round on to my lee side. Handled with great skill, it made one or two trial runs with a bows-on approach, during which I handed over my emergency bag. They shouted to me to climb out over the lifelines – not an easy task as we were heeled over and still pounding. The *Tochterboot* had a steel post forward, against which the crew member braced himself with both arms free and outstretched. On the next run I was able to jump for it and was caught in his arms. While the boat backed off, he opened a forehatch and I was bundled below. It was rather claustrophobic, with no head-room, but at least there was a bunk to lie on.

■ LESSONS LEARNED

There can be no doubt the 351b CQR anchor that Robin Gardiner-Hall was using on *Pentina II* was man enough for the task. The fact that it held in the shallow waters of the Elbe is clear when its cable sheared the port samson post off at deck level. Having then transferred the chain to the other samson post, Gardiner-Hall veered extra cable and the second samson post sheared as the chain ran out, ripping out the bitter end lashing in the chain locker. The whipping end even cut the lower starboard lifeline!

This incident offers a frightening reminder of the enormous snatch loads involved in rough weather. Perhaps a stronger lashing would have prevented the cable going overboard, but at least this incident reminds us to check that the bitter end of our chain is made fast with a long lashing that can reach the deck and be cut in an emergency – but is not likely to break. How many sailors have secured their anchor chain by a lashing? It's an essential facility in dire straits when you may want to intentionally part company with your anchor because it is holdng you into danger.

Gardiner-Hill was given sound advice by the captain of the German lifeboat that rescued him and advised that flares should always be let off in pairs, at an interval of about 10 seconds, in case someone sees a distress signal and assumes it was his imagination.

twenty three

THE LAST HOURS OF *WINDSTAR*

Yacht	*Windstar* (29 ton Bermudian rigged cutter)
Skipper	Captain Bertram Currie
Crew	Peter Combe
Bound from	Lowestoft to Cowes, UK
Time and	
date of loss	approx. 2200, 29 July 1956
Position	somewhere between the Kentish Knock and Outer Gabbard shoals

Windstar was built in Mevagissy in 1937 and had served during the war as an anchor to a barrage balloon; she had just returned from a cruise to Scandinavia, during which she was under the command of a paid skipper, with the owner, Peter Combe, and two others as crew.

For the final passage back to Cowes, there were only two on board and Captain Currie was an invalid from recent illness as well as a diabetic. His doctors only allowed him to make the trip under protest, so long as he did not 'overdo it'.

Peter Combe takes up the story, describing his skipper as 'a man of astounding imperturbability and apparent nonchalance, with complete disregard for the possibility of hazard ... he seemed sublimely and blithely content to sail on indefinitely so long as there seemed to be water under his keel'.

WE MOTORED OUT OF LOWESTOFT harbour with the jib furled and bent on ready to hoist and the mainsail uncovered, and took the inside passage south from the harbour mouth before heading to sea. At 2200 hours the first gale warning had been broadcast. Neither of us had heard it.

After 2 miles we had cleared the coastal shallows and set course to southward. 'Well, chum,' said Bertram, 'we're going to be pretty sleepy by the time we get to Cowes. You'd better turn in for a while.'

The situation then, if not too attractive, presented no cause for anxiety. We knew where we were, the night was clear, and the journey, which should have taken about 80 hours, was well marked and lit all the way. We had enough fuel to motor the entire distance, if necessary, and I was confident I could hoist the mainsail alone if we had a fair wind in daylight.

I did not expect to get much sleep. After we had started I had also some qualms about abetting the skipper in undertaking this tiring run at the end of his holiday, but he was determined to go, and eager to get the boat back to Cowes for the regatta week. There was something of an anticlimax about the run home at the end of the summer cruise and since leaving Oslo, the nearer we approached England, the colder and wetter and drearier had the weather become. The challenge and amusement of taking the boat home alone did, in fact, enliven what would otherwise have been a rather flat finale.

After sleeping a while I found we were quite a bit to shoreward of our course, due to confusion about lights, and while Bertram took a spell below I ran out to Shipwash Light Vessel from which I had laid the course for a clear run down to Kentish Knock.

At 0700 hours we passed Sunk Light Vessel, the tide having carried us eastwards towards the Thames Estuary, and I laid a new course for Kentish Knock. It was not worth the effort of trying to hoist any sail to hold us steady, as the wind was only a few points off our starboard bow. By now it was as rough as the North Sea passage had been, and even a little more choppy. Apart from the lack of Calor gas it was impossible to do anything in the galley, so we lived that day on some chocolate and biscuits and hard liquor. In any case, I was now feeling far from well, tired, a headache, slightly sick, and sorry that we had let ourselves in for another beating. I had hoped that by the time we reached Dover Bertram would be tired enough to agree to put in there to sleep. As the prospect of a hot, dry lunch in Dover receded, I became anxious about Bertram being able to go on without making himself ill, or taking a bad fall. He had managed to give himself his daily injection of insulin – no mean feat in that weather – but there seemed little chance of his eating his accustomed fill to balance it.

By midday the gale was at its height, the seas growing very big and the surface streaked with foam. Visibility grew poorer as the volume of wind-driven spray increased. It was now difficult to steer. Our course fortunately lay into the wind, but we could only hold it spasmodically. There was no question now of a sail holding us steady. We could steer fairly steady about 15 degrees either side of the wind until a strong gust blew her head away, when she would take a long while to come back up again.

At 1245 hours we passed Kentish Knock Light Vessel very slowly, making possibly two knots. For a moment, it looked as though we would be carried down on to her, the tide or the weather taking us still to the eastward. Dover seemed a very long way off. It was now a question of holding our head into the weather and riding out the gale, which was so freakish for the time of year as to seem incapable of lasting. By now it was only possible to hold our head against the wind with the wheel hard over and watching for the ticklish moment when the wind was more or less dead ahead, when, if we were carried off to starboard, it had now become impossible to bring her up again into the wind – the propeller being on the starboard side and the thrust being weaker from that side. Each time she fell away to starboard and kept falling with the weather abeam we now had to wear her right round and start again. Fortunately, we were never badly pooped doing this, but each long lapse to starboard brought us nearer to the Goodwins.

We had the canvas cockpit cover rigged, inside which whoever was not steering could shelter from the wind, although the water was everywhere coming through it. Whoever was at the wheel, sitting abaft this cover, was obliged to sit up quite high to peer over it – which occasionally seemed a good idea, in case we might be running into danger. In fact, it became almost impossible to watch the seas ahead, as every time you raised your head you received a discouraging blast of salt shot in the eyes. Despite the fact that one shivered more, I found it more agreeable to steer, as it occupied my mind and distracted me from the disagreeable state of my head and stomach. Facing thus fore and aft with my hands on the wheel, I seemed in a better position to balance. As in the North Sea passage, it was a rather exhilarating sensation, like riding a big high-mettled hunter, as *Windstar* plunged and reared, occasionally taking the seas with a sharp leap like a dolphin. Bertram took one or two crashing falls during the course of the day. In fact, on our return, his doctor discovered three fractured ribs.

A day or two before, I had been reading about the forces and symptoms tabled in the Beaufort wind scale, and discussing it with Bertram – shouting conversationally at the top of my lungs – I added that, as far as I could see, this bore all the characteristics of a hurricane. 'It very likely is,' he replied calmly and we lapsed again into silence for another half-hour or so. We later learned that hurricane Force 10 had, indeed, been recorded.

By now we were still holding our head more or less into the weather and making some way through the water. We were able to stay on starboard tack and away from the direction of the Goodwins most of the time. The engine was well able to keep pumping out any water we were making, and we were riding the seas well, only occasionally shipping a big sea on to the decks at more than a minute's interval which splashed into the cockpit and drained overboard before the next. My only anxiety was that we should be able to have some indi-cation of where to turn westward up channel as soon as possible, to try to make Dover. I had little faith in the good fortune of seeing the East Goodwin Light Vessel on our present course, and hoped that we would see the coast of France before being run on to it. Presumably it would be dark by then and lights visible. The radio direction finder receiver was not operative with the engine running, and it was impos-sible to hold steady into the weather without this.

I was also growing a little anxious about our ability to hold on indefinitely without rest, or something to eat, if this wearying, weak-ening, utterly dreary grind continued without a single glimmer of hopeful change.

At about 1400 hours there was a radical change in our situation, though far from welcome. Three things happened almost simultane-ously. First, the engine failed. A moment later – and I presume it to have been later, as we swung out of the wind without steerage way though I cannot swear to it – a really big sea broke over our starboard side, and for a while I looked through a pale green world of pouring water. I was at the wheel, and held on confidently for the boat to lift, and the sky to reappear, for what seemed some time. When the water stopped I saw the cockpit quite full of it, and Bertram, who had been carried from the starboard side together with the cockpit cover, clear through the cover on the port side, perched between the metal struts, like a bird in a bush, with his behind on the deck. I helped him back, apparently unhurt, and we set about fetching back the lengths of main and jib sheet that were trailing outboard, and cleared away the mess of the cockpit cover.

Although the engine still started and ran, it stalled when we tried to coax it into gear, even astern. While we were still shaken at all this, the jib, which I had earlier doubly secured to keep it quiet in the gale, flung off both its lashings and hoisted itself. Presumably the changed direction of the gale's attack enabled it to get a better purchase. I watched fascinated as the canvas ran practically to its full and correct height and promptly blew to bits with a flapping and crackling most painful to the yachtsman's ear. It would have been madness to try to catch hold of any part of it under those conditions, so we just waited, hoping that it would destroy itself as soon as possible. In doing this, the flailing sheets carried away the attached block, the lowest port-side mainstay (a half-inch wire hawser), the for'ard portion of the port side deck rail, together with two stanchions – the next one remaining was bent double over the side as if it had been made of tin – and also the spinnaker boom, which had been secured there.

'There goes the spinnaker boom!' I shouted at Bertram as it floated past us. He treated this excited comment with the contempt it deserved, there being no possible rejoinder, except perhaps that we probably would not require it this trip. The yacht now began to look sorry and unshipshape with these first wounds.

So strong was the gale that she sailed, to my wonder, for ten minutes steady upwind on the few tattered ribbons of jib, but not close enough, so that the seas were dangerously abeam.

'What do we do now?' I asked Bertram, after pointing out this interesting phenomenon. 'Run before the wind under bare poles,' he replied, and I heard the ring of trumpets in his voice. This thrilling phrase, often read in the books of sea adventure which I had devoured as a boy, made me chuckle with surprised delight, yet it seemed quite reasonable. I did not feel disposed to secure the loose stay which was waving about crackling things with the wooden sleeve it wore. Eventually I think it fouled something below the mast and stayed quiet. I was certainly not eager to try to construct a sea anchor. Later we were told we should have done this, but even had the ship's company been more up to it, the gear easy of access, and conditions more sympathetic to efficient and seamanlike movements, I think it would have been an error.

There is something so very helpless about being at the mercy of a sea anchor, and our hull would have taken a worse beating holding into the seas. As it was, we were driven along at an astonishing speed, which we later calculated to have been about 6 knots. We could thus steer quite well, sustaining less strain on the hull, as we carried along with the weather, sometimes like a surfboard on the crests.

We expected to be badly pooped, but only twice do I remember really big waves breaking in over the stern, which rose wonderfully to each oncoming sea. These did not come in exactly parallel waves, but after a while I found it less tiring and unnerving to steer in the general direction of the weather than to look over my shoulders and try to line up our stern to receive each approaching sea. I am prepared to swear that they varied from 30 to 40 feet high at their worst – there are few witnesses to contradict me. One of the advantages of running like this was that we could keep a fairly steady course, which was about north-east, and from where I thought we had been when we turned. We had plenty of sea ahead until we reached the north-west coast of Denmark, or missing it, found ourselves back in Norway – by which time we could only hope that the gale would have blown itself out.

The weather was now less vicious in our faces, but we were fully exposed to the following wind, and I noticed both of us shivered violently all the time we were at the wheel. Earlier in the day I had changed once, but was now quite drenched again. Over blue jeans and a thick cotton shirt, I wore a sweater and a light skiing anorak – chiefly because of its hood which protected my ears – and on top of this an oilskin, more to keep the wind out than the wet. On my feet I had a pair of fleece-lined snow-boots, also completely soaked but nevertheless quite cosy.

Strangely enough, the sea and the wind were not very cold; it was only the force of the latter which chilled us, driving right through our backs. We were quite pleased to take a spell below, where everything was now wet and disordered with books, clothes and cushions and other gear all over the floor of the cabin and the saloon. The crew space forward was even wetter, and the galley a fine jumble of smashed crockery, tins and pots which had broken loose. When I went below to enjoy, without much success, a damp cigarette, and find a little peace, I kept throwing things back off the deck, but eventually gave up. Whoever went below shut the door from the cockpit after him to keep out the splashes, and the man at the wheel was left alone in the water.

Occasionally we bailed for each other with biscuit tins – chiefly for the sake of morale. The cockpit was quite isolated, in the watertight sense, from the rest of the craft, but the self-draining part of it had some sort of valve trouble. Having effectively removed the water, it had the habit of belching back as much again with a merry gurgle. We had accordingly plugged it with a champagne cork some days before. I found the large glass binnacle cover more useful for bailing the cockpit, and developed a handy technique of holding it in the corner with my foot while steering, and after a good roll hoisting it up full of water, with my spare hand. I had already discovered the uselessness of putting a quick temporary lashing on the wheel while I left it for a moment to do anything. She just kicked it off in about three sharp jolts.

At some time after 1500 hours – I do not remember looking at my watch at any time after we started running north-east, the situation became timeless and immediate – I began to check the bilges when I went below. There was a good deal of water, but as I had not had occasion to look into it myself since leaving Oslo, I had no idea what would be considered normal. On a previous occasion, when water had been showing on the lower part of the deck by the galley door on a return trip from Deauville, it caused little alarm as I remember, and this was not yet apparent. This time, however, we could not pump it out with the engine, the drive being off the shaft. I pumped a while by hand, but it was difficult to tell how much difference I was making – if any. I told Bertram that we had a good deal of water inboard, and he was naturally not surprised. I pumped some more, and later, when it seemed to me that the hand pump was achieving very little, I told him this. Later, when he took a spell below himself, and had been through similar motions, he confirmed my fears that we were gradually making water.

The situation then, although we did not discuss it, took on a more doleful aspect. It became colder as the day faded, and we were both quite eager to take a turn below pumping. It seemed to me from the bore and the feel of the pump's action that it might be able to hold the water we were making in various ways above water-level as it filtered down into the bilges; but what was happening below the waterline one could only guess.

At about 1600 hours, while I was at the wheel, I suddenly saw a trawler off to port on a parallel course up weather about 300 yards, and yelled at the top of my lungs, to Bertram, 'Do you want to signal her?'

'Oh, I don't think that's necessary,' he replied, and disappeared again below.

It seemed to me, since we were alone and helpless, that we might have asked for a tow, or at least made our predicament known to the outside world, but although I waved wildly with my spare hand there was no answering sign. In fact, I believe that she would have been unable to turn out of the wind and come to us without getting into difficulties herself. It would have been a good idea to have been wearing a signal to say at least that our engines had failed, and were under no control, if anyone could have noticed and read our tiny signal flags. The only other thing I had seen that afternoon was a large dolphin which came gambolling down the side of a big sea to meet us like a puppy, and apparently quite undismayed by the weather.

It gradually became clear that we were making water much faster than we could pump, if, indeed, the pump was achieving anything. I selfishly took long spells at the pump believing that I could pump a great deal faster than Bertram.

It was strange below, comparatively quiet, comparatively dry and warm, and gave one a strange sense of security, while the movement of the ship itself seemed less violent. It seemed so remote, I kept wondering whether I would open the doors of the cockpit and find Bertram had disappeared over the side without my knowing, and as I looked at them, bolted to keep them shut, it was hard to realise how easily a really big sea coming over the stem could stave in their frail wood like cardboard.

I arranged the cockpit cushions on the deck by the pump, and pumped hard and long with my right arm stiff, rolling my body back and forth, which seemed a less tiring method, for an indefinite period. There was no comparable method possible with the left hand, the pump being hard against the port side of the engine space, but I used my left arm on occasions to save fatigue. I did not fancy having my arms too tired to pump before the rest of my body was too exhausted to care.

I kept thinking petulantly, 'This is such an utterly dreary and stupid way to die,' as I lay there damply rocking, confronted with a confined prospect of darkly swirling bilge water and the stink of diesel oil.

Towards 1900 hours I thought of putting on the radio and enjoyed complete unreality for a while from the smugness and patronising *bonhomie* of the BBC. Then a news bulletin followed in which the announcer tritely announced 'unprecedented gales in the English Channel,' – at least our perils were authenticated. The *Moyana*, returning triumphantly from winning the Torbay to Lisbon race, had sunk in the early morning – gusts of 80mph were registered in Cornwall. A steamer had capsized with the loss of one life. Out of 24 yachts in the Channel Race, only ten had been accounted for. Lifeboats and distress calls all along the Channel. I began to feel proud that we were still afloat. Apples had been flying off the trees in Kent (too bad), and a dozen people had been killed ashore by falling or flying objects. Perhaps we were safer here!

With this happy news, I relieved Bertram at the wheel. I asked him if he knew where the distress flares were and suggested we should have them handy. He agreed. I also asked him to switch on the navigation lights while he was below, so we were ready and visible when it got dark. We started the engine, running it slowly, to keep the batteries charged. It was somehow heartening that Bertram now seemed prepared to admit that we were sinking, and should make the fact known if we met anyone who was interested.

I had hitherto always been sustained by a sort of metaphysical confidence that it was not yet my time to die, believing in a kind of eternal 'rhyme and reason' or poetic balance – whereby there was something for me in this short life before my card was full and ready to hand in. Taking account of the futility of my life to date and my lack of conviction for the future, I realised that this confidence in my own purpose and capacity had of late faded. Bertram, who seemed to have lost all zest for life since his son died, and seemed to show little will to live, would have been rather happy, I think, to have gone down in *Windstar,* which he loved. It did in fact seem devastatingly right – or at least agreeable to sublime rhyme and reason that *'finis'* should be written here. I took a few sharp pulls of the brandy bottle, which imparted a more direct, if temporary, glow before I took over the wheel as dusk was falling.

I was quite looking forward to a little more dark, as it would increase the chances of seeing a light, or having ours seen, at greater range. I did not want to burn our few flares until we definitely saw something to show them to, after which I planned to let the pump take a position of secondary importance while I made a distress signal with the masthead light, and kept on making it until something happened.

When we got low enough in the water for the seas to start breaking inboard seriously, and accelerate matters, I could not somehow see us making brave and stirring valedictory gestures to each other. Should I suggest putting a note in a bottle to keep the records straight and say goodbye to our friends? We would have to drain a bottle first. Happy thought!

About 2100 hours I suddenly saw for a moment a large vessel bearing green 130 about 3 miles off, and yelled for the flares. Bertram, after a short argument with the cabin doors, leant out on to the seat with a red canister which had a screw cap on one side, and seemed to take an age to unscrew. He then tried to get out a flare through a small hole, and after a great deal of probing and pulling, produced a piece of rumpled newspaper packing. This went on for some time until he had fished out quite a few newspaper scraps with some difficulty. At last a flare permitted itself to emerge. We then had to discover what to do with them. 'They are self-igniting,' said Bertram. But how, neither of us knew, hoping faintly they would burst into flames when they understood what we wanted. Neither of us could see very well by this time, yet when I found light and spectacles I could make out the far from striking printing, which said, 'Tear off cap, and rub inside smartly against head of flare.' This produced absolutely no result, and as it seemed to smack rather of Aladdin's lamp. I tried it several other ways, even pulling one flare entirely to pieces. Eventually I went to the galley and found a packet of matches which did work, and striking a whole box at a time held the exploding heads against the wretched things. One flare, at length, did give a slight sizzle, and I kept working at in the shelter of the cabin – to absolutely no purpose.

Under the stress of these exercises I remember my language grew unregrettably unparliamentary, and I even spoke quite sharply to Bertram. It was curious though, as we remarked afterwards, that throughout this entire adventure we remained ridiculously polite to each other, if a little curt, without any of the, 'For heaven's sake, grab that, you bloody fool' kind of dialogue, usual in such emergencies.

I then soaked a strip of the driest piece of cloth I could find with a can of lighter fuel, and wrapped it round a flare. This also was too damp, and wouldn't burn. I gave up on the flares, briefly thinking of starting a bonfire with them on the deck.

Our rescue ship seemed to have disappeared. I went for the Aldis lamp, which I plugged into the masthead light socket at the foot of the mast, there being no other place for it. It didn't work. When I told him, Bertram said, 'It worked the other day,' and I put the masthead fitting back. No masthead light either. This, anyway, had been suffering from mysterious fits of failure which the electricians had been unable to cure. I checked the other navigation lights. None of them was burning – nor would they.

All this time I was moving very fast about the deck, and below, slipping and bumping in my hurry, and increasing the mess in the galley looking for matches, and in the saloon looking for the lighter fuel, and something to burn. The inside of the yacht was now a terrible mess. Even the bottom boards had been thrown out of the bunks, and the decks were a mad jumble of clothes, cushions, books, charts, and tins and pots of food, two food lockers having burst open to pour their contents into the muddle, and the water was now splashing up out of the bilges as she rolled. In the middle of it all the swinging Tantalus attached to the saloon table ticked happily back and forth with its cargo of bottles, as though nothing were amiss. I took the hint and some more brandy, and found a wet biscuit on the deck.

Looking again for our ship, I eventually found her a little for'ard of our beam. Her lights were now showing clearly and it was getting darker. A little later I realised she was another craft. I could then also see what I took to be the original ship in about the same position as before.

While below I had put on every inside light we had to show as much of us as we could. And then, to my amazement, when I switched on the stern light it lit – although it had been unshipped by the seas, and had lain banging about the deck at the end of its flex for most of the day. I got up on the deck aft and seized it. With one hand on the back stay I stood holding it as high off the deck as I could, and began to flash S.O.S. in a wide arc between the two ships. The light had flickered out once or twice rather sickeningly, and, not knowing how far above the water the batteries were, I started looking for some other light. Our rubber torch had gone to ground among the rubble on the cabin floor, but Bertram told me where to find an old army pattern map reading and signalling torch in a leather cover. With this spare light between my teeth, I went on flashing. It seemed that the smaller vessel was approaching, and at last she quite definitely flashed back to us.

It was a wonderful moment to be in contact at last with someone else in the world.

I was now anxious not to lose them. It was strange how, as rescue became a more tangible possibility, I became more anxious and impressed with the problems involved. I feared for our battery system and that we might lose each other, playing hide and seek among the troughs of the sea. I kept flashing to her to dispel any doubt they might have about our signals, and to keep our position well in view.

The East Gabbard Light Vessel, now visible to them 13 miles off beyond us, did in fact confuse them for a moment. Now that they were definitely coming in to us I rested my right arm with the stern light, and kept on flashing with the torch, which had a morse button. As the urgency eased a little, I began to grow ridiculously self conscious, and wondered if it might not be more professional to send a proper message. I sent our signal letters a few times in between SOSs, so that they could relay our identity in case of mishap.

We found we could steer towards the ship fairly comfortably, and eventually I saw she was a small vessel of about 100 tons coming in quite slowly with a nice big Aldis lamp on the bridge searching among the waves for us. I began to realise the difficulties ahead, of getting from a comparatively helpless yacht on to a steamship, in the dark, in a hurricane.

I asked Bertram – who, by this time, had been continuously at the wheel since I started playing with the distress flares – whether he wanted to try to take a tow, or whether I should try to board her as soon as possible, and organise some means of transit for himself. This was my gravest worry, as I did not see how he could be expected to perform any violent gymnastics.

'Yes,' he said, 'you had better do that.'

As she got closer I went below, found my briefcase among the rubble, and put my address book in the pocket of my oilskin, ignoring my passport and wallet which were next to it. This was a completely superstitious gesture. It seemed that I would be lucky to get my body out of it alive; what else could I not dispense with in the circumstances? It seemed to be tempting fate to put anything else in my pockets, but to lose an address book, as I had done before, breaks a great number of human contacts, cutting off some for ever, so I had decided to go and fetch this.

While I was below, Bertram shouted that she was flashing to us. Let her flash, I thought, this is no time for conversation and, in any case, I would probably not be able to understand. I expected her to be a French or Belgian, or even a Dutch coaster, and only hoped that we would understand each other when we got within range for yelling instructions.

She came round very slowly and carefully astern of us. I tried to wave her on in the direction of the weather, since that was the only way we could steer and shouted to Bertram to hold her there. He replied that he couldn't see. The cabin lights dazzled him, and as all this time he had sat very quietly, I thought he was pretty tired out. I think now, considering this eye trouble, that he was probably suffering from an overdose of insulin as well as everything else. I directed him from the stern as well as I could until the ship came in alongside.

It was the most admirable piece of seamanship. She came in very slowly, carefully and deliberately, in that appalling weather, and laid herself alongside us as though we were a pier on a fine day instead of an erratically bobbing yacht.

They began to throw us lines, and eventually we were close enough for them to land aboard. I cannot exactly remember everything which took place from this moment in fast frenzied succession. I leaped and clawed my way about *Windstar*'s deck as swiftly as I could, trying to secure and make ropes fast. They threw me the heaviest hawsers they had, which made it even more difficult to find anywhere to belay them effectively on such a craft.

It was difficult to see in the dark punctuated by the dazzling glare of her searchlight. They had thrown oil on the water, which covered the hawsers and splashed aboard, so that I slipped and slithered more than ever, and at one moment heard myself sobbing with the effort like a wounded cowboy in an action-packed western – a dramatic exercise in which I had never before believed.

'Put a line round the mast,' someone yelled, and I thought vaguely how clever of them to have noticed our ensign and taken the trouble to speak English. I led one hawser round the mast which jammed some-where before I could get enough rope round and make more than a half-hitch with a bight. I dropped the eye of another round the anchor winch forward, and then found that we were moving forward. In fact, the steamship had sternway and was slipping back. We had taken some violent bumps against her side already, but moving forward under the sheer of her bows was even more alarming.

I expected to be pounded under at any moment as we both plunged up and down. To complicate matters, two wire stays caught behind her anchor, where they began to saw up and down, making a horrible noise like a mad violin. The bo'sun told me afterwards that I swung myself up and wrenched these free, kicking against her plates, but I really don't remember. I was too preoccupied with the urgency and concern of having made only one line properly fast forward, and nothing aft to stop us sliding away like this. Her bow looked very sharp and vicious, glistening black and silver in the dark and wet as she chopped up and down. Imagine being a mouse on the block at Tower Hill, whom a drunken executioner is trying to behead, at night, during a thunderstorm and an earthquake.

We moved apart quite quickly, while I tried to make fast the hawser, which had pulled free of the mast and was now running out over the stern. I got it through the fairlead, but couldn't hold it, nor find anything strong enough to suddenly jump it on to. I considered the binnacle for a moment, but it wasn't stout enough. It would have been useless to damage the boat any more, ripping out stanchions, or stays, or the binnacle, in the hope that it would check our flight. The bar on which the main sheet block ran would have been ideal, but the hawser was too thick to push through it easily as it ran out like a live thing, and the block itself slamming from side to side as we rolled could have removed my fingers very easily. I watched the rope snake away overboard.

We were driven forward and across the steamer's bows while she slid backwards and round our stern until she seemed to be about 100 yards off or more, over our starboard quarter, and still holding us on the remaining hawser like a badly harpooned whale. Her rope was thus around all the standing rigging from just forward of the mast on the port side to just forward of the cockpit on the starboard side. As the strain increased it seemed impossible that she could reel us back in, or fail to bring down rigging, boom and mast on top of us. The hawser stood between us in a stiff, straight line. There was a sharp series of vicious cracks, whangs and creaks, and eventually the hawser parted with a snap. I think only two stays had carried away, but I didn't bother to check.

I was now afraid that after the beating we had taken against the steel hull we must be filling with water even faster, and for a while feared that the steamer would or could not return to us again. For an unreasonable moment I even thought perhaps she might be more interested in salvage, and wiggled the stern light at her again in what I hoped was a winsome fashion. As she eventually came in again I made ready multiple loops from the tangle of sheets, made fast at several points to bend her next hawser on to. Bertram, I noticed, had finally left the wheel and was sitting in the cockpit looking rather dazed. 'The steering's jammed,' he said, and went below to collect ship's papers and one or two valuables. I tried to shift the wheel, and after a hard heave it spun out of my hand like a catherine wheel. Something had either broken or jumped out of gear as we bumped against the steamship. We were now completely helpless.

I stood on the stern again with the stern light in my hand to watch how the ship came in again. As we swung helplessly about I tried, ineffectually, to keep the ensign from flapping in my face, and then caught hold of the jackstaff to put it out and clear it overboard. This suddenly seemed not the thing to do, apart from looking like an unlucky gesture of despair.

As I had plenty of time to indulge in romantic gestures, I went and searched for my knife in the cabin, and then climbed aft again to cut the ensign down, stuff it into the collar of my oilskin like a scarf, and jettison the jackstaff. I wonder if I would have made this quaint gesture had it not been for a nostalgic respect for the white variety of ensign.

As the steamer approached I yelled that we could not now steer to help in any way.

A voice shouted back, 'Do you want to come aboard?'

'Yes!' I shrieked in amazement.

Apparently they had noticed Bertram sitting at the wheel in an attitude of such unconcern that they were in some doubt that we wished to leave!

A few moments later we struck her side head on, smashing in the stem and carrying away the forestay. As we rocked crazily alongside again I heard them yelling on deck to look out for the mast as it swung over her deck. I managed to secure another hawser around all the winches forward and it then seemed high time to leave.

Bertram was now on deck, wearing a spare cap (we had both lost ours overboard during the day), and seemed ready to abandon ship. I had noticed the previous time, as the two vessels soared up and down alongside like a pair of demented elevators, that her deck rail forward came within reach now and again. This time I did not intend to let the opportunity slip, and made my way forward to wait until we were scraping alongside again in the same position. For a pessimistic moment I wondered if I still had the strength to pull myself aboard. Everything felt numb and weak. I stood for a while trying to take a deep steady breath and relax, hopefully looking at my hands as I flexed my aching fingers. I needn't have worried. When her deck ducked within reach I found myself up and over before I had time to think about making any effort.

As I picked myself off the steel deck I heard someone cry out, 'There's one of them aboard!' and then repeat it again to the bridge in such a wild tone of voice that I felt for a moment they were going to throw me back! I joined three or four of them by the rail below the bridge and explained at the top of my voice that Bertram could not be expected to do anything violent.

'He's sick!' I bellowed, which seemed the simplest formula to inspire a more complicated plan of rescue.

Meanwhile, they had thrown several lines down to him, and were shouting at him to tie one around himself. Luckily, the line I had secured forward was well secured and fortunately placed so that *Windstar* towed alongside very nicely as the steamer moved forward just enough to keep her there.

I watched from the dark deck of the steamer and an entirely new viewpoint. I was now safe – so small a phrase and so minute a difference of time and place to denote so vast a change of state – like a spectator watching the brightly lit stage of *Windstar*'s deck from which I had now stepped.

Bertram stood upright with difficulty on the slippery, heaving deck. Luckily the remaining section of portside rail was in front of him as he tried to hold his balance and secure a rope at the same time. Three times the boom swung over and caught him on the back of the neck – a sharp blow which looked as though it could fell an ox. He lost his spare cap overboard too, while tying the rope round his middle. He seemed to make, as best he could, a sort of half-hitch with the end. which none of us who were watching believed to be really secured. Another line he held in his hand taking a turn around his arm, and we tried to catch his hands as the two decks rose and dipped towards each other. Twice we nearly had his hands, and then as *Windstar* plunged down and away the lines jerked him overboard and he fell between the two hulls.

It was a quite sickening moment, and I think I tried not to see. I know that for some moments I didn't dare to pull on the rope to prove to myself that he was not on the end of it. The bo'sun, who was on the rope with me, deliberately let as much slack go as he could, so that Bertram could either duck below the hulls as they came together or, if not attached, try to secure more line. The gap, however, widened for a moment, and we eased in the line. There was a weight at the end and, expecting any moment to lose our prize, we pulled him aboard in about three heaves, suspended by the middle, like a sheep being loaded, and lacking all the dignity of a captain leaving his sinking ship. When we bundled him over the rail and said, 'Thank God… we never thought the rope was fast!' he replied at once, 'Nonsense – tied it myself!' After he had been dragged across the deck and into the saloon he at once began to make quips about knowing how a walnut felt in a cracker, and remarking that he had no need to be a frogman to know what a ship's bottom looked like. He had no right to be capable of either speech or movement at all.

Five minutes later *Windstar*'s mast snapped off about 10ft above the deck and vanished over the side, but we never went to look at her again. The captain asked Bertram if he should try to tow her, but he told him to let her go. This he did, with great regret.

The ship, we found, was MV *Alouette*, of the General Steamship Navigation Company, and had only been passing because she had been unable to hold her anchorage while sheltering in Margate Roads.

The ship's company were extremely kind and, I think, thoroughly enjoyed the whole business. The captain, Captain F. Baker, a youngish man who had the air of a P&O liner captain, and sucked a curved pipe in a stately way, had a great time talking to us. The second night, when we had docked in Harlingen, the crew wanted me to drink with them in the fo'c'sle, which I did with considerable glee, got thoroughly drunk very quickly, and began to relax a bit for the first time.

Our trek across the dykes to Amsterdam, through the kind assistance of the shipping company's agent in Harlingen, was fairly comic, though frustrating to my impatience to get home. We looked like a pair of brigands in our salt-caked clothes. Bertram wore his inflatable blue jacket from which a long rubber nozzle (for inflating) reared itself under his right ear.

We startled two young ladies at the British Consul's office considerably, but were very ably and sympathetically supplied with identity papers, money and air tickets to London at Consular speed.

We made a splendid entry into the reception hall of London Airport, first and alone, being without baggage, except for the tattered ensign I still carried bundled round a small piece of *Windstar* which had been found the morning after, jammed in one of *Alouette*'s hawsers, while the customs officers glared sullenly at our retreating backs. A small party of friends and relations burst into a welcoming sound more like guffaws than the brave and resounding cheers more appropriate to this momentous occasion, but we saw their point.

┌─────────────────────────────────────┐
│ ■ **LESSONS LEARNED**   │
└─────────────────────────────────────┘

Finding out how your emergency equipment works when you are battling the elements in a real-life state of emergency is a recipe for potential disaster – especially with pyrotechnic distress flares. When Peter Combe saw a large vessel 3 miles off, the skipper had difficulties extracting the flares from their storage canister.

Next Combe admits 'We then had to discover what to do with them... neither of us knew.' They hoped 'they would burst into flames! At night, neither of them could see very well and even with torch and reading glasses, Combe had difficulty reading the instructions. It's basic good seamanship that the skipper should make sure he and his crew are familiar with the use of all safety equipment – from lifejackets and liferafts, to distress flares, gas for the cooker and radio procedure etc. Drills in daylight, and in the safety of a harbour, or inshore waters, are preferable to discovering in your hour of need that things won't work. It could make the difference between the survival of your boat or yourself.

Even greater difficulties arise when a yacht is abandoned alongside a big ship. As can be seen from other accounts in this book, the yacht is invariably damaged and often sinks soon after being dropped astern of the vessel. Peter Combe graphically describes the two vessels soaring up and down alongside each other 'like a pair of demented elevators'.

Peter Combe must have been constantly worried that his skipper would succumb to diabetes, having only been allowed on the voyage under protest by his doctors provided he did not 'overdo it'. In the event, Currie proved a remarkable man, who 'managed to give himself his daily injection of insulin – no mean feat in that weather'.

Running before the wind under bare poles, they feared being badly pooped, but in the event 'only once did a large wave break over the stern, which rose wonderfully to each following sea'. As Combe admits, he was not eager to make a sea-anchor, which could have slowed them down in the big seas, though Combe believed 'it would have been an error. There is something so very helpless about being at the mercy of a sea-anchor, and our hull would have taken a worse beating holding into the seas.'

The dangers for a yacht caught in a gale among the channels and swatches between the coast of Essex and the north coast of Kent, are graphically described. But there is one vital lesson: if the gale is from the south-west, which it so often is, and a yacht can clear the Kentish Knock, then it may be able to run away safely into the deeper water of the North Sea.

When the crew of *Windstar* had to resort to pumping by hand, the job was made more difficult because the pump was installed 'hard against the port side of the engine space'. A reminder that careful attention should be given to the positioning of bilge pumps.

twenty four

THE FATAL REEF

Yacht	*Merlan* (43ft Bermudian sloop)
Skipper	WL ('Lance') Curtis
Crew	Keith Douglas Young, Eric Walker, Brian Shaw
Bound from	Georgetown, Tasmania, to Geelong, Victoria, Australia
Date of loss	16 January 1949
Position	on rocks off Phillip Head, near Melbourne

Merlan had competed and been just beaten into second place in the Sydney–Hobart race of 1948. For the race she had a crew of nine, but only three of them, together with an additional volunteer, were left to sail her back to Geelong. The voyage of 250 miles across the Bass Strait is described by Keith Douglas Young:

WE LEFT GEORGETOWN AT THE mouth of the Tamar River, in Northern Tasmania, at about 1330 on Friday 14 January. Not, as events later proved, a particularly auspicious day on which to have sailed. The weather forecast promised a good voyage ... fine weather with southerly winds veering to south-east, which would give us an easy run to the Heads. According to the radio reports, all barometers in Tasmania were rising; and with the weather seemingly assured, we felt no forebodings as we set out under full sail on what should have been a simple and speedy passage of one and a half to two days, for the approximately 250 miles distance.

Fine weather stayed with us for the first day. We made good time with a favourable wind and a gentle swell which set the reef points jigging against the inward curve of the sail. The smooth racing hull of the *Merlan* porpoised forward in a series of powerful lunges while the towering mast described a pattern of arabesques and circles against the sky. It was perfect sailing weather.

The log reading after the first 24 hours showed us to be considerably more than halfway home. However, during the afternoon of the second day our barometer began to fall, slowly at first, but with increasing rapidity as evening approached. At the same time a dirty black scud began to build up in the sky. The almost hourly stream of planes which had been in sight as they sped overhead were lost to view in the rapidly forming cloud-wrack. These planes, in addition to relieving that sense of mid-ocean loneliness and isolation, had served as a good check on navigation. It was comforting, however, to be able to hear them still.

By midnight Saturday our glass, which had been steady at 30.05, had dropped to a menacing 29.5 and showed signs of falling still further. A good fresh breeze was blowing, but at that time not yet strong enough to cause us any real discomfort or worry. *Merlan*, still under full sail, was giving a good account of herself, although solid water and spray were being hurled aboard in some of the gusts. It was obvious to us that the worst was still to come. We carried on under these conditions for a further hour or so, when the decision was made to take the mainsail off altogether and set the storm trysail. This was accomplished without much difficulty as the wind lulled temporarily while we were shifting sails. Hardly had we made everything secure when it really began to blow. The advance-guard of the gale, as forecast by the rapid and steep fall of the barometer, finally menaced our ship.

Shortly after the gale struck we sighted our first light on the Victorian coast. This was identified as the Cape Woolamai Light. Here it became necessary to change course to the west in order to stand up to the Heads. Our position was confirmed some little time later when the unmistakable 22½-second flash of Cape Schank was sighted in the murky distance.

By this time the wind had veered round to the west. We decided to get away from the land and stand in once more in the morning. With the night pitch black and the coastal lights periodically blacked out in driving rain squalls, it was scarcely a safe risk to approach the land too closely.

There was no rest for any of us that night. Those who tried to snatch a little sleep found it almost impossible to wedge into a bunk securely enough to avoid being pitched out as *Merlan* fell heavily off some of the more precipitous seas. In addition, it had become bitterly cold and all our clothing was thoroughly saturated. It was impossible to prepare any sort of hot meal or drink. The best we could do was to snatch a handful of biscuits, an orange or an apple and perhaps a bit of chewing gum. I had quite a battle keeping my cigarettes and matches dry, but succeeded by wrapping them securely in a spare oilskin.

It was a thoroughly miserable night. Next morning found us under trysail and jib ploughing through a lumpy grey sea with the wind coming in gusts and sometimes petering out altogether before coming in just as freshly from another quarter. We were still, at this time, some considerable distance offshore and making slow progress under reduced sail. Again we changed course to make directly for Port Phillip Heads, whereupon the wind began to build up until in a short time it was blowing half a gale directly out of the west. This was rather disheartening, as it meant we had to drive *Merlan* right into the teeth of the wind under trysail, not a particularly efficient sail at the best of times.

By midday the wind had mounted to storm-force – about Force 10 or 11. Some of the gusts we estimated at from 70 to 75mph, a figure which was later confirmed by Weather Bureau observations made at the time ashore. This state of affairs prevailed for the next few hours, during which we tried to battle our way to the west under the inefficient trysail. Then the wind helped us by backing to the south so that we eventually found ourselves making heavy going against a full sou'westerly gale along the Victorian coast between Cape Schank and the Heads.

Huge seas rolling up Bass Strait were making it difficult and dangerous for those of us who found it necessary to remain on deck. In spite of efforts to ease her over some of the worst of the seas, our decks were being continually swept. There was hardly a moment when the self-bailing cockpit was free of water; for as fast as it could drain the contents of one sea another would pour aboard. Much of this water was finding its way below, where, to add to our troubles, both pumps had gone out of action. Soon the water below reached a level several inches over the floorboards and it became necessary to bail with a bucket, which we continued to do for the ensuing several hours.

In the early afternoon of Sunday it was decided to take in the trysail. Even that small patch of canvas was more than the boat could safely stand. With an almost continuous series of breaking seas hurling themselves feet deep across the decks, this was a hell of a job. Blinded and almost choked by the tumultuous waves, Lance, Brian and I clawed our way forward where, on looking aloft, I was somewhat startled to see the mast trembling and vibrating like a plucked harp string. We returned to the cockpit for a trick at the tiller. At the end of an hour it was time for another spell at the bucket. To our dismay, the water was gaining on us and starting to splash up over the mattresses on the bunks. It was now a matter of getting into shelter quickly, or having the boat founder under us. It was too late to turn back and run for shelter at Flinders or anywhere in the lee of the Schank. Heaving-to was also out of the question, owing to the size and force of the seas. With the deadness of the sloop occasioned by the terrific weight of water in her, there was always the danger that they would overwhelm us.

Merlan had behaved magnificently in all that we had come through, and any boat less honestly built would, I am convinced, have foundered long before. But there is a limit to what even the best craftsmanship in wood can stand, and it was apparent that *Merlan* was tiring. The bucket bailing was by far the worst of all our previous ordeals. Not only did the bucket become progressively heavier as it was handed up full each time, but the crew handling it had to brace themselves against the unpredictable dips, lurches and wrenches of the yacht.

Meanwhile, under the single jib, we had gradually closed the land until *Merlan* was not more than a mile or two off shore. The height of the seas and the flying spray was such that we could catch only brief glimpses of the nearby coastline. By mid-afternoon we estimated that we could be only a short distance from the Heads. We expected the entrance to be hazardous, but our condition was such by this time that it would have to be attempted in spite of the risks.

At about 1600 I wedged myself securely against the boom and strained to catch an identifying glimpse of the shore. At the moment I was about to give up, I caught one brief glimpse of the white shaft of the Lonsdale Lighthouse on the western side of the Heads. This momentary peep was sufficient to give us a bearing, and on checking our position we discovered we were about a mile due south of the Heads. It was a simple matter then to ease our sheets and begin the run for the Heads and what we earnestly hoped would be shelter, safety and rest.

As we drew closer to the entrance we could see the tidal signal flying from the yardarm of the Lonsdale Light. It informed us that the tide was adverse – that it was ebbing. There was no turning back. We would have to try and force our way through. The regular steamer channel in the centre of the Rip was a churning, boiling maelstrom in which I am convinced no small boat could possibly have lived. Further to the east lay the dreaded Corsair Rock, unseen in the welter of white water that was the Heads, but still a lurking menace. Our best, in fact our only plan was to carry on as we were – as close as possible to the Lonsdale side.

With gigantic seas sweeping up under our stern as we stormed along on a northerly course, we were picked up and literally hurled ahead at terrific speeds as we skated on the crests of some of the waves. A breaking sea would almost certainly have meant our end; and though many times it did look as though we might be overwhelmed by water hurtling up astern, none broke upon us.

The next greatest danger was the possibility of a broach, and this actually happened during our hazardous dash through the Heads. I found myself grabbing for grip on something as *Merlan* was picked up by a monster sea charging up astern and hurled ahead at a speed we estimated to be in the vicinity of 15mph. As the yacht began to slide down the almost perpendicular slope of the wave to the great bulk of water which had forced its way below, all ran to the nose of the boat. This, of course, left the helmsman with no control and we had a ticklish minute before the yacht was brought back on her course. But this single broach, as it turned out later, had been sufficient to bring us within the orbit of the Lonsdale reef, quite lost to view beneath the boiling surge. Next moment we struck the reef! It was a mortal blow for *Merlan*. That much was obvious after the first shock. I was standing at the foot of the hatch with a just-filled bucket which I was about to hand up to Brian. To the accompaniment of a horrible grinding sound

I was pitched the full length of the cabin, where I picked myself up, dazed and shaken, with the bucket still in my hand. The dreadful tearing, rending, crunching sound as the yacht drove on the rocks is something quite impossible to convey.

Picking myself up I began to fight my way to the hatch and escape through an indescribable confusion of sodden sails and clothing, charts and navigation instruments, mattresses and tins of food which had been flung out of burst lockers. My one thought, I suppose naturally enough, was to get on deck.

Just as I reached the foot of the hatch (about five seconds after the initial shock) *Merlan* struck again. Once more I was hurled the length of the cabin, to end up even more bruised and battered at the foot of the mast. A second time I clawed my way through the hatch just in time to see and feel a really terrific sea lift *Merlan* bodily and hurl her forward on to the reef. Brian, who had apparently secured a firm grip on something substantial, seemed to be all right. Eric, tightly lashed in the cockpit, had likewise emerged unscathed, though the heavy bronze fitting at the rudder head had snapped completely off, leaving him with the now useless tiller in his hands.

But we did appear to have one casualty. At the moment of impact Lance had been flung violently against the doghouse at the after end of the cabin and his face was a mass of blood which poured from a nasty gash near the bridge of his nose. The effect was pretty ghastly. Apart from the shaking up and a few bruises and scratches, I seemed to be in working order.

The jib had blown itself out at the moment we struck. After a moment Brian and Lance went forward to lower it. However, they found the halyard in such a tangled mess that they were forced to abandon the attempt. In the meantime I had returned below, where I managed to retrieve four life-jackets. We put them on. Just as well we did, for beyond doubt those lifejackets saved our lives in the struggle which was to come shortly afterwards.

Within minutes, a large crowd of holidaymakers had begun to gather on the shore about half a mile away. There was, of course, absolutely nothing they could do, but we must have provided them with an interesting spectacle. The keeper of the Lonsdale Light had witnessed the entire happening and had telephoned at once for the lifeboat stationed at Queenscliff to be launched to come to our rescue.

Before long the lifeboat appeared, but because of the tremendous sea running, the adverse tide and the treacherous currents and tide-rips it could not be brought close to the wreck. At that moment things never looked more hopeless. We held a bit of a conference to decide what our best course of action might be and whether we might, by our own efforts, save ourselves. It was clear to us that so long as the gale prevailed there was absolutely no hope of a boat approaching us. It seemed, therefore, that we would have to take to the water and try to make for the lifeboat cruising up and down about a quarter of a mile away in the lee of the reef.

It was now about 1700 and since the tide appeared to be at low water slack we determined to make our effort before darkness set in. On the cabin top was a small plywood dinghy. Though none too optimistic about its chances of supporting the four of us in the waters swirling and boiling over the reef, we did hope that it might perhaps carry us some of the way. It did – about 6 feet. We had barely left the stricken *Merlan* when our cockleshell dinghy was swamped and we were left struggling in the powerful, sucking tide-rip.

Within seconds the seas had taken complete control and we had been swept dozens of yards apart. The same gigantic wave which had engulfed our tiny dinghy seemed, once it had us firmly in its grasp, to sweep each one of us in a totally different direction. Then began what was really a nightmare struggle before the eyes of some hundreds of people.

We had swamped in one of the labyrinthine channels of the reef, a channel through which a vast volume of water was swirling at a terrific pace. I began swimming as desperately as possible, but like the others, was entirely at the mercy of the currents. The most fortunate of the four, I managed to crawl through a mass of slimy kelp on to a more solid portion of the reef. Actually I crawled part of the way on to the reef three times, only to be washed off by seas sweeping across. But on the fourth attempt I contrived to hang on. Clinging grimly to the reef for a few minutes to catch my breath, I recovered some strength. Then began a staggering walk to the leeward side where I knew I would once more have to take to the sea for a swim to the lifeboat. Before doing so I turned to see how my shipmates might be faring.

I was elated to see Brian dragging himself on to the reef, but was quite alarmed to see Eric and Lance, supported solely by their life-jackets, being swept out past the wreck into a position which seemed fatal. Then, as I watched, Eric was swept by a wave into a favourable current and began to approach the reef. He began to struggle once more and by dint of furious efforts was at last able to clamber on to the water-swept rocks. Somewhat later, Lance, nearly spent, made it also.

By this time a group of Queenscliff fishermen had succeeded in launching a dinghy and by a marvellous combination of seamanship and courage had brought the boat right up to the reef from which we had expected to have to make another swim to the waiting lifeboat. One error of judgement, one unpredictable sea sweeping aboard their dinghy, and they too would have been struggling for their lives.

It was a comparatively simple matter to pile into the dinghy, a solidly built 15-footer, but there was still the dangerous quarter-mile pull to the waiting lifeboat. The seas had not abated, and with eight men aboard, even a 15-foot dinghy is somewhat crowded. But our rescuers displayed faultless seamanship; we got a line to the lifeboat and were hauled alongside. In a matter of moments we were wrapped in coats and blankets and a man-sized pannikin of rum was thrust upon each of us. First aid was applied to our cuts and scratches received on the boat and more especially from the jagged rocks on the reef. And so we were rescued.

■ LESSONS LEARNED

- Having an effective, self-bailing cockpit, with ample drain holes, is demonstrated when Young says 'there was hardly a moment when the self-bailing cockpit was free of water; for as fast as it could drain the contents of one sea another would pour aboard'. Much of the water found its way below, where, with both pumps out of action, it was soon over the floorboards. Despite bailing with a bucket for several hours the water was soon splashing up over the mattresses on the bunks.
- The importance of preparing hot food in advance, perhaps in

a Thermos flask, when bad weather is expected, is underlined when Young describes the barometer dropping to 'a menacing 29.5' on Saturday night and later says 'it was impossible to prepare any sort of a hot meal or drink. The best we could do was to snatch a handful of biscuits, an orange or an apple and perhaps a bit of chewing gum.'

- It was now a matter of getting into shelter quickly, or having the boat founder. The terrific weight of water in the sloop made her unresponsive, and the danger that seas would overwhelm them came true when they made for Port Phillip Heads with a fast ebbing tide. 'As the yacht began to slide down the almost perpendicular slope of the wave to the great bulk of water which had forced its way below, all ran to the nose of the boat …' This single broach was sufficient to bring them near the reef, where the mortal blow was struck.

- Luckily, Young managed to get below to retrieve the lifejackets which saved their lives in the struggle that followed. Again, in such adverse conditions it is sound seamanship to insist the crew are wearing lifejackets before it becomes necessary. In such cases, tying crew members together to avoid being separated is also recommended.

twenty five

STRUCK BY A UFO

Yacht	*Easting Down* (38ft ex-RNLI wooden lifeboat)
Skipper	J S Robertson
Crew	Mary Robertson, Andrew Robertson, Rachael Robertson, Alexander Robertson, John and Ruth (two friends of the children)
Bound from	IJmuiden to the River Humber
Date of loss	August 24 1965
Position	approx. 45 miles W of IJmuiden

Easting Down was an ex-RNLI lifeboat built for service in the Portland Bill area. When the Robertson family and their two young friends set out in 1965 to cruise in Holland, she had been re-rigged as a gaff-cutter, with twin diesel engines and spacious accommodation in three separate cabins. They left South Ferriby Sluice on Sunday 15 August and reached IJmuiden at 2100 the following day. From Amsterdam, they spent a week cruising the IJsselmeer. On Monday 23 August they left IJmuiden to begin the return passage, having heard Scheveningen Radio forecast south-westerly 4–5 becoming north-westerly 4–6 later.

WITH A WIND OF FORCE 4 we were able to point our course for the Corton Reef Light Vessel, closehauled on the port tack, making 4–5 knots. Gradually, the wind freshened and headed us slightly. By 1600 hours we were logging 5 knots under mainsail and staysail and jib only. The wind continued to freshen. At 1800 we furled the jib. The wind was now Force 7. Shortly after handing over the watch at 2000, I was called out on account of some puzzling lights. At this time all seemed well. The ship was sailing and behaving very well. An hour later, however, we heeled so far that I could not remain in my bunk, and was horrified to find water where the cabin floor should be.

Dressing hurriedly, I went out, to find my crew enjoying the sail, and quite unaware that anything was wrong. With the log reading between 6 and 7 knots, and the lee rail awash for the first time in its career, the ship was creaming along and a joy to handle. The wind was now very strong, and the sea rough, and we had a struggle to stow the mainsail, but we had to do so to reduce our list and allow the pumps to work. Starting the Thorneycroft engine we maintained our course and pumped. The water level did not fall. The standby pump was rigged, but soon both pumps became blocked by shavings left by the shipwrights. From 2200 hours onwards the bucket brigade laboured intermittently, filling buckets in the cabin, passing them out to the cockpit for emptying. Once we had got the level down we were able to keep it down to floor level by bailing alternate hours only.

Seasickness took an increasing toll. At first the duty watch continued to sail the ship while the others bailed. By 0100, however, it was impossible to steer owing to the wind and sea. Engines were stopped, and we lay ahull.

A fix placed us at Lat. 52° 40' N Long. 03° 00' E at 0600 hours, but we were drifting back towards the Dutch coast at an unknown rate. The wind was very strong, and still increasing. Daylight disclosed an impressive scene. We measured a wind speed of 35 knots only 5ft above sea level. Big breaking seas bore down on us, but the ship rode them magnificently. To reduce inflow of water alongside the lifting cable, I had pulled up the centreplate just before dawn. Lying beam on to wind and sea we slid sideways down the face of each sea, leaving a slick of smooth water to windward. This protected us from the worst of the seas. By now the wind had moved towards the NW and cross seas produced occasional pillars of water which blew down onto us, crashing onto the deck, and finding hitherto unknown ways inside, round the edges of closed hatches.

Charts and log had deteriorated into a sodden mess. Dividers and parallel rules, flung from the table, disappeared in the bilges.

I experimented, trying heading into the seas with both engines on, but this proved hard work, uncomfortable, and impossible to maintain.

At the crest of each sea, the wind caught our bows and blew them off to port or to starboard, and way was only regained as the next sea approached. Running downwind towing warps was also useless, creating risk of pooping and broaching. I know now, beyond doubt, that in a vessel of shallow draught it is safer to lie ahull broadside to wind and sea, even with a non self-righting hull like *Easting Down*'s. It is also relatively comfortable. Our only fears were that by the time the gale abated we might be too exhausted to sail the ship or we might have drifted onto the shoals of the Sheldt estuary. We had to keep the water bailed down to floorboard level lest it reach the unprotected batteries and short out our power, rendering us unable to use radio or engines in time of need.

At 0805 I attempted to send a Mayday, but there was no answer. The aerial relay was jamming. At 1105 I tried again, and was answered by the British ship *Etterick* and by Scheveningen Radio. I estimated that by now we must have drifted near to Browns Ridge. The distress frequency was busy, and we had to wait for signals concerned with the German timber ship *Tanenberg* in distress 25 miles SW of us, near the Outer Gabbard, to finish before we could talk. We maintained radio contact with *Etterick*, which was heading for our position at the time of the signal. A submarine passed within a mile to the north of us, but failed to answer our signals. But *Ossendrecht*, a 16,000-ton ship bound for Hudson Bay, picked up our call relayed by Scheveningen Radio. Her master estimated our probable rate and direction of drift so well that he sailed straight towards us. Due to the height of the seas he did not see us until very close. At 1300 hours he steamed round us and hove to a cable to windward. We started the engines and motored alongside his pilot ladder. As the shipping forecast now promised further gales, and Hurricane Hilda was also approaching to our north at over 30 knots, it seemed wise for an exhausted crew to leave a leaking ship. We had drifted 7 miles in the two hours since our distress call.

I was grieved to learn that *Ossendrecht* could not take *Easting Down* in tow. John volunteered to stay aboard with me and try to sail the ship to shelter, but I considered the risk too great. The children, who had been confined to their bunks for safety, climbed the ladder, followed by the women, while I attempted to salvage clothes, binoculars, cameras and radio. Then John and I also climbed the ladder.

While we were abandoning *Easting Down* she dropped into a trough, pulling the bow rope tight and wrenching a mooring cleat from the foredeck. Then, as *Ossendrecht* got under way and started to leave the yacht, a big sea rolled *Easting Down* and her mainmast struck *Ossendrecht*'s hull and broke. With sorrow we watched her, with the broken mast drooping to starboard, as we steamed away. In a few minutes she was lost to view, her white hull hidden among the white breakers.

Next morning we learned that *Easting Down* had sunk only 15 minutes after being taken in tow by a tug some four-and-a-half hours after we had abandoned her.

Whether she could have been saved had I stayed aboard to bale we shall never know. The cause of the leak was never found. It may have been from the centreplate case, but the North Sea was full of baulks of jettisoned timber, and we had struck several pieces. One of these, thrust against the hull by a propeller blade a few miles from IJmuiden, may have damaged the hull. While such hazards abound it would plainly pay to fit an engine-driven pump. Had we had one this tale would have had a happier ending.

■ LESSONS LEARNED

- Collisions with UFOs (unidentified floating, or partly submerged objects) are a significant risk to yachtsmen, as the losses of *Easting Down*, *Dorothea*, *Windstar* and other incidents in this book demonstrate.
- It is not clear from his account whether Robertson actually tried running downwind and 'found it useless', or whether this was simply his belief based on earlier experience. In any case, it was the realisation that they could not keep the water at bay, and that when it reached the batteries it would short out their power, that made Robertson decide to send a Mayday while the radio worked.

- Robertson concluded that in a vessel of shallow draught it was safer to lie ahull broadside to wind and sea. His only fears were that by the time the gale had abated they might be too exhausted to sail the ship or they might have drifted into the shoals of the Schelde estuary.

- When to abandon a yacht is a matter of judgement, based on individual circumstance, but the fateful decision must always be made by the skipper. *Easting Down* did not sink until more than four hours after being abandoned, as a result of being taken in tow. 'Could she have been saved had I stayed on board to bail?' the skipper asked himself. But even an engine-driven pump is fallible, particularly if it is driven from the propeller shaft and the stern gear becomes damaged.

- A yachtsman requesting help from a big ship should always remember that although the captain of that ship is bound by maritime law to come to his assistance, he is not similarly bound to save the yacht – in fact, the very act of coming alongside risks the yacht being badly damaged, or sunk, if there is any sea running.

- The skipper of a yacht in trouble will often be so relieved at seeing help that his instinct may tell him to get alongside without delay, and the captain of the ship may do nothing to dissuade him. From the bridge of a large freighter or tanker, perhaps 100ft above the water, the captain may not be able to assess the danger that will arise as soon as the yacht is alongside. If she is to windward to provide a lee, nothing can stop the big ship from bearing down on the yacht. The yacht's skipper must make his own decision – should he go alongside, and irrevocably commit himself and his crew to the hazardous task of getting aboard the ship? Or should he steel himself to take some other action? If he has reason to believe that other help is on its way, then he could request the big ship to stand by. When no other help seems likely, and if he can talk to the ship's captain, they can weigh up the possibility of using a liferaft or one of the ship's lifeboats to transfer the crew of the yacht.

- Once a decision has been made to get alongside, a hawser from the ship must be made fast to the strongest point on the foredeck of the yacht – and this may prove to be the first problem. Modern yachts are seldom fitted with substantial bitts or a samson post. If the mast is deck-stepped, it may serve to make the rope fast to the base of it. The yacht is now effectively at the mercy of the big ship and the crew of the yacht should realise this and not waste time trying to fend off. Instead, they should concentrate on organising the safest possible means of evacuation. If the ship has a pilot's hoist, then it may be possible to use that, otherwise lifelines or scramble nets from the ship are essential. Crew should be wearing safety harness.

twenty six

THE LOSS OF *SEA BREEZE*

Yacht	*Sea Breeze* (49ft Bristol Channel pilot-cutter)
Skipper	H W Tilman
Crew	Brian Potter, Mike Clare, Brian McCleagan and Dougal Forsyth
Bound from	Lymington, Hampshire to the west coast of Greenland
Time and place of loss	2100, 21 August 1972
Position	in entrance to Sermilik Fjord, Greenland

Bill Tilman, the renowned English explorer, sailor and mountaineer, was offered the chance to buy the Bristol Channel pilot-cutter, Sea Breeze, a month after returning from Norway following the loss of another pilot cutter, Mischief (see 'Mischief's Last Voyage' in Total Loss (Adlard Coles Nautical)).

Despite being advised by a surveyor not to buy her, Tilman could not resist the temptation, although he knew 'that much renovation and rejuvenation' would be needed. She was only one year younger than Tilman, who was 70 at the time.

The first voyage in Sea Breeze, in 1969, did not go well, and within 25 miles of Scoresby Sound, Tilman's crew 'mutinied'. He had to return, sadly reflecting that 'Once before I had had the melancholy experience of sailing homewards with a disillusioned crew.'

In 1970, Sea Breeze was short of a complete crew and, to augment it, Tilman placed an advertisement in The Times which became much quoted: 'Hands wanted for long voyage in small boat. No pay, no prospects, not much pleasure.' Tilman's plan was to voyage to the south-west coast of Greenland, where 'there are plenty of mountains of the order of 5,000 to 7,000 feet!'

In 1971, with another crew including 'two guitar players and their instruments, a bugle and a mouth organ', Sea Breeze attempted to reach Greenland again, but was stopped by ice 70 miles off the coast.

In 1972, Tilman's plan was to take Sea Breeze to the west coast of Greenland, to Baffin Bay and Ellesmere Island. Having left Lymington on 1 May, they met 'dirty' weather in the Atlantic and while some 500 miles east of Greenland's Cape Farewell, suffered a broken boom which made it necessary to 'set a topsail abaft the mast as a sort of trysail and alter course for Reykjavik in Iceland, 300 miles to the north'. They arrived there on 2 July and a new boom was made by 'laminating together eight lengths of one-inch planking'. While in Reykjavik, the crew was rearranged to include a student from California and they left on 10 July, intending to call first at Jan Mayen Island. Tilman takes up the story:

WITHIN A COUPLE OF HOURS the unfortunate Californian had retired to his bunk, retching and groaning, where he lay for the next five days in a sort of coma, a bandage over his eyes, neither eating nor drinking, nor even moving. We thought he was dead. So we put into Isafiord to land him, and no sooner were we alongside but he was up and about, looking remarkably sprightly considering his five days' ordeal. Brian promptly telephoned his friend and secured the son whom he did not know but guessed would be in his early twenties with considerable sailing experience. Two days later, on returning to the boat after a walk in the hills, Brian and I learnt that Dougal Forsyth had already arrived and that he was a schoolboy of 16. This rather staggered me but there was nothing to be done, and young Dougal, sturdy for his age, proved to have the makings of a useful hand.

We sailed from Isafiord on 18 July and reached Jan Mayen on the 25th. Some 70 miles north-west of Horn we sighted our first ice, a field of heavy pack-ice close aboard to the west. There was no ice anywhere near Jan Mayen this year. The steep cliff that marks the south-west cape was sighted from 40 miles away, the ship happily pointing straight at it. We anchored first in the small bay off the Norwegian base, the bay of evil memory where *Mischief* took such a battering from the ice in 1968. One of the small party awaiting Mike and me as we rowed ashore greeted me with, 'Mr. Tilman, I presume?'

He had been on the island in 1968 and seeing our yellow hull had put two and two together and concluded it was 'that man' again.

We hung about for several days while all the ice disappeared except that inside Scoresby Sound where, from Cape Tobin south to Cape Brewster, it remained chock-a-block. Along the coast, too, north from Cape Tobin there remained a belt of shore-fast ice so that we were unable to anchor anywhere, and it was the more frustrating because at one time we were within 3 miles of the settlement and could see the wireless masts.

On 8 August when we tried the engine it started reluctantly, made a queer noise, and finally refused to start at all. A friend who knows the engine diagnosed the trouble as a broken valve spring and thought the engine could have been run on one cylinder had we had on board anyone able to cope. So we gave up Scoresby Sound and went south to Angmagssalik, where, by the time we arrived, which was not until 21 August, there should not be much ice. The entrance is long and narrow but would be possible to sail through were there no ice; we needed water and stores for the voyage home and having come so far the crew deserved something more than a view of Greenland. It would have been prudent to go home.

The absence of ice off the Sound led me to think that the coast to the south would be ice free, and we started off with the pleasant thought of keeping this magnificently mountainous coastline close aboard all the way. However, south of Cape Brewster we began meeting ice, and the further south we went and the further away from the coast – for the coast falls away to the south-west – the thicker the ice became. When a field of close pack ice showed to the east it became clear that this was no place for a boat with no engine. So we sailed north again, rounded the pack to the east, and gained open water. It was a slow passage and we had another unpleasant encounter with ice in thick fog only some 70 miles north-west of Iceland, probably the remains of the field we had seen on the outward passage. Unusual, too, were the number of bergs we kept sighting from a point 30 miles west of Iceland right across Denmark Strait to Greenland.

On the night of 19 August, when some 30 miles east of Cape Dan, we met a north-easterly gale, the hardest blow of the voyage, which went on for 24 hours. Hove-to and reefed down with only some 8ft of luff on the mast we lost a lot of ground to the south-west, and on the 21st, the gale having spent itself, a bank of fog over the land made it difficult to identify.

I intended spending the night at sea but when an opening appeared in the floes, decided to sail through in order to anchor in Sermilik fiord which lay temptingly wide and open to the south-west. Having reached the open water with nothing but a few bergs about, we thought our troubles were over until the wind became fluky and finally died when we were still a mile or so from the shore. Towing with the dinghy did little to help – a couple of long sweeps would have been more use.

After the gale, the glass had risen smartly and was high and steady so that the fierce blast of wind that came in about 9pm, when it was getting dark, the herald of a dirty night, was quite unexpected. The first blast laid her over until the lee deck was half under water. The boat shot ahead and was soon within a quarter-mile of the dimly seen shore. She had plenty of way on, and the rate we were going and the fear that we might hit something induced me to get the sails off in a hurry – prematurely, as it happened, for we found no seabed with the sounding lead. By then a lot more ice had come down the fiord, too much to sail among with safety in the wind then blowing. So for the next three or four hours we drifted slowly away from the shore, the crew hard at work fending off floes. We had not even enough respite to get the dinghy on board. When a rock islet loomed out of the darkness to leeward we set the staysail in an effort to clear it, and might have done so, had not a floe got under the lee bow and stopped her. Her heel caught and she swung round to be pinned by wind and wave broadside on against the rock with the cranse iron at the bowsprit end striking sparks off the rock face.

Dropping the staysail all hands shoved desperately and vainly with boathooks. She could not be got off and was taking a terrible hammering. Fearing she would break up, or fill and slip off into deep water, I told the crew to abandon her. A little later she did slip off so that at first light only a few feet of mast showed above the water.

Mike got ashore first with a rope which he anchored to hold Dougal while he jumped. We should have secured the rope on board to serve as a handrail. Without waiting for the rope to be thrown back Brian followed, slipped on the rock and was washed back almost under the boat until the next wave took him forward to be grabbed by Mike, wet from head to foot.

The only loose rope handy was the lead line so young Brian got ashore on this while held by me. This left me with the weight end and thinking that 7lb of lead round my waist might be a hindrance if it came to swimming I had to go below for a knife to cut it off. After being first thrown violently to the deck with a crash that made me think the deck above was caving in, I found a knife and presently joined the others, wet only from the waist.

I'm ashamed to confess that my faculties were so numbed by the sudden disaster that while all this was happening it never even occurred to me to collect such valuable and portable things as diary, log book, films, camera, money and sextant. The crew were no better. Sleeping bags were all that most of us got ashore. A sack of food had been thrown ashore but a wave washed it away.

The wind continued throughout the night and in the morning rain set in, to continue throughout the day. At daylight we moved to the top of the rock. Mike had brought a very light bivouac tent into which we put Brian and Dougal who were wettest and coldest. The rest of us, having looked into every nook and cranny and found nothing – our rock was rich only in pools of water – spent the day pacing up and down, speculating on the chances of a boat passing and, if one did arrive, wondering whether we would be seen and on the number of days a man could last without food. There was a small settlement a few miles up the fiord and no doubt communication between this and Angmagssalik, but how frequently or infrequently was the question.

But our luck was in. Late that afternoon we saw a small local boat bound up the fiord. She was passing a good mile away and visibility was poor on account of the drizzle. All five of us stood on top of the rock waving sleeping bags and even shouting – a perfectly futile exercise, since her three man crew were warmly ensconced in the wheelhouse. For several agonising minutes she held steadily on until at length to our heartfelt relief she began to turn towards us. The Green-lander crew acted smartly. Two jumped into their big dinghy, brought it close to the rock stern-on and, in spite of the swell still running, took us off in turn without mishap.

■ LESSONS LEARNED

The lesson of this sad story for me – at present no one else seems likely to profit by it – is not to mess about in Greenland fiords without an engine, especially when they are full of ice. Nevertheless I think they were the victims of an unlucky chain of circumstances – first the failing wind that prevented us from anchoring, followed by a wind of such strength that we could not safely sail among ice, but for which we would have come to no harm.

twenty seven

ODD TIMES AT SEA

Yacht	*Odd Times* (23ft gaff-rigged cutter)
Skipper	Peter Rose
Crew	Paul Sheard
Bound from	St Pierre Island, Nova Scotia to Cornwall, England
Time and date of loss	0655, 28 July 1967
Position	approx. 200 miles SE of St Johns, Newfoundland

Odd Times *was designed by John Leather and built for Peter Rose in 1958. Having sailed in her 'from her native Essex shores to the Aegean and from Scotland to the Caribbean',* Odd Times *was in Barbados in January 1966. During that year, Peter Rose, sometimes with a crew and sometimes single-handed, sailed up the east coast of the USA, as far as Ivesterly, Rhode Island, where* Odd Times *remained for the winter of 1966–67. The return voyage to England was to be made during the summer of 1967, with Paul Sheard as crew, but a few weeks before their departure from Nova Scotia, Peter Rose began to suffer serious seasickness:*

AT SYDNEY WE TOPPED UP with provisions before sailing for St Pierre. The fogs that had delayed us earlier caused us to omit southern Newfoundland from our itinerary as we wished to be on our way from St Pierre by about the middle of July. It seemed to me that it would be wise to be away from the north Atlantic Ocean well before the end of August so as to have a better chance of avoiding gales and even the odd long-distance wandering hurricane. On the other hand, to be much earlier would mean increasing the chance of encounters with ice on the western side of the ocean. So we sailed for St Pierre, and I was afflicted by seasickness of a worse sort than I had ever previously experienced, except perhaps in the worst of conditions. But our conditions were good and it was not only unpleasant, it was also very worrying. I was able to help Paul with the navigation, but other than that he sailed *Odd Times* on his own, and made a very good job of it, too. We arrived at St Pierre on the afternoon of 14 July (a big day there, of course) and, off the heaving swell, I recovered.

The French government runs a small but well equipped hospital on the island and I was examined by a competent young doctor who had various tests and X-rays carried out to try and find the reason for the extreme seasickness. The result of this was that I seemed quite healthy but that there was strong circumstantial evidence that I was allergic to a particular type of drug contained in some anti-seasickness tablets – the type that I had taken on the crossing from Maine to Nova Scotia and then again on sailing from Sydney to St Pierre. This was a great relief and we prepared to sail from St Pierre, this unique and isolated bit of France in North America, eight days after our arrival. We were both feeling much more confident and we jettisoned all anti-seasickness tablets: Paul, lucky chap, doesn't need them anyway, and I would cope with the 'ordinary' dose of this affliction and get over it in the normal way after a day or two.

After lunch on 21 July we sailed. It was a fine day, though, as usual, the fog was hovering a short way out to sea. The wind was light to moderate and fair and we easily sailed our course, a little east of south away from the island. For the first 24 hours progress was good and all seemed to be going well in favourable conditions. I was slightly seasick but this caused only minor discomfort and I got over it rather more rapidly than usual. And yet all was not as well as it seemed.

It is, of course, normal to have some fatigue on the initial stages of a long passage; getting one's system used to four hours on, four hours off, watch and watch, is bound to be a bit of a strain until one becomes acclimatised. Previously this had taken me two or three days to achieve. On this occasion I just did not begin to get there, and as the days went on the fatigue increased and changed to exhaustion for no apparent reason, conditions remaining generally favourable other than the all-pervading fog. It was not even particularly cold.

Paul coped splendidly with the increasing burden as I became less and less capable of doing anything at all other than remaining supinely horizontal.

One week out from St Pierre came the time for a momentous decision. Up until then we, or rather Paul, had carried on, either letting the boat self steer herself when he needed rest, or heaving-to when conditions were such that *Odd Times* would not hold to a reasonable course. Until then we both hoped and rather anticipated that I would recover but, as time passed, this hope seemed increasingly remote. Fog had prevented the possibility of obtaining sun sights as, although it was sometimes sunny, the horizon was never visible. I could have instructed Paul how to obtain a noon latitude sight at least, though at this stage of the crossing a lack of knowledge of our exact position would not have mattered. As it was, we discovered later that we were considerably in error in our dead reckoning as we had not passed from the west-flowing to the east-flowing current despite the very considerable increase in water temperature which we had thought of as signalling the change from the Labrador current to the North Atlantic Drift.

There seemed to be three possibilities open to us. To carry on, to turn back towards Newfoundland, or to seek assistance. If we carried on our next assured possibility of obtaining help, assuming we did not meet a ship, was ocean weather ship *Delta*, stationed near our projected course about 500–600 miles ahead and on to which we could home by means of our radio direction-finding equipment when within about 100 miles. Beyond *Delta* lay the Azores, about the same distance ahead but 200 hundred miles to the south of the course for England. This possibility seemed all very well, providing the conditions remained fair – a possibility but, in those waters, very far from a certainty. What would Paul's position be if called upon to cope single-handed with bad conditions, as well as with an invalid who seemed to be getting weaker every day?

The next possibility was to return to Newfoundland. This would have entailed a probable continuous beat to windward against the prevailing wind, back in cold conditions. At this stage I felt hardly able to trust my own judgement and made the decision that I will long continue to ponder. We would seek assistance if possible.

Now the fog cleared and we had overcast skies with intermittent rain squalls. The barometer was going down and this doubtless had its influence. We both felt very depressed but there seemed to be no alternative to the decision.

A few hours later, shortly after noon, Paul sighted two trawlers. He started the engine and motor-sailed towards them; they were proceeding very slowly with a net strung out between and astern of them. Somehow I managed to crawl up on deck and into the cockpit. Paul took in all sail. The trawlers turned out to be Spanish and we had some initial difficulty in making ourselves understood. Eventually, they realised that something was wrong and we manoeuvred under the lee of one of the vessels and managed, despite the heavy swell, to get *Odd Times* close enough for Paul to jump aboard the trawler and to get clear again without touching.

Then commenced a few hours that I hope never to repeat. I was not at all sick, just exhausted, and I was finding great difficulty in maintaining my equilibrium, both physically and mentally. While Paul explained the problem first to an English-speaking Spaniard and then by means of their radio to the St John's, Newfoundland, Coastguard, I tried to keep *Odd Times* in the lee of the slow-moving trawler, without getting too close. Recurring spells of dizziness did not help.

Paul eventually got into direct communication with a ship carrying a doctor that was about 15 hours from us, and with a Dutch survey vessel and ocean-going tug that was only about four hours away and which was bound for St John's. It seemed that immediate rest rather than a further night followed by medical aid would be wiser and the tug was diverted to come to our aid. When the tug, the *Smit Lloyd II*, hove in sight, Paul rejoined *Odd Times*, somehow or other again without damage.

Soon after 2000 in the failing light we went alongside the *Smit Lloyd*. It was now that *Odd Times* received her first damage, superficially. The noise as we struck in the large swell was utterly heart-rending, with splintering wood predominating as part of the rubbing strake and the starboard navigation light was wrenched off. A heavy nylon warp was passed from the tug and made fast round *Odd Times'* mast with a bight taken round the samson post. Paul passed up an emergency bag that he had earlier packed containing irreplaceable papers, the photographic slide record of the voyages of *Odd Times* and our various cameras. I was hauled aboard the tug, and would have lost some fingers between the rigging and the tug's side in the process but for some quick thinking and shouting by a member of the tug's crew. Paul jumped and *Odd Times* was taken in tow. I was half led and half carried below.

Odd Times, still perfectly sound, except for the already mentioned superficial damage, fell into position astern and the tug proceeded at about 5 knots. *Odd Times*, with her helm lashed amidships, followed docilely.

At about 0200 the line to *Odd Times* was seen to be chafing and was replaced with a wire rope by a member of the tug's crew. Apparently at this time she was in good shape and completely dry down below. All seemed to go well for the next few hours but the wind freshened to 30 knots or more and the swell increased – both coming from a couple of points of the port bow. The *Smit Lloyd II* slowed to about 4 knots, the minimum speed at which she could maintain adequate control.

At 0655, at 45° 00' N. 51° 41' W, the disaster occurred. Either the bight of the wire rope had come off the samson post or else, under the enormous strain of being towed in the then heavy swell, the samson post had carried away, but, either way, the strain of the tow was taken directly on the mast and before anyone on the tug could do anything about it *Odd Times* started sheering wildly and was pulled right over.

She filled, and sank. All of this in little more time than it takes to say it. The master of the tug had done all that he could and had no option but to sever the tow line and proceed.

■ **LESSON LEARNED**

There are always dangers in being towed, except perhaps by the professional crew of an RNLI lifeboat who are well practised in such rescues. It's an operation of apparent simplicity which can be fraught with danger. A small vessel must be towed at a speed low enough to allow her to rise to each wave, especially in a heavy sea. The results of towing a yacht at too high a speed can prove disastrous.

Odd Times was lost under tow at about 4 knots, the minimum speed at which the tug could keep control. Despite the apparently low speed, the bight of wire rope either slipped off the samson post, or, under the enormous strain, the samson post carried away. Suddenly, the strain of the tow was taken on the mast. *Odd Times* began sheering wildly and was capsized and sank.

The lesson learned here is that to take the strain of towing from the foot of the mast, the rope or wire must also be strongly fixed at the yacht's stemhead or bow roller, otherwise she will sheer about unmanageably.

In 1967, before the days of reliable seasickness tablets like Stugeron, Peter Rose thought he had been suffering from the side effects of a particular type of drug in some anti-seasickness tablets. Before leaving Nova Scotia he 'jettisoned all anti-seasickness tablets'.

In the end, it seems that Rose's seasickness greatly accelerated the onset of his exhaustion – both physically and mentally. This also affected his judgement. Modern sailors are lucky to have drugs to prevent or slow up their reactions too seriously. Don't forget your medication if you are prone to this debilitating malady.

twenty eight

SURVIVING A HURRICANE

Yacht	*Island Princess* (48ft Bermudian ketch)
Skipper	Barry 'Finbar' Gittelman
Crew	Michael Munroe, Bob Harvey and Matthew 'Doc' St Clair
Bound from	Marathon, Florida, to Belize, Central America
Time and date of loss	0415, 6 August 1980
Position	approx. 40 miles S of Santiago de Cuba

This account of the loss of the ketch Island Princess *is based on the comments of her skipper and crew, linked together by* SAIL *reporter, Bob Payne.*

ISLAND PRINCESS WAS BEING SAILED from Florida to Belize by a delivery company based in Key West. The yacht was a strongly built wooden ship with 2-inch planking that had been refastened prior to the trip. Both masts had been removed and checked, all standing rigging replaced and the engine put in 'top running order'. Skipper Gittelman reported: 'She was in just about perfect condition. And as far as equipment goes, I would say we had a full complement of the very best safety gear available.' This included a 4–6-man Givens Buoy liferaft with a water ballasted stabilisation chamber.

The skipper and two of the three-man crew were experienced offshore sailors, but the fourth man, 'Doc' St Clair, was making his first deep-water passage. However, *Island Princess* had two characteristics that were to prove fatal to her. Her internal ballast was in the form of lead pigs and her companionway hatch was offset to starboard, which meant that if she were knocked down to starboard that hatch remained under water for a long time.

Gittelman and his crew had given thought to the possibility of encountering a hurricane, and they had chosen the much longer route round the eastern end of Cuba, instead of heading directly across the Gulf of Mexico and down the Yucatan channel. This route offered more chances of shelter in hurricane holes.

Island Princess left Marathon on 27 July, but the first word they had of Hurricane Allen was on Sunday 2 August, when a weather station reported that a low had developed into a tropical storm, had officially become a hurricane and was moving west on a course that would probably take it south of Jamaica.

Bob Harvey remembers hearing a report on 4 August that said the storm would pass south of Jamaica and had been downgraded. Those aboard *Island Princess* heaved sighs of relief. What they didn't know was that at that very time Hurricane Allen was making a move that would put them directly in its path. Nor did they know that it had been downgraded from Category 5 only to Category 4. Being caught in a Category 4 rather than a Category 5 hurricane would be rather like being hit by a train that has slowed to 60 miles an hour. As it turned out, the hurricane was soon to be upgraded again. Munroe said: 'At 1000 on the fifth we sighted a grey wall of clouds. But we weren't worried, because from the reports we'd been getting we thought it must have been a local depression.'

As the wind and seas increased, they decided to put a reef in the main, but by the time they were finished, they knew they didn't want the mainsail at all. Slowly, they began to suspect the truth. What they were experiencing was the front edge of a hurricane.

'My thoughts at that point were that the hurricane was still probably going to pass south of us,' said Gittelman. 'I reasoned that the best thing to do was turn to the north. First, because we wanted to avoid the centre, but just as importantly, if we did get into it and were dismasted or anything like that we would be driven down on the north coast of Jamaica. And the north coast of Jamaica is a rockpile.'

By sunset the wind had reached 50 knots out of the north-east and was building fast. The seas were 10 to 15ft high. The *Island Princess*, with her engine turning over slowly in forward gear, was close-reaching under a tiny forestaysail.

Gittelman was at the wheel and Harvey and Munroe sat with him in the cockpit. They all wore lifejackets and safety harnesses. In the dark, Harvey had rigged safety lines all over the boat so that there would always be something to clip on to. He had criss-crossed the cockpit with heavier lines, so that if the boat was knocked down no one would have far to fall before he could grab hold of something.

St Clair was below in his bunk, seasick.

Just before 2200 Harvey went below to listen to the weather report. When he came back he said things sounded bad and were going to get worse. The wind was already blowing over 100 knots.

At midnight the forestaysail blew away.

'Even then I don't recall being particularly worried,' Gittelman recalls. 'Even under bare poles she felt stable and the engine was driving her to windward controllably. I told myself that it was blowing like stink, but I'd seen it bad before, and we could get through this. We just had to grit our teeth and do it.

When the wind got up to somewhere around 125–130 knots, the boat was still stable. The seas were ugly, but they weren't that high, maybe 20–25ft, because the wind was blowing the tops off them. The boat would rise up and be stable at the top and then she'd come back down and rise again. We were real happy with her. I was just hanging on, gritting my teeth, pretty well all consumed with driving the boat. I had little else on my mind.

Then it got up to somewhere around 150 knots – I'm guessing at this point – and I'm saying to myself: '"Jesus, I had no idea it could get this bad. But it can't get any worse, so all we have to do is hang in there."'

And then it did get worse.

About 0300 Gittelman began to have doubts. The boat didn't feel stable any more. In fact, all 30 tons of her were being lifted off the crests and thrown sideways into the troughs. Gittelman thought it was time to try trailing warps.

Clipping into the safety lines, Munroe and Harvey crawled forward, taking about ten minutes to get from the cockpit to the rope locker, and dragged all the anchor lines aft. They streamed them over the stern, along with all their chain and a 45lb anchor. How long that took they have no idea. 'Nobody was stopping to make log entries,' Gittelman said.

'It took me about two or three minutes to realise it just wasn't going to work,' Gittelman said. 'She was doing 8 knots and was broaching, rolling her sides under. She was squirrelly as hell, and we were getting pooped. So in a relatively smooth patch we brought her back up into the wind and dragged all the lines back aboard.'

How they managed such a mammoth task under those conditions, even they are not sure.

'All I know is that anybody who says he can't do something never had it standing between him and survival,' said Harvey.

'She did all right for another half-hour, but then things got worse,' Gittelman commented. 'And at that point I couldn't tell how much. It was beyond my comprehension. I've been 20 years going to sea, and I just couldn't imagine these things were possible.'

When they were first knocked down, St Clair was still below and, inexperienced sailor that he was, still not sure how bad things were. Half an hour earlier Harvey had come below and told him to get into his foul weather gear, lifejacket and safety harness because the boat looked as though she might not have long to live.

'He didn't sound like he was kidding,' St Clair recalls, 'so I got up.'

When St Clair was dressed he got on the VHF radio and started calling for anybody who might be listening. He told them who they were and their approximate position, and that they were experiencing hurricane-force winds and didn't know how much longer they were going to be afloat. He did that for four or five minutes but got no response.

'Then I told myself it couldn't be that bad or they would have called me. So I lay down again. About the time I got stretched out good the boat suddenly slammed over and everything on the starboard side fell straight down. I was standing on the port side of the cabin doghouse watching a two-foot-high geyser of water coming in the porthole. I couldn't believe it. I had to touch that geyser to convince myself it was there. As soon as I was convinced I knew it was time to get on deck.'

On the way out he grabbed two things: his good-luck hat and a rigging knife on a lanyard, which he slipped round his neck. As he bolted through the companionway he mockingly chided the rest of the crew for the mess they had made of the inside of the boat.

Then he looked around at what was outside and almost went into shock.

In the orange glow of a sky lit with sheet lightning, he saw the boat lying on its side with water halfway up the cockpit. Gittelman was hanging off the boom gallows, screaming something to Munroe and Harvey, who, covered with lines, were on the high side of the mizzen, with their feet dangling down into the cockpit. Water, glowing orange from the lightning, moved horizontally through the air. Waves struck the boat from all directions. The noise of the wind had gone beyond loudness – it was simply a 'dull white sound'.

In the next 20 minutes the *Island Princess* was knocked down three more times. The crew would be swept over the side to the end of their safety harnesses. Then they would drag themselves back aboard, only to be swept over once again. They were constantly swallowing sea water. Water was coming in the boat's engine air intake, her portholes and her companionway.

On the fourth knockdown – which was to starboard – her ballast shifted, putting the companionway under for good. Three or four minutes later the glow from a submerged but still burning deck light was all that marked the spot where she had slipped beneath the waves.

'When Finbar yelled for us to abandon ship,' said St Clair, 'I suddenly realised that this was no movie, so I kicked the liferaft free and fired the bottle to inflate it.'

The liferaft inflated upside down. St Clair and Munroe scrambled onto its upturned bottom and fought desperately to push it away from the boat, which was flailing at it with the wildly rolling mizzen mast. St Clair thinks that may have been when he broke his ribs, but he isn't sure, as he wasn't aware of the pain until several hours later.

Meanwhile, Harvey and Gittelman were fighting desperate battles of their own. For what almost proved too long, Harvey couldn't get to the end of his safety harness to unclip himself from the sinking boat. He finally had to unclip from his end, and – attached to nothing – leap for the liferaft from the mizzen. Only a fingertips grab by Munroe prevented him from being swept away. Gittelman, it seemed to St Clair and Munroe, who watched him from the overturned liferaft, had decided to go down with the ship.

'I'm not sure what possessed me,' Gittelman said. 'But I just sat at the wheel and tried to steer the boat. It was already under water, everybody else was on the liferaft. I was clipped to the liferaft's painter. But I tried to drive.'

Perhaps the boat slipping beneath him finally convinced the skipper to abandon the helm and jump for the liferaft.

'As soon as I climbed onto the bottom of the liferaft I realised that something was tangled with it and that the boat was pulling it down. I needed a knife, but couldn't get to mine because it was inside my foul weather gear. So I shouted for a knife and before the words were out of my mouth, Doc slapped his into my hand. The blade was already open.'

'I'd lost my good-luck hat in the first five minutes,' said St Clair, 'but that knife saved our asses.'

Once the liferaft was free of the boat, a wave crest immediately flipped it right side up and the ballast chamber filled. Everyone scrambled through the opening in the canopy.

Gittelman's order to abandon came at approximately 0415 on Wednesday, 6 August. By comparing weather service advisories with the *Island Princess*'s position, which was between Port Antonio, Jamaica, and the extreme south coast of Cuba, it appears that the four men took to the liferaft in 175-knot winds.

They had no way of estimating the wind strength, but they do remember that the wind-driven spray sounded like buckshot hitting the canopy and that the 30ft seas were cresting and breaking on them from all directions.

'Every time one of those 30-footers decided to collapse on us it would fill the liferaft with water and drive it so deep that my ears popped,' said St Clair. 'At that point we would have to push down with our feet and up with our hands to make an air space at the top of the canopy. We were constantly up to our necks in water, and there were even fish swimming around inside the liferaft. The only thing that helped us to realise we were still alive was a little light glowing at the top of the canopy. '

It was around this time that Gittelman, who was slightly claustro-phobic, said: 'To hell with this; I'm going outside where I can breathe.' The others made sure he didn't go.

Despite the buffeting they were taking and despite their skipper's claustrophobia, the crew felt that once in the liferaft they had it made.

Harvey said: 'Once the ballast chamber filled, which didn't seem to take any time at all, the liferaft settled right down. You'd feel it pitch over when we were hit by a wave, but as soon as the pressure came off it would come back up again. It was like being in a womb. We were floating around in there, sometimes with our feet off the bottom. We didn't feel comfortable, but we did feel secure.'

Soon after they had entered the liferaft, the roaring and frothing suddenly ceased. The seas stopped breaking, the wind subsided, and in the darkness overhead the men could see broken patches of sky.

They were in the eye of the hurricane.

Gittelman said: 'We could hear the roar recede into the distance, and then there were five or ten minutes of perfect silence while we just sat there staring at each other.'

St Clair can still remember how the others' faces looked drawn, tight, and with eyes that were big and glistening, and he is sure that his face looked the same. He also remembers saying: 'Finbar; this is another fine mess you've gotten me into!'

Fifteen minutes later the storm was upon them again. They described its approach as sounding like that of a thousand freight trains: 'But we don't know what it looked like; nobody volunteered to look out.'

At about 0600 the sky started getting light, but St Clair remembers: 'I didn't want it to, because I was afraid of what we would see. But I finally pulled down one corner of the Velcro – and wished I hadn't. Waves were collapsing on top of waves that were collapsing on top of waves. Everything was grey and white and screaming. It was insanity.'

But then they discovered a new problem. Munroe had begun to throw up blood. Later, Gittelman – seasick for the first time in his life – would follow.

St Clair had charge of the survival kit, in which he found a knife, six ten-ounce cans of water, two cans of candy and other survival rations, a fish line and hook, a first-aid kit, a whistle, six hand-held flares, eight small pen-type flares, a signal mirror, a repair kit, a sponge, and four or five packs of soggy tissues.

Harvey observed: 'If we needed papier-mâché for anything, we would have had plenty.'

In addition, St Clair had three more pen-type flares that he'd been carrying with him since his days in Vietnam. The liferaft also contained two paddles, a sea anchor, a life ring, a pump and a two-part EPIRB, with the battery pack separate from the transmitter. The wires between the two had pulled out, making the EPIRB inoperable.

'I opened two cans of water and let everybody drink a fair amount,' said St Clair. 'We'd all swallowed a lot of salt water, and the kidney and liver damage that can result from that is no fun.'

While Munroe and Gittelman rested, Harvey and St Clair spent much of Wednesday hanging out of the opening in the canopy with the paddles, trying to keep the opening to leeward of the breaking seas, which, even after the wind subsided, remained large and dangerous. Occasionally, Harvey would remove his seaboots and bail with them. 'The liferaft kept filling, but at least we were doing something.'

On Wednesday the liferaft's two inflatable ring sections began to separate from each other. Using line from the sea anchor, the men lashed them together again.

That evening they drank two more cans of water; and St Clair, noticing signs of hypothermia, encouraged the men to huddle against each other for warmth.

'We were experiencing cold and little pains,' he said. 'Every time we'd get the water fairly warm from our bodies and start to doze off, a wave would come in and make it cold again.'

Thursday, before daylight, the hallucinations began. St Clair saw what he thought were the lights of Jamaica. He was picking out street-lights and cars driving along the shore. 'There it is, guys, we've got it made, it's right there – look.' The others looked and saw nothing there. Harvey heard a dog bark and people talking. Munroe saw comic books.

Later, St Clair spent much of the day talking to a bird that had landed on the top of the canopy. 'The bird was real,' said Gittelman. 'But it couldn't talk.' That afternoon they drank their last can of water and, because Munroe's condition seemed to be worsening, they gave most of it to him.

St Clair recalls: 'At that point I took one long look at Michael and told myself he would be dead by that time tomorrow. He was starting to get incoherent. His eyes were sunken in. I've seen men like that before, just one step away from death. And that would be it. He was going to be the first. Finbar had been throwing up a lot of blood, too, so I figured just from blood loss alone he would go next. I had some broken ribs; that made me the next weakest, so then I'd go. And Bob would probably go just from the psychological shock of watching us three die.'

Harvey, however, had no intention of seeing the script played out that way. He'd slept most of the day so that he could stay awake through the night, when he figured they'd have the best chance of signalling any ships they spotted. That's how he came to be staring through the canopy opening at about 2200 when a light appeared on the horizon. He watched it for a while; then, in a low voice, almost without emotion, he announced: 'There is a ship.'

Instantly, the other three were at the opening. As soon as they all agreed that what they saw was a ship and not a low-lying star, St Clair fired four red flares, one right after the other. Then he lit a hand-held flare. Harvey, who knew Morse code, began to signal with the flashlight. Among other things, he signaled 'SOS' and 'Out of water'.

On the bridge of the Norwegian tanker *Jastella*, the second mate spotted a red pinpoint of light to the north. At first he thought it might be a lighthouse on Cuba, but his chart showed that light to be white and 40 miles away. He figured that it must be a fishing boat. Then he saw a blinking white light; somebody was trying to signal him. He picked out the word 'water'. He tried the radio and did a radar sweep. Nothing. It had to be, he reasoned, a liferaft.

Two days later, the crew of the *Island Princess* were in hospital in the Cayman Islands – the *Jastella*'s destination – and after a week's stay, they were home again in Key West.

Afterwards, Gittelman said: 'It has played on our minds, sure; but we are sailors, and it won't keep us from going back to sea. What we'll do is go back with a few lessons learned. We learned about liferafts, about survival, and we learned about what it takes to sink a boat. But most of all we learned where not to be when. We learned to stay the hell out of the Caribbean during hurricane season.

■ LESSONS LEARNED

- In such extreme survival conditions the lessons learned aboard *Island Princess* and the liferaft are somewhat unique. When the wind reached 50 knots, Harvey rigged safety lines all over the boat, making sure there would always be something to clip on to. He even criss-crossed the cockpit with heavier lines so that in a knockdown the crew could grab hold of something.

- When the wind got up to more than 100 knots and all 30 tons of boat was being lifted off the crests and thrown sideways, Gittelman thought it was time to try trailing warps. But after dragging all the anchor lines aft and streaming them over the stern, along with all their chain and a 45-pound anchor, he realised it wasn't going to work.

- Abandoning ship, St Clair grabbed two things: his good-luck hat and the rigging knife on a lanyard, which he slipped round his neck. Once again the importance of a knife was demonstrated. The liferaft was being dragged down by a line from the ketch and Gittelman couldn't get to his knife inside his foul weather gear. Luckily, Doc had a knife handy. 'That knife saved our asses,' said St Clair.

- The crew were rescued by the tanker only because Bob Harvey knew Morse Code and signalled 'SOS' and 'Out of Water' with the flashlight. The second mate aboard the tanker 'picked out the word "water" ... It had to be, he reasoned, a liferaft.'

- The boat's downfall, literally, was her internal ballast, in the form of lead pigs, plus the companionway hatch, offset to starboard, so that in a knockdown to starboard the hatch was under water.

twenty nine

THE SINKING OF *TERN*

Yacht	*Tern* (36ft gaff-rigged yawl)
Skipper	H S Carter
Crew	P Woodcock
Bound	from the Beaulieu River, Hampshire to Poole, Dorset
Time and date of loss	approx 1200, 11 April 1928
Position	in the entrance to Poole Harbour

Tern, designed by Albert Strange, was homeward bound from the Beaulieu River in the Solent to Poole during the Easter weekend of 1928. She had made a fast run before a strong south-easterly and, as she reached the bar, the lumpy sea grew confused as they met the first of the ebb running out of the channel, so that the skipper was intent on keeping Tern *on course and did not notice a coasting collier coming up astern:*

THE MATE, WHO HAD BEEN below for a few minutes, now appeared in the companionway.

'She's going to pass us pretty closely, isn't she?' he said.

The skipper glanced round. The collier was nearly up with them, a little on their port quarter. She was close, but would pass them at a distance of 40ft or so. There seemed to be no cause for alarm. She would probably give them a heavy wash which might slop aboard, but that would hurt no one.

She was a steamer and an overtaking vessel. It was her duty to keep clear, so the skipper steered tranquilly on, while the mate joined him in the cockpit.

Slowly but steadily the collier overhauled them. It was after high water and she was pushing along at full speed. She was, in fact, in a hurry to pass the bar, for, in those days, it had not been dredged to its present depth and her draught was almost as great as the depth of water, so that the clearance under her keel could not have been more than a few inches.

She passed to leeward of the yawl, drawing out ahead until her counter was just clear of the end of the latter's bowsprit. Her bow wave rolled harmlessly under the canoe stern, a mere bucketful of water topping the rail to fall inboard on deck. The danger, if any, seemed past. Only the quarter wave remained to be negotiated.

Owing to the collier's draught and the comparatively shallow water, this wave was something of an outsize one. Very steep and with a curling foam-capped crest, it rushed along, an angry mass of drab-coloured, sand-filled water. This roaring quarter wave lifted *Tern*'s stern. Higher and higher she reared and then she began to be carried forward with the wave.

Trouble at sea is apt to crop up at unexpected moments, and when things happen, they often happen quickly. They did so now. Like a bolt from the blue came disaster. From sitting at his tiller steering his ship before a big but by no means dangerous sea, the skipper suddenly found himself in the midst of a smother of foam which boiled up and slopped aboard on either quarter, while the tiller, from being a live thing under his hand, lost all feeling and became a useless, dead piece of inanimate wood, as the yawl, her rudder buried in a mass of moving water, tobogganed along on the face of the wave.

Faster and faster she went, so fast indeed that the main boom came right inboard with the wind's back draught. In a wild burst of speed she charged ahead, rushing up on the collier and overhauling her until she was once more level with the bridge.

Though from the beginning of her wild rush she had been entirely out of control, she had run straight, but now, under the influence of some irresistible power of suction and in spite of the hard-down helm, she suddenly sheered in towards the collier. There was a fearful splintering crash as the bowsprit snapped off short like a carrot and then, with a sickening thud, the bow drove home against the steel plates.

For a moment there seemed a lull. The collier drew ahead, the yawl fell astern. Then events again moved swiftly in this mad minute of misfortune.

'Are we leaking?' asked the skipper.

The mate started to run forward to see what damage had been done. He did not get far. Between the fore end of the self-draining cockpit and the companion was some five feet or so of deck. As the mate passed the hatch, he glanced below to see to his amazement and consternation the water already over the cabin seats and level with the table.

'We're sinking!' he cried.

'Launch the dinghy, quick,' ordered the skipper.

The dinghy was lashed on the small cabin top and, whipping out his knife, the mate started to cut the lashings. The skipper sprang to help, but in vain. There was no time. Even as they worked there came a long-drawn whistle as the invading water drove the air from the lockers round the cockpit, and less than half a minute after receiving the fatal blow, the little ship took her plunge.

Just before she sank the skipper tried to tear loose the lifebuoy which was lashed in the rigging, but the seizing was too strong and he found himself struggling in the heavy seas. He very quickly realised that, hampered as he was by his heavy coat, he had not the strength to keep afloat for long. As he struck out, he felt something solid, grasped it and held on. It was the head of the mizzen mast which supported him, but in such a position that he was completely submerged by every wave.

The mate, intent on freeing the dinghy, worked on her till the last moment and was sucked under when the vessel sank, but, young and strong, he quickly bobbed to the surface again and, getting rid of some of his clothes, swam close to the skipper and encouraged him to hold on.

The crew of the collier had not seen the accident and the skipper and the mate had the mortification of seeing her cheerfully steam way up the channel while they fought for their lives. Luckily for them other eyes had been more observant and a motor launch was driving at full speed to the rescue. The skipper had almost resigned himself to the end when the mate sighted her approaching.

'Hang on,' he cried to his skipper. 'There's help coming. They'll soon be here.'

Between his duckings the skipper also caught a cheering glimpse of the launch, but even then doubted his ability to last out.

The launch approached and stopped, fearing to strike the wreck and knock a hole in her bottom. Her crew threw a lifebuoy. It fell short by a dozen yards, but the mate retrieved it and swam with it to the skipper who, abandoning the mast, dropped thankfully into it and was towed to the launch. The mate clambered aboard and, with the help of the solitary youth who formed the launch's crew, managed to haul the skipper over the rail into the well where he subsided on to the bottom boards – exhausted, but safe.

Tern sank in the afternoon. She lay right in the fairway on the Poole side of the bar. During the night another steamer entering the port steamed over her in the darkness, snapping off her hollow mast and crushing in her hull.

A few days later the wreck was raised and taken to Newman's yard at Hamworthy. Her mainmast and bowsprit were gone; the stem was practically torn out of her, the butt ends of the planks gaping wide on either side to the forefoot, while the hole in her port side made by the keel of the steamer reached well below the waterline. On survey she was pronounced a total constructive loss and her name disappeared from the Register of British yachts.

■ LESSONS LEARNED

Keeping a lookout ahead is common seamanship sense. But remembering, also, to keep to a good lookout astern can all too easily be forgotten. As Tern reached the Poole Harbour bar in lumpy, confused seas, the skipper was concentrating on maintaining his course and failed to look over his shoulder and see the big ship astern. As the overtaking vessel he assumed it was her duty to keep clear.

Always add a margin of safety to any information in charts or pilot books. In this case, the bar not been dredged to its normal depth and the ship's draught turned out to be 'almost as great as the depth of water'. The clearance under the keel was thought to be just a few inches.

Combined with the shallow water, the collier's draught created an angry, outsize quarter wave which lifted Tern's stern and propelled her forward. Tern's tiller, became 'a useless, dead piece of inanimate wood' as the yacht sped along on the face of the wave out of control. Surfing on a wave can often cause the rudder to lack directional control.

The skipper describes an 'irresistible power of suction' which, despite his best efforts on the hard-down helm, suddenly sheered Tern towards the collier with a terrible splintering crash. With steel against wood, the little ship plunged to her death.

Safety equipment is useless if it cannot be used. In this disaster, the skipper found the lifebuoy lashed so tightly in the rigging that he couldn't free it. In heavy seas, his heavy clothing threatened to down him and he struggled to stay afloat. Mercifully, when he felt something solid and held on. It was the head of the mizzen mast which saved him – though he was submerged by every wave. As the skipper and mate fought for their lives in the tubulence, the vigilance of a passing launch plucked them to safety.

STORM FORCE 10 IN THE
IRISH SEA

Yacht   *Gwendoline* (19ft Sterte sloop designed by Fred Parker)
Skipper   Geoffrey Toye
Crew   Tracy
Bound from Cardigan, Wales, to Dunmore East, Southern Ireland
Date of loss August 1978
Position   approx. Near Tuskar Rock in the St George's Channel

---

IT WAS TEA TIME ON a fine Sunday afternoon in August when we sailed over the bar at Cardigan in a light north-easterly breeze. We planned to make a crossing to Dunmore East, in Southern Ireland, and conditions, it seemed, could not have been better. The forecast was good.

Gwendoline was a 19ft Gins carvel sloop, a Sterte, designed by Fred Parker and built by Kitsons at Poole. When she came into my possession she was badly in need of a refit. Most of her ribs were cracked, her keel-bolts had rusted thin as needles, and patches of her transom were soft enough to poke a finger through. It was a labour of love, and when she was relaunched every defective part had been restored.

She was a very pretty boat, white with a gold sheerline. Her boot top and deck were red, her brightwork newly varnished. She was a gleaming example of brass and mahogany, heroine of a marine survey and the darling of my eye.

Nor was she just an ornament. I remember reading about a Sterte that had crossed the Atlantic twice, and I can well believe it. During the three seasons that I sailed her, on several occasions in the sudden and violent conditions frequently found off the West Coast, I never once doubted her ability to take care of herself in bad weather. She was sometimes stubborn in stays, but she was fast, weatherly and could be trusted to steer herself on most windward courses.

For several months we had planned an Irish crossing. The plans began over a dinner at Bristol, where Tracy, my volunteer crew, was an art student. My feeling of good fortune at acquiring such an attractive crew was tempered with some doubt as to the wisdom of accepting one so inexperienced. However, she proved a remarkably quick learner and, in the event, I believe I may owe her my life. She was pleasant company, a natural sailor, and infinitely forgiving when things went wrong. If this paragon had a fault it was that she was a vegetarian. The meal she cooked us before we set sail upon the foamy wastes was a kind of undercooked dough whose Marmite aroma was reminiscent of sweet and sour All-Bran. It was awful.

Off Cemaes Head, the sea was confused. It often is, just there. I streamed the log, took the departure and arranged the chart on the plotting board, making a few calculations for the effects of tide in advance. Tracy was quiet and when I looked up from my work I noticed she appeared rather green. Coincidentally, I did not feel too wonderful myself and since I had never before been seasick, I put our mutual queasiness down to the lunch, aggravated by the choppy sea off the headland. I was soon to discover the foolishness of that piece of reasoning.

It was still light and I turned in to snatch a couple of hours before the night watch. When I awoke, night was falling and the land was well astern, the Strumble Head light clearly visible on the quarter. We chatted and shared a hot drink in the cockpit. After my nap I was feeling a little brighter, but Tracy was still sick. She took my place in the bunk.

Then followed the best sail of my life. The breeze strengthened to perhaps Force 4 and under full sail *Gwendoline* danced along, throwing up clouds of phosphorescent spray that set the sails aglow. I was wearing a reefer jacket which shone brightly as the droplets were trapped in the wool. I was startled to see the back of my hand glowing, emitting enough light to illuminate surrounding objects. A steamer overhauled us and passed by a couple of cables to starboard, her lights shining brightly and her wake a blaze of phosphorescence. All of this beneath a perfect canopy of stars on a night I shall never forget.

Just before dawn, the wind began to increase. Tracy had been feeling sick most of the night, so I had left her in her bunk. However, the time had come to reef, so she took the helm while I put a couple of rolls in the main. Now Tracy was feeling better but, once again, I began to feel sick and unable to do very much.

The wind was still rising and visibility was poor. Dead reckoning put us near Tuskar Rock. Not wishing to close that inhospitable coast in uncertain conditions, I decided to trust the DR and swing south, hoping to resume a westerly course towards the Coningbeg Light Vessel once our reckoning put us south of the rocks.

I turned in below and, just as I was dropping off to sleep, there was a severe jolt and a crunching noise from below. My first thought was that we had run on to the rocks, but Tracy could see none and the echo sounder put us in very deep water. Then there was another impact and a loud bang. The centreboard case, to which my bunk was fastened, quivered violently.

I should have sprung from my bunk and gone on deck, and sitting in my study now, years later, it seems incredible that I didn't. I remained in my bunk for two reasons, or rather one reason and one cause. Tracy had announced that she could see a large fin just off the bow. By the description it must have been a mature basking shark and I guessed we must have grounded upon its back and it had responded angrily. The sighting of the fin explained the impact against the keel. It seemed futile to go on deck since there was nothing that could be done. Also, I was very sick and the lethargy which accompanies that sensation has to be experienced to be believed.

Peace returned and I fell asleep. When I awakened about an hour later I no longer felt sick, I felt wet. Water was lapping against my bunk. I worked the pump for about 20 minutes, until the bottom boards were dry, but it was obvious we were making water fast. No leak was visible inside the hull and the weather was worsening rapidly.

Our charts were soaked and any navigation would have to be from memory and the odd rescued scrap of soggy chart. We sighted a fishing vessel. I called him up on the radio and discovered that he was French. I managed to make myself heard over his conversation with a friend with the aid of the alarm button, explained our plight and requested a position. They treated this as a joke, mimicking the sound of the alarm. I shall not dwell on this, except to record that it happened.

The leak was getting worse, so was the weather. We hove to while I furled the mainsail and replaced the working jib with the storm jib. As I was returning to the cockpit, the yacht rolled heavily and I was knocked on the head by the boom. It was a sickening blow and I fell on to the cockpit sole. I remember trying to break my fall and, although I thought I got up again, it seems I lay there stunned for several minutes while Tracy, with a correct sense of priority, examined me to see that I was still breathing and left me there while she made sure the boat was all right. Nor was I particularly refreshed when I did get up. On the contrary, I was sick and a little irrational. I gave a few course instructions, which Tracy wisely ignored, and returned to my bunk.

The situation was grave. We were somewhere to the south of Ireland in a sinking yacht with an injured skipper, during a gale that was to become a storm. When I recovered my senses sufficiently, I sent out a Mayday on the radio. All I heard in reply were three more Mayday calls from other vessels in distress. The air was full of urgent evidence that we were not the only crew caught out. Then the earth wire of the Callbuoy radio parted. Despite its lead sinker, it had been blown out horizontally by the force of the gale and had snagged around the propeller of the raised outboard. This rendered useless both the radio and the engine.

There was now a full gale from the north and we had no choice but to run off before it. Cornwall lay far to the south and the North Cornish coast is a place to be feared in a northerly gale. The problems of getting around Land's End with no charts were overshadowed by the knowledge that we would not survive long enough to get there. We were cold, wet and weary and we would never have been able to keep pumping her out that long.

Motoring against that gale with the outboard was out of the question. We had on board an inflatable dinghy, but with the wind shrieking across the deck I do not believe we could have secured the dinghy, even if we had succeeded in pumping it up. It would have flown like a kite.

I brought the outboard engine into the cockpit. It was a Seagull, and removing the propeller would not be too difficult. I went below to get some tools and, as I was on my knees and out of sight of my crew, I said a few prayers. I am afraid my maker only hears from me when I am in trouble. I needed Him then. I was frightened, sick, and feeling the weight of my responsibility for involving another person. As I later discovered, Tracy had taken advantage while I was below to say a few words herself. It was not that we were embarrassed, but rather that neither of us wished to damage the other's morale.

A few minutes later, while I was engaged in removing the propeller, the miracle happened. Tracy sighted another yacht. It appeared out of the mist and spray about three-quarters of a mile off the starboard bow and crossing our course.

I went below for the distress flares and grabbed two parachute rocket flares. The other yacht, a large ketch-rigged Westerly, was already disappearing off the port bow as I braced myself in the fore-hatch and took aim. My plan was to explode the rocket above the other vessel so it would parachute down in her vicinity, since her skipper could hardly he expected to notice a red flare the best part of a mile upwind and up-spray.

The first rocket streamed in a beautiful trajectory, but carried away to the right. It may be of some use to the reader, should you ever be in a similar position, to know that initially at least the rocket turned into the wind. This is the opposite to what one would expect, although once in stable flight it does get carried downwind.

Correcting my aim, I fired a second rocket which flared above the other yacht's cockpit. He could not have failed to have seen it, but yet the ketch sailed on and disappeared. I began to feel very guilty about bringing Tracy along, and was starting to say as much when she pointed into the distance. The ketch was motoring towards us.

It turned out that her steering gear had been damaged by the storm and the crew had rigged an emergency tiller in the after cabin before turning her about and very gallantly returning to our aid.

The skipper was understandably reluctant to risk coming alongside in such violent conditions, but when I shouted an explanation of just how bad the situation was, he agreed to take us aboard.

We kept both boats sailing and as we came alongside I told Tracy to be ready to jump. Typically, she had offered to let me go first and before agreeing to obey orders and precede the skipper, she extracted a promise that I would not remain aboard to try and save my boat. She got her promise, together with the threat of a thick ear if she hesitated and on the word, and as the decks were coming level, she jumped. Friendly hands pulled her to safety.

When it was my turn to jump, the boats were separating, so I did not quite make it. I missed the top guardrail, caught the second and smashed my knees against the hull. The sea closed over my head. Finally, I looked over the rail and everyone rushed to haul me aboard. Unfortunately, they got my arms either side of a mizzen shroud and confused my reluctance to be sawn in two with saturated body weight, or perhaps narcosis of the deep. They pulled harder until finally I managed to get one arm free of its tug of war team and I shot around the stay and over the rail like a cork from a bottle.

The skipper was a doctor. He examined me and diagnosed concussion. We were given mugs of coffee, hot soup, and a couple of berths.

Norman and Sheila, and their son and nephew, were making for Penzance. The two boys had been carrying on, although seasick and needing to rest, and had stood watch for some time. I was asked if I would be up to standing a watch. Norman came into the forecabin to ask this while I was in my bunk. Tracy was asleep on the opposite bunk and I think I must have slept for a while too, because I felt much better.

That night Norman and I sailed through the worst conditions either of us had ever experienced. He decided to try to make some easting, in the hope of getting a lee from St David's Head, with a view to making Milford Haven.

The wind, I believe, reached a steady Force 10 and was gusting over that. Most of the night it would have been about Force 8. The seas crashed into the cockpit and several times I awakened from dozing on the sole to find myself afloat in my lifejacket, tethered by my harness and still in the cockpit. When the tiny jib was caught aback, such was the force of the wind that the deck vibrated up and down visibly. At times there was a complete 'whiteout' when the air was full of brilliant white spray and you couldn't tell up from down, or sea from sky, only the gimballed compass giving any indication of the horizontal. It was a nightmare.

Like most nightmares it ended with the morning. The wind eased and we closed the coast. One of the boys took the helm and I collapsed into my bunk. At noon I awoke to find we were picking up a mooring at Milford.

We took our leave of this family of quiet and hardy people with just a brief exchange of thanks and courtesies. We shall never forget them.

Once ashore, hunger took over and we headed for the smell of steak and chips. It was a nice restaurant. Full marks to the waitress, whose face betrayed nothing in the way of a reaction to our appearance. Tracy wasn't too bad, but as we left I caught sight of myself in a mirror, caked with salt and dried blood on my forehead. In the pocket of my torn reefer jacket I found the brass pin from the Seagull's bracket. My thoughts went back to my last sight of *Gwendoline*, my boat, her orange storm jib still set, low in the water and sailing fast towards the open Atlantic.

■ LESSONS LEARNED

Looking back, the author, Geoffrey Toye, admits to marvelling at the courage of his crew and himself and also wonders at the judgement of youth. The navigation was good, as was, by and large, the boat handling. But the vulnerability of the low centre-board casing and the lack of a self-draining cockpit was, he admits, 'a misjudgement never to be repeated.'

From one incident, a chain reaction often grows to make the situation worse. In this case, when the yacht rolled heavily the skipper was knocked on the head by the boom – a sickening blow which stunned him for several minutes and left him sick and a little irrational. His crew wisely ignored his course instructions.

When the moment came to fire a distress parachute flare, it streamed in a beautiful trajectory into the wind, to the surprise of the skipper. It was the opposite of what he expected.

Flares should be pointed outboard and downwind away from your body. They will always turn into the wind slightly and should be fired at arm's length and about 10 to15 degrees downwind of the vertical.

It's a good idea to fire flares at five minute intervals. If the first one is glimpsed by a watchkeeper on a ship out of the corner of his eye, he might question his own judgement. But the second flare will confirm your position.

It's the skipper's responsibility to make sure he gives his crew a thorough safety briefing so they are familiar with how to operate distress equipment.

Flares should not be used after their expiry date, when they should be disposed of in accordance with regulations.

INDEX OF BOATS AND YACHTSMEN